Ritual and Social Dynamics in Christian and Islamic Preaching

Also Available from Bloomsbury

Young Muslims and Christians in a Secular Europe, by Daan Beekers

Inventing the New Dispensation in Zimbabwe,
edited by Ezra Chitando, Lovemore Togarasei and Joram Tarusarira

Charismatic Healers in Contemporary Africa,
edited by Sandra Fancello and Alessandro Gusman

Ritual and Social Dynamics in Christian and Islamic Preaching

Edited by
Ruth Conrad, Roland Hardenberg,
Hanna Miethner, and Max Stille

BLOOMSBURY ACADEMIC
LONDON • NEW YORK • OXFORD • NEW DELHI • SYDNEY

BLOOMSBURY ACADEMIC
Bloomsbury Publishing Plc, 50 Bedford Square, London, WC1B 3DP, UK
Bloomsbury Publishing Inc, 1385 Broadway, New York, NY 10018, USA
Bloomsbury Publishing Ireland, 29 Earlsfort Terrace, Dublin 2, D02 AY28, Ireland

BLOOMSBURY, BLOOMSBURY ACADEMIC and the Diana logo are trademarks of Bloomsbury Publishing Plc

First published in Great Britain 2024
Paperback edition published 2025

A catalogue record for this book is available from the British Library.

A catalog record for this book is available from the Library of Congress.

ISBN: HB: 978-1-3504-0884-5
PB: 978-1-3504-0888-3
ePDF: 978-1-3504-0885-2
eBook: 978-1-3504-0886-9

Typeset by Newgen KnowledgeWorks Pvt. Ltd., Chennai, India

For product safety related questions contact productsafety@bloomsbury.com.

To find out more about our authors and books visit www.bloomsbury.com and sign up for our newsletters.

Contents

Acknowledgments vii

Introduction: Topic, Contributions, and Perspectives for Future Research 1
Ruth Conrad, Roland Hardenberg, Hanna Miethner, and Max Stille

Part 1 Preaching and Social Dynamics

1 Are 1,000 Sermons Representative Enough? Political and Social Dimensions of Sermons and Religious Speeches 1800–1950 in Germany and Some Methodological Problems 19
Olaf Blaschke

2 The Struggle for Hope Continues: The Christmas Sermons of Archbishop Thabo Makgoba, 2009–19 39
Cas Wepener and Marileen Steyn

3 Moral Exhortation in Islamic Discourse: Performance and Ethics in Islamic Sermons 63
Abdulkader Tayob

Part 2 Popularity and Normativity in Sermons

4 Unity and Justice and Freedom: Preached Religious Staging of Political Values in the Public Sermons on the Day of German Unity (*Tag der Deutschen Einheit*) 89
Jan Hermelink

5 Joel Osteen's Prosperity Gospel and the Enduring Popularity of America's "Smiling Preacher" 105
Maren Freudenberg

6 A Case on Behalf of the Routine Listener 127
Julian Millie

Part 3 Ritual and Religious Speech

7 "Words against Death": Religious Speech—Perspectives from Ritual Ambivalences and Trends 143
Paul Post

8 Arabic Oration in Early Islam: Religion, Ritual, and Rhetoric 156
Tahera Qutbuddin

9 The Rain Rogation *Khuṭba*: A Case Study of the Reciprocal Relationship between Islamic Ritual and Religious Speech 173
Linda Gale Jones

Appendix 1: Bishop Dr. Wolfgang Huber (Berlin-Brandenburg) 193
Appendix 2: Bishop Johannes Hempel (Sachsen) 196
Appendix 3: Bishop Dr. Christian Stäblein (Berlin-Brandenburg) 199
Contributors 203
Index of Names 205
Index of Subjects 207

Acknowledgments

This volume is the outcome of an international online conference held from 25 to 27 in March 2021. It took place within the framework of the Collaborative Research Centre 1070 "Resource Cultures" of the University of Tübingen (Germany) and was organized by Ruth Conrad (Humboldt University Berlin), Roland Hardenberg (Goethe University Frankfurt; Frobenius Institute for Research in Cultural Anthropology), and Max Stille (formerly: Max Planck Institute for Human Development, Berlin; now: NETZ Partnerschaft für Entwicklung und Gerechtigkeit e.V.). We would like to thank the Collaborative Research Centre 1070 and the Frobenius Institute for generous support in the planning and realization of the conference.

As editors of the volume—together with Hanna Miethner (Humboldt University Berlin)—we thank Matthias Mader and Tilman Asmus Fischer for the organization and formal editing of the volume, Lucy Duggan for the professional editing, and, last but not least, the authors for their contributions and patience.

Introduction: Topic, Contributions, and Perspectives for Future Research

Ruth Conrad, Roland Hardenberg, Hanna Miethner, and Max Stille

In many religions, sermons are sociocultural practices that initiate, create, and accompany social dynamics. It is argued that sermons as public speeches create, legitimize, stabilize, and transform social groups and identities. They are often key elements of religious and social developments because they communicate certain values as normative, impart religious viewpoints, administer exclusion and inclusion, and constitute as well as transmit religious knowledge. Sermons can combine religious, social, economic, and political dimensions in ways that are often subject to negotiation. In many societies, sermons stimulate debates and gain a considerable degree of popularity, especially when they become part of popular media. The embeddedness of sermons in popular media, among other phenomena, tends to generate specific local patterns of religious speech.

This volume evaluates religious speeches in relation to their diverse and far-reaching effects by analyzing Christian and Islamic sermons and preachers in the past and present. We gather research on sermons from various countries and different historical times. In addition, multiple forms and occasions of sermons come into view. We are explicitly interested in the highly diverse cases of Muslim and Christian preaching in order to identify concrete similarities and differences. We combine local studies with a general, comparative perspective, because neither suffices alone to grasp the rich complexities drawn from studying preaching as a sociocultural practice. If local practices and broader perspectives are not brought into conversation with each other, the specific local conditions are either overestimated in their importance or overlooked. For example, Christian preaching in Germany largely takes place in the context of a relationship between churches and the state and is thus regulated by state-church law (cf. Blaschke; Hermelink), while the evangelical preaching of America can be located in an economic and communitarian system of religious providers (cf. Freudenberg). In Islamic preaching, the local, concrete congregation is of great importance as well as the occasion, be it a festive one or the regular Friday *khuṭba* (cf. Jones, Millie vs. Qutbuddin, Tayob). On the other hand, when the sermons are described without reference to concrete practices, studies of this kind either become normative or lack the actors' point of view. The comprehensive research we aim at, research that combines the analysis of local contexts and general perspectives, requires an interdisciplinary approach. Therefore, the methods, approaches, and types of analysis gathered in this volume come from anthropologists, scholars of Islam, Christian theologians, and historians. With this interdisciplinary, cross-religious—but not multireligious—and cross-epochal research and discourse on preaching, we hope to make a significant contribution to the present state of research on sermons.

In this volume, the chapters address three main perspectives in three parts, each highlighting one aspect and focusing on specific issues. However, all three perspectives are brought into conversation with each other throughout the volume. Given the complexities of preaching as a cultural phenomenon, these perspectives partly overlap to some extent. In each part, one more general essay is combined with two case studies of concrete sermons.

In Part 1, the focus is on the explicit contribution of sermons to processes of sociocultural transformation. This perspective examines the religio-rhetoric situation from the outside. We particularly think about the social norms imparted by sermons and how precisely such norms become effective. Because of the speeches' connection to holy texts and the religious norms of each specific group, a tense relationship often arises between sermons and the respective sociocultural present.

The second perspective brings the dynamic tensions between normativity and popularity into focus. Rather than juxtaposing the normative stances of sermons with their popularity, we see that normativity can itself contribute to popularity and the quest for popularity entails its own normative stances.

Third, sermons are mostly embedded in rituals. Speech and rituals are, in our view, part of a reciprocal relationship, where the sermon, its own performative character, and its positioning within religious practice are interwoven and inform one another. Thus, we are looking at a practice that in turn has its own bearing on the sociocultural dynamics of religious speech. This ritual perspective takes into account that the sermon as a speech act transcends the realm of audible language but is part of and shaped by a complex setting that is local and corporeal.

In order to be able to generate comparative perspectives within these three topics, we limit ourselves to sermons from diverse Christianities and from different Muslim communities. Moreover, our main questions about the relationship between preaching and social dynamics, the relationship between popularity and normativity, and the ritual embeddedness of religious speeches are reflected particularly well in both Christian and Muslim sermons. Thus, preachers in Christianity and Islam are currently often so successful precisely because they can combine normative claims with pop-cultural rhetoric and performance patterns, and also because they seek to provide answers to social challenges in concrete societies and communities.

In the following, we will unfold the themes of the three perspectives in more detail and briefly introduce and contextualize the corresponding contributions of the parts and their authors. At the same time, we show points of comparison and entanglements.

Preaching and Social Dynamics

Our volume shows that sermons trigger, promote, and constrain sociocultural transformations and are therefore of great societal relevance. This holds true, as described above, both historically (e.g., war sermons; cf. Blaschke) and contemporarily (e.g., sermons by leading bishops; cf. Wepener and Steyn). Sermons oscillate between the fluid borders of the political and the religious and enable processes of social, political, and economic change. They are embedded in the horizon of values of a religious community and its transformations. Sermons share religious knowledge and take part in shaping various identities. They spur mechanisms of inclusion and exclusion and thereby simultaneously give shape to shared values and attitudes. This works in at least three modes: first, through the mediation of specific religious contents and the targeted transformation of theological models of interpretation (e.g., the "prosperity gospel" in both Pentecostal and Muslim communities; cf. Freudenberg). Second, through a particular performance that draws on local traditions, merges them with translocal or even global aesthetic patterns, and builds on emotionalizing effects of religious speech. The construction of authority, its legitimization, and the specific appropriation of the content by the listeners plays a fundamental role here. Third, actions that accompany the religious speech and the specific ritual are very important for its social impact. This can be observed in religious group gatherings, social facilities, and educational institutions.

Questions that are raised in this part are: Which specific sociocultural dynamics are addressed by the religious speeches? How can one describe those dynamics and the specific and therefore "non-substitutable" function and task of the particular religious speech? Which values are communicated, which are not? How are those values justified and socially legitimized, for example, by tradition, sacred texts, experience, and the like? What ideas and concepts of community and of society can be identified? What kind of community do the sermons propose? Are the sermons designed to promote social change or is social change a product of the speeches' social embeddedness? When preaching is understood as a social practice, how then are the fluid borders of the political and the religious contoured and actively modeled? What factors contribute to sermons' social impact and how do they achieve that impact? That is, practices of emotionalization, aesthetic performances, certain theological models of interpretation, and so on? What role does the speaker have (e.g., charisma, authority, and popularity)? Are there differences between Muslim and Christian preachers in the way certain topics are addressed?

The ways in which sermons relate to social issues and are woven into political conflicts can be shown particularly well and exemplarily in Christian sermons of the nineteenth century in Germany. Olaf Blaschke's chapter is dedicated to this task. Due to widespread industrialization and urbanization, considerable social conflicts arose in the course of the century within the area of the later German Empire, to which the churches and religious communities reacted in different ways. Against this background, the chapter from Blaschke introduces the central issues of this part: First, he discusses the questions of where and how sermons touch on sociopolitical issues and what political and social power is attributed to them by the state, and the churches. For this purpose, he delves into the German-language sermon cultures—Protestant and Catholic—of the nineteenth and early twentieth centuries, uncovering rich material. He suggests distinguishing between several social and political periods of preaching from Napoleonic times to the 1950s. In these periods, sermons emerge as both the subject and the object of political conflicts. In dealing with this material, important methodological questions arise, which Blaschke discusses in a second step—the questions of the quantitative and qualitative representativeness of the material, of the relevance of confessional preaching in the face of secularization and religious pluralization, as well as the evaluation of the reception and impact of sermons. Blaschke presents basic methodological challenges of historical as well as empirical sermon research that are relevant throughout the volume. The chapter also discusses the essential methodological questions of an interdisciplinary cultural theory of preaching: On the basis of which material is it developed? Due to the almost infinite material, the question of selection is anything but trivial. How can the significance of individual studies be justified within the framework of an overall theory? At the same time, Blaschke shows that the relationship between the state and religious communities is central if we are to adequately determine the function and social significance of preaching. If, for example, laws prohibit certain sermon content, then it is possible that its presence can no longer be proven historically, although this content may have been the most important at the time.

The two case studies in this part are set in contemporary South Africa, a country where the fields of the political and the religious have traditionally been closely intertwined.

Cas Wepener and Marileen Steyn analyze the eleven Midnight Mass Christmas sermons delivered by the Anglican Archbishop of Cape Town (South Africa), Thabo Makgoba, from 2009 to 2019. Thabo Makgoba is currently bishop in the same diocese where Desmond Tutu was archbishop during the time of struggle for freedom and preaches from the same pulpit, but addresses new struggles in South Africa. Because of their media exposure, these Christmas sermons have considerable public visibility. The guiding question of the chapter is: What is the relationship between Archbishop Thabo Makgoba's Christmas sermons and the South African social dynamics of the past decade? Over a period of ten years, the form of the sermon remains stable, but its function and content change. Wepener and Steyn show that the sermons reference society with growing frequency, becoming more and more confrontational, more political, and more demanding. The focus of their content shifts—away from questions of apartheid to the growing social challenges in shaping a "new *societas*." As in Blaschke's work, state interventions intended to prevent political references in sermons are also addressed in this chapter. If sermons influence the social dynamics of a society, they can also create conflicts with the political elites. Wepener and Steyn understand pre-sermons as "public ritual performance" and connect the questions of the social dynamics addressed in and through sermons with the ritual dimension of religious speech. Because of this ritual-theoretical perspective, this chapter links particularly well with the chapters in Part 3.

Abdulkader Tayob understands the Islamic Friday sermons in South Africa (*khuṭbah* and pre-*khuṭbah*) as part of the discourse around Islam that is characterized by plurality, contestation, deliberation, performance, and critique. He offers an analysis of the moral exhortations in sermons as creative interventions in the discourse of Islam that neither sacrifice their link with the past nor their engagement with the present. The *khuṭbah* and pre-*khuṭbah* should not be read as an indication of the uniformity of Islam, nor of its modernity or anti-modernity. To illustrate this, Tayob focuses on one sermon given in a prominent Friday mosque in Cape Town that was simultaneously broadcast on YouTube on February 5, 2021. The sermon celebrates and reflects on the mosque in Muslim communities. Like other sermons given in the past two years during Covid-19, it addresses a rupture in the discourse of Islam created in this time. The preacher consecrates the role of mosques in modern times, and then describes how it was affected by Covid-19 regulations. He tries to maintain what he considers a fundamental place for mosques in Muslim societies. The pre-*khuṭbah* moral exhortation offers an opportunity to appreciate how a religious discourse engages with the past and the present in critical times. Tayob thus succeeds in showing how a religious community reacts to and participates in social dynamics with the means of the sermon. The sermon not only comments on a current given situation but thereby also reflects the religious community's indebtedness to a tradition while staying connected to the present-day situation at hand. Preaching is not only a practice of positioning oneself in and toward an outside world prone to regular social changes. It also offers a way for a community to assure itself of its own values and norms facing transformations or to enter into a discussion about them. The sermon also serves the religious-political will formation of the individual and the group. A good sermon succeeds in reconciling the social dynamics of the present with the tradition of the form.

From a comparative perspective, these case studies point to an interesting difference: While Christian preaching, according to Wepener and Steyn, locates itself in society by participating in political-social discourse and directly addressing political actors, Islamic preaching, according to Tayob, describes the congregation's internal and self-understanding as a way of locating itself in society. The first case study presents a preaching style that addresses politics and society pointing outside of its own inner realm; the second portraits preaching events that are pointing inward to what consolidates the own community by referring to its traditions and identity.

Popularity and Normativity in Sermons

The second chapter discusses the dynamics of popularity and normativity in sermons. The contributions analyze the extent to which religious speakers make claims of collective validity and the linguistic and rhetorical means they employ to substantiate these claims. We understand "claims of collective validity" to encompass norms, values, and traditions that speakers assert as being mandatory and true for the group to which they are speaking. In this respect, the chapter seeks to paint a detailed picture of how sermons make collective claims. Reconstructing validations of certain forms of thought, feeling, and acting gives us an insight into mechanisms of inclusion and exclusion and the role of tradition and revelation in justifying them. We pay particular attention to processes of popularizing normative ideas and values. In so doing, we inquire into how sermons attain vividness and perspicuity for their listeners, and which shared aesthetic models are employed by speakers to connect normativity and popularity. Thereby, the chapter aims to qualitatively reconstruct how religious claims are negotiated in religious speeches.

Questions that are addressed by the chapter include: Which claims of collective validity can we reconstruct from sermons and how can we do this? Which rhetorical and linguistic means do speakers use to attain plausibility, establish norms, and set boundaries and distinctions? Which forms of inclusion and exclusion can we identify? Which models of life, thinking, feeling and behavior are promoted or discouraged? How do the speeches produce vividness and intelligibility and how do speakers connect normativity and popularity in their speeches? How do they, by rhetorical and linguistic means, connect to culture, experiences, and commonplaces? Are there specifically religious strategies of legitimizing collective claims of validity? What is the function of religious tradition and revelation in collective claims? And again: Are there differences between Christian and Muslim preaching or do they work comparably?

The contribution by Jan Hermelink is the first to attempt answers to some of these questions, referring to the special religious-political situation in contemporary Germany. Due to the provisions of state-church law in Germany, churches and the state are separated, which still does not make German society laicist. Interfaces between politics and religion and between state and religious communities remain in need of joint negotiation and compromise (e.g., religious education in state schools or training of pastors at state universities). Against this background, the relationship of the sermon to the political sphere is discussed particularly intensively and critically in Germany. This is already pointed out in the contribution by Olaf Blaschke (see above). While Blaschke describes the historical development, Hermelink discusses sermons marking German reunification (on October 3, since 1990). He examines how sociopolitical values are invoked and affirmed in the sermons that are held at the annual festivities on the Day of German Unity by bishops and other leading clerics. October 3 is a sensitive date. It is linked solely to the administrative act of the former GDR's accession to the Federal Republic of Germany. The day is not the celebration of a large demonstration in East Germany in the run-up to the opening of the Berlin Wall, nor does it commemorate an event in common German history that is filled with positive emotions. Thus, the festive date itself does not communicate any common values. These must be generated in the course of the official celebration. An official service led by the bishop of the respective regional church is part of this celebration program. The sermons delivered there are expected to have a strong sociopolitical normativity, since they affirm the key values of Germany's democratic system. Values such as thankfulness, solidarity, mutual acceptance, and a sense of responsibility are emphasized by using popular formats of speech; for example, a commemoration address, personal testimonial, or motivational talk. Due to their location within a festive program, the sermons have a distinctly "popular style." They produce normative effects by using what Hermelink calls a religious-political "double coding" of key symbols, central metaphors, selected traditions, and basic gestures, for example, pleading, careful listening, amazement, or relishing. As with Wepener and Steyn, Hermelink also shows that the quantity and quality of references to the social situation change depending on local conditions and biographical imprints. Popularity is always situated popularity.

While Hermelink starts from the aspect of normativity and analyzes how popular elements are integrated into sermons by German bishops for reasons of reception, Maren Freudenberg's contribution shows that among neo-Pentecostal preachers, popular style is an integral part of their concept of normativity. Her chapter is devoted to Joel Osteen, head pastor of America's largest megachurch, Lakewood Church, in Houston, Texas. Osteen enjoys enduring popularity among his followers. His weekly sermons are broadcast on television to reach approximately ten million viewers, in addition to the tens of thousands who attend his services in person. He preaches a distinct version of the prosperity, or health and wealth, gospel that advocates claiming one's "dues" from God through positive thinking and positive confession, paired with faithful adherence to the Bible and unwavering trust in the Holy Spirit. Presenting a carefully crafted and highly professionalized image of himself as successful, accomplished, and happy, he encourages his followers to develop a mindset of constantly expecting and asking for "more," both in material terms and in terms of well-being. In sermons, this normative narrative of personal gain is carefully constructed, on the level of content, not only through biblical references, but mainly through frequent references to everyday life that render Osteen's version of the prosperity gospel immediately relevant for believers. On the level of form, he uses the rhetorical devices of repetition and humor to drive his message home. By way of a sleek, stylized performance and by appealing to his followers both rationally and emotionally, he manages to substantiate the claim that God favors those who cultivate a mindset of forever demanding more, never "settling for less." The result of this performative and rhetorical approach combines popularity with normativity to establish personal health and individual wealth as the perceived ultimate goals of human existence. When we look at the sermon under the focus of popularity, it becomes apparent once again that form and content cannot be separated.

While Hermelink and Freudenberg describe the relationship between popularity and normativity from the perspective of the preacher, Julian Millie focuses on the reactions of the listeners and begins his argumentation by looking at their role at the preaching event. He distinguishes between two forms of listeners: The first is the "agentive listener," who has received a great deal of attention in research. Millie, however, directs his view to the "routine listener." This "routine listener," with her or his incidental listening and learning, is integral to the formation of religious identity. Preachers have always targeted this group of listeners by means of rhetorical and performative strategies, for example, by picking up on shared cultural knowledge or telling jokes. For such sermons, which take place in the context of larger religious events, the aspect of the physicality of listening, of being physically present, is crucial. During his fieldwork in Bandung, West Java, Millie came to know many Muslims who frequently attended preaching events, but who only did so at times of heightened collective practice, such as celebrating the conclusion of the fasting month, *'id ul-fitri*, when people would make extended journeys to their hometowns and villages. By directing attention to incidental listening, Millie simultaneously counteracts the possible hierarchy researchers of religious practices might establish between agentive and non-agentive listeners, privileging the former over the latter.

Comparing these perspectives on preaching reveals how preaching can productively be described as a relationship between the sermon and listener. The popularity of a preacher and the sermon is partly generated by the specific setting, for example, the German reunification ceremony that Hermelink describes, the festivities millions of people travel long distances to attend as is the case for *'id ul-fitri*, or the stadium performance given by megachurch pastors as Joel Osteen. In all cases, one could observe a strikingly similar relationship between popularity and normativity: Events such as state festivities, megachurch services with broad additional online audiences, and religious festivities are successful in numbers because they are also very normative in content, reaffirming state-approved values (cf. Hermelink), demanding a certain faith and even mindset from their respective congregation (cf. Freudenberg) or being simply a mandatory part of a larger religious festivity (cf. Millie).

Furthermore, the case studies allow for reflections on religious speech and its different notions of publicity and the public. In the mainline Christian settings researched, religious speech played a vital role in facilitating and shaping an official state act, and thus expressing collective memory. The neo-Pentecostal case study adds the notion of a wider public reached through different media channels, with preaching taking on commercial value. The perspective on Islamic preaching, however, showcases how the family festivity *'id ul-fitri* can bind the private and public together and how attentive listening is not necessarily a reliable, let alone the only way to determine the popularity of a sermon.

Ritual and Religious Speech

Part 3 focuses on the relation between rituals and sermons. It asks about the role of sermons in religious rituals and the way in which religious rituals alter religious speech. Quite often, speech is qualified as religious speech because of linguistic, spatial, and performative conventions that mark this speech as closely related to religious ritual. In a ritualized setting, rhetoric and action such as movement, gestures, or the voice might be more limited or, conversely, expand what would be possible in everyday situations. In both cases, rhetoric and action are part of ritual knowledge, which is unequally distributed among those assembled, but whose scripts and grammar are shared at least to the degree that each participant can fulfil her or his role. In this environment, ritual knowledge can open up specific possibilities of communicating with the divine, remembering and reenacting situations that pertain to religious or communal values, and fulfilling duties that are of religious and often salvific significance.

Questions addressed here are: What is the ritual significance of the speech vis-à-vis other parts of the ritual setting? How is speech ritualized, how does it refer to ritual? What are the important verbal markers and linguistic shifts, for example, set phrases or quotations from or depictions of ritual action, objects, gestures, and shifts in voice? Which roles does a ritual allow for or assign? How are the preacher and the audience conceptualized in a specific ritual setting?

Do their roles change over the course of a ritual? Are there intermediaries, for example, ritual experts who carry authority but do not speak themselves? How does ritualization, which often encompasses redundancy, rigidity, and stereotypes, affect the experience of the listeners? What is the effect of repetition for the efficacy of each speech act? What role does ritual context play here? Does it focus on communication between the human and the divine? What are the different degrees of ritualization, for example, between different religious traditions? To what extent do rituals change, or do they only conceal historical change in speech forms? Are speech and ritual seen as reaffirming one another or are they seen as competitors, with one gaining in importance when the other is downplayed?

The first chapter in Part 3 (Chapter 7), by Paul Post, gives an overview of the questions that Christian ritual research poses when observing the connection between speech and ritual. Starting with the example of a memorial service speech given after an air disaster in Eindhoven (Netherlands) in 1996, this chapter explores the ritual dimension of religious speech through two specific ritual studies lenses. First, Post explores the perspective of ritual ambivalences and ambiguities, especially traditional versus new; cold versus warm; individual versus communal; inclusive versus exclusive, and useful versus useless. Second, he assesses current trends that influence and characterize ritual, such as "casualization," the problem of explaining and the emergence of what Post calls the "Basic Sacred." He introduces his approach to ritual criticism, a critical and normative ritual studies view. Instead of concentrating on some ambivalences and trends in depth, he opts for a broad overview to map the field of rhetoric and ritual. He argues that religious speech can be described as a "spoken word performance." The ritual dimension is constitutive for religious speech and is not merely its backdrop. The speech itself has a ritual character. The chapter thus offers additional perspectives on the research of Millie, Freudenberg, Qutbuddin, and Jones presented in this volume.

The interplay of speech and ritual can be demonstrated particularly well in early Islamic sermons. For reasons of comparability, two case studies from the field of early Islam are presented here. Chapter 8 by Tahera Qutbuddin addresses in detail the issue of the ritual character of sermons in early Islam. The Friday sermon that is an intrinsic part of Muslim ritual across the globe today has a long history rooted in the first Friday sermon delivered by the Prophet Muhammad in Medina, and more broadly in the multifunctional orations of the early Islamic world. Across the mosques, homes, battlefields, and open town spaces of the Middle East in the seventh and eighth centuries AD, religion, politics, and aesthetics coalesced in the richly artistic public performance of spontaneous Arabic oration (*khuṭba*). Praised for their rhetorical craftsmanship, interactive speeches and sermons by Muhammad, 'Alī, and other political and military leaders were also the major vehicle of policymaking and persuasion, and the primary conduit for the dissemination of ethical, religious, and legal teachings. A separation of religious and secular spheres cannot be established for this period because the sermon communicates beliefs (*taqwā*) in the public sphere.

While Qutbuddin shows the ritual character of speech itself, Linda Gale Jones reflects on the interrelation and mutual influence of speech (language) and ritual in the case of festival sermons. As a rule, Islamic liturgical orations are embedded in rituals since they form an obligatory part of the Friday worship and canonical feast day celebrations. They are prescribed as ritual responses to crises affecting an entire community, notably extreme prolonged drought as well as solar and lunar eclipses. They also typically feature in para-liturgical celebrations, such as *al Mawlid al Nabi* (Prophet Muhammad's Birthday). Jones analyzes chronicle accounts of the Rain Rogation *khuṭbas* that the Grand Qadi and chief Khatib of Cordoba Mundhir b. Sa'id al-Balluti delivered at the behest of the reigning Umayyad caliph 'Abd al Rahman III. The Rain Rogation *khuṭba* constitutes a particularly apt manifestation of the ritual and social dynamics of religious speech. By reading Moroccan chronicler Ahmad al-Maqqari's depiction and reproduction of Mundhir b. Sa'id's rogation *khuṭbas* in light of ritual theory and sociocultural theories of emotions, Jones comes to the conclusion that the Islamic Rain Rogation ceremony is a communal penitential ritual. Its success depends, on the one hand, on the reciprocal relationships forged between the preacher, the caliph, the community, and the deity and, on the other hand, on the performative aspects of the preaching event. A vital component of the ritual performativity of these *khutbas* entails the arousal of intense collective emotions of debasement, humility, and contrition for one's sins. She concludes with a brief consideration of the political implications of the preacher's deployment of religious speech as an effective instrument for the ritual humbling of the caliph.

These chapters, as far apart as they may be geographically and historically, are bound together by how speech is embedded in ritual settings. Examples can be found of how life in different societies seems to require a liturgical form of dealing with and reflecting on social events. A vital part is played in these rituals by speeches addressing current issues, and by being at the heart and center of these liturgical processes they guarantee the efficacy of the respective ritual, be it letting the victims of a tragedy find peace and consolation, educating people on military and state matters, or invoking the rain after a dry period. The speech is part of the ritual, but at the same time it is itself a ritual and contains ritualized elements. The "ritual" speech is part of the effectiveness of the ritual and interprets it, too.

Perspectives for Future Research

The multiple perspectives and contributions in this volume allow for viewing and understanding sermons comparatively. This also opens up perspectives on future research. Comparative sermon research is a broad field of research that is experiencing many new developments. This concerns both historical and contemporary sermon research. The significance of sermons and preaching for societies, religious groups, social transformations, and cultural dynamics has so far only been explored in rudimentary fashion and rarely in comparative research designs. This volume aims to make an innovative contribution to the exploration of this field of research. It thus facilitates a conversation between previously separate fields of research and thereby generates new perspectives and inspires future research. The diachronic scope corresponds to the variety of sermons that manifests itself in the religious practices we witness throughout the centuries, transcending territorial and societal borders, shaped by the people involved on the ground.

On the one side, the various studies in this volume illustrate that Christian and Islamic sermons occur in numerous contexts, have many variants, and are subject to multiple conditions. Preaching, both in Christianity and Islam, is always a local practice that can only be described appropriately in its respective local and cultural context. At the same time, preaching is a global phenomenon. In many instances local preaching is interwoven with global transformation processes. When considering major global shifts in medialization and digitalization, one can observe how also local preaching cultures, both in Christianity and Islam, are influenced by those transformations. This is where comparative research can come in.

For—and this is the other side—the bringing together of research on sermons from different religions, epochs, and countries makes it evident that, despite all their differences, the individual forms of preaching have a surprising number of things in common. A sermon is a sermon and as such it is distinguished from other forms of speech by certain characteristics. We explore the conditions and characteristics of these recurring formal features in the three perspectives outlined—the reference to the concrete social situation and society, the tension between normativity and popularity and the embedding of sermons, as performative forms, in ritual contexts.

While appreciating the breadth and diversity of the sermons, we have found that the contributions to this volume also demonstrate that we are indeed dealing with similar constellations when analyzing the material. Sermons are highly socially embedded. Apart from being communal events themselves, they verbalize and sometimes shape social dynamics, and thus play a significant part in community-building and in processes of exclusion and inclusion and accompany or comment on social change. A good example is the role of preaching during the Arab Spring, which challenged long-term dictatorships in four countries and held out the possibility of social and political change. The perspective we have developed in this volume can be useful for further research exploring the role of sermons in commenting on the protests of that time.

Preaching, however, is a decidedly religious activity where listeners gather around a preaching person expecting guidance, orientation, or religious invigoration. A sermon thus often has a normative element to it. Nevertheless, the normative quality of a sermon does not take away from but rather enhances a preacher's popularity: surely a tension that makes research into sermons not only relevant for subjects in the realm of theology or religious studies but also highly interesting for anthropological or sociological quests. Future research could ask how religious groups position themselves in plural societies by means of normative and absolute truth claims. It could also take into account the growing importance of charismatic personalities through social media.

Last, sermons often take place as part of a ritual setting. They are rarely given as singular events but are recognizable by the context that anchors them in, for example, a memorial service, a rogation ceremony, or religious festivities. The ritual seriality of the sermon occurring each Friday or each Sunday gives rise to observations about the forms of sermons that can be described along spectrums between stability and innovation, tradition and cultural dynamics, or aesthetics of production and reception. Future research could seek to link the dynamic changes of rituals with the dynamics of rhetoric, especially in social media, and interrogate them for interactions.

We have chosen these three perspectives, knowing that there would be others and more. However, the three perspectives we propose juxtapose recurring formal features and local sociocultural adaptations, examine historical and contemporary preaching cultures for unifying features and help to evaluate the meaning of preaching in different religious traditions and social formations.

We hope this volume provides the reader, be it the scholar or virtually anyone taking a keen interest in the religious languages, codes, and practices of Christianity and Islam, with a fresh take on how two religions can be studied with regard to their shared—albeit uniquely executed—practices of preaching.

Part 1

Preaching and Social Dynamics

1

Are 1,000 Sermons Representative Enough? Political and Social Dimensions of Sermons and Religious Speeches 1800–1950 in Germany and Some Methodological Problems

Olaf Blaschke

Let us start with a story. Preachers like to start with stories—stories with a personal touch—entertaining and instructive. The story is about a man who studied in the 1980s, when I was also a student in Bielefeld (Germany). This man revealed something he and his fellow students used to do while studying Protestant Theology at the renowned faculty in Bethel, a district of Bielefeld. When they met up in private, these theology students played an interesting game. It went like this: Someone suggested a noun, anything that popped into their mind. And someone else had to give a spontaneous sermon that absolutely always had to end with Jesus. The fun part was to maneuver to Jesus from a noun like "alarm clock" or "taxi-driver," "forest" or "cheeseburger." Though the starting point and the stories differed, the outcome was always the same: Jesus. Anyone with some memories of sermons might confirm this observation. Though sermons always differ, the result is always the same message, already anticipated: that Jesus loves us or that he saved us.

And indeed, homiletics teaches what these students transferred into a party game. The eminent encyclopedia *Lexikon für Theologie und Kirche* defines homiletics as a subdiscipline of Practical Theology.

> It understands the sermon as an effort to unlock the current situation (of individuals, of the Church, or of society) in the light of the gospel, into the horizon of hope in God's promise, which inviolably has opened to all humans

> in Jesus' life and death. (Klöckener 2009: 246–8; all quotations translated by the author)

Does this mean sermons are boring because they all have the same message? If we are interested in what happens between the first sentence and the outcome, Jesus, they are no more boring than many political speeches or Hollywood movies. Furthermore, sermons have changed in the course of history, with regard to their content and their performance, which makes them a challenging subject to study. Sermons can influence people's biographies and reflect social and political change in history (on the relationship between politics and sermons, cf. Braune-Krickau and Galle 2021).

As a first step, this chapter suggests a few social and political phases of preaching from Napoleonic times to the 1950s in German-speaking Europe. In three periods, sermons were particularly concerned with the social question, for example, around the 1848 Revolution. In six other periods, between 1800 and 1950—for example, in the 1870s, during the culture war *(Kulturkampf)*—sermons can be described as both the subject and object of political conflicts.

Certainly, it is interesting to interpret printed sermons hermeneutically, but it is much more challenging to assess sermons as spoken texts truthfully and evaluate their social and political effects in history. Thus, the second part of this chapter raises methodological questions, discussing problems of quantification, representativity, and relevance.

Sermons in Changing Political and Social Situations

In the sixteenth and seventeenth centuries, sermons in Europe naturally reflected on the political system and whether God and the Bible could serve as justifications to stabilize or criticize political power (cf. Schorn-Schütte 2021). The baroque sermon, the sermon in the age of enlightenment, and later sermons (Schneyer offers these historical categories but none for the past 200 years) could reflect and foster political and social change. At times they touched upon social questions, while at other times they could be involved in political and legal conflicts. Let us try to highlight three phases since the nineteenth century in which the social dimension of sermons played a prominent role.

1. The decades between 1840 and 1871 were shaped by the social question. The Protestant preacher Johann Wichern is still remembered in Germany today. Already in 1835, he founded a home for poor children in Hamburg,

known as *Das Rauhe Haus*, and was committed to the inner mission in the decades after 1848 (Wichern 2014). On the Catholic side, Wilhelm Emmanuel von Ketteler, bishop of Mainz from 1850, was fighting poverty and social inequality. In his sermons of 1849, he emphasized that property carries with it social responsibility (Ketteler 1849; cf. Aubert 2003). When the eminent social reformer Franz Hitze gave his talks about the social question as a young priest in 1875, he complained that the topic was overshadowed by the culture war (Hitze 1877; cf. Blaschke 2021).

2. Beginning in the 1890s, sermons once again addressed the social question more vehemently. Pastors were concerned about low wages for the working class and social injustice. Another concern was the growing impact of socialism. The Social Democratic Party in Germany was the strongest in the world, and in 1912 the biggest party in the German parliament. Social and political aspects cannot be separated here.
3. Another period in which bishops and priests used the pulpit to preach for those who suffered was in the years after the Second World War. Bishops even encouraged people to steal: Famously, in the cold winter of 1947, Josef Cardinal Frings in Cologne said that coal robbery from the wagons transported by the Allies from the Ruhr to France should not be judged a sin. Thousands went there and stole coal to heat their homes. Frings later had to explain his attitude to the Allies (see Fring's sermons in Helbach 2012: 957, 1101).

The second perspective of this chapter is to distinguish critical phases in which sermons aimed to be a motor of political change and at the same time were under surveillance from political authorities—though of course, the social question also always had implications for political demands.

1. In Napoleonic times, two preachers gained enormous prominence: On the Catholic side, Clemens Maria Hofbauer, the so-called Apostle of Vienna, whose sermons were observed by the police, and on the Protestant side, Friedrich Schleiermacher in Berlin, who supported reforms in Prussia and whose patriotic sermons were also placed under police observation (Schnabel 1987: 314–16; Wolfes 2004).

   After the Napoleonic era, in certain parts of the German-speaking world, a movement of awakening emerged. The protagonists regarded ecclesiastical life as superficial. They wanted to touch their audience and reach them. People had to convert from materialism and outward

Christianity to inner faith. Some Catholics in southern Germany around Bishop Johann Michael Sailer had begun this process already twenty years earlier. In Württemberg in the 1820s, Ludwig Hofacker exerted an enormous influence (cf. Hofacker 1842). The sermons of these pietists did not aim to teach, they did not aim to edify but to awaken.[1] They worried about salvation and insisted on the role of personal decisions. "It was always the same topic," wrote Franz Schnabel: Here is the lost sinner, there the path from ruin to salvation. "Come to Jesus, he gives you everything." Because they preached the same content again and again, people understood and liked it. For this strategy, the preachers didn't even need to prepare a manuscript, which makes it harder for historians to analyze their performances (Schnabel 1987: 394–9). The post-Napoleonic awakening movement cannot be labeled a political phase, on the contrary. Pietist sermons were not in favor of political or social revolutions, nor were Calvinist, Lutheran, or ultramontane sermons,[2] though ultramontane texts in Germany could find some positive aspects in the Belgian Revolution of 1830 (cf. Schneider 1998).

2. The second political phase began in 1837. Because of the upheavals in Cologne when the archbishop was arrested, these years saw the rise of a self-confident Catholicism, protesting against the suppression of the Church by the state. Sermons had their share in this Catholic movement, attacking the policies of the state but also other Christian denominations. The new confessional age began in the 1830s (Blaschke 2000, 2002). Catholic preachers increasingly spoke disrespectfully about Protestants, while Protestant pastors intensified their anti-Catholicism. The situation was particularly unpleasant for confessional minorities: For instance, Protestants in Catholic Trier were a tiny minority. In July 1838, the Trier District Synod turned desperately to the Prussian King to ask him to defend the provisions of the 1648 Peace of Westphalia and "to forbid Catholic pastors, on pain of a heavy fine, to present the Protestant religion as a non-salvific or non-Christian one and their fellow Protestants as apostates" (Meyer 2000: 424–5). But degrading Protestants could also be achieved more subtly. Joseph Ehrler, Cathedral preacher in Munich from 1867 and bishop of Speyer from 1878, expressed pity for the poor Protestants in his printed sermons in 1873 and 1874, because they were not with the Pope. He argued that Catholics should meet those who fight against the Church, which was naturally the Catholic Church, with love, since they had lost their way (Ehrler 1873: 429, 438, 504–5). Ehrler

published seven volumes of his sermons. In the period we are discussing, the 1830s and 1840s, some states introduced pulpit paragraphs in order to prohibit sermons attacking other denominations or the state. In 1839 article 447 of the criminal code of the Kingdom of Württemberg stipulated: "Clergymen who misuse their office to utter invective or dishonorable insults against existing religious societies in public lectures are" to be punished with two years' imprisonment or "in particularly serious cases or in the case of the second recidivism, with dismissal from the service" (Hufnagel 1839: 110).

Article 449 of the criminal code states that "clergymen who denigrate the existing state constitution, the state government or the administration in official speeches shall be punished by a fine of fifty to two hundred guilders" and in serious cases by dismissal from service (Hufnagel 1893: 110). Braunschweig in 1840 introduced a similar paragraph (Das Criminal-Gesetz-Buch für das Herzogthum Braunschweig 1840: §282, 118).

Clearly, the pulpit was a place from which Catholic priests attacked Protestants, whom they called heretics, and Protestant pastors attacked Catholics as stupid papal subordinates (Blaschke 2013; Dittrich 2014). In addition to this, stereotypes against Jews found their way into sermons. Nevertheless, The Preacher and Catechist (*Der Prediger und Katechet*), a prominent periodical of sermons, tended to avoid any kind of denominational or political provocation. The periodical hardly mentioned contemporary Jews but mainly referred to Jews in biblical times (Langer 1994: 170–207). In 1873, it complained that the Jews didn't accept the Messiah and remained blind and obdurate (Joseph Ziegler 1873: 86). Although Catholics, and not only Protestants, promoted modern antisemitism (Blaschke 1999), the pulpit was not the favored platform to perform it.

After 1848, the Catholic renewal was strengthened, when the German bishops decided to unleash an extensive missionary campaign. Between 1848 and 1872, Jesuits, joined by Redemptorists, Franciscans, and other religious orders, led more than 4,000 "missions to the people." They held mass, they performed exorcisms, but the most important instrument for restoring Catholic faith were their theatrical and sensational sermons. Although the missionaries avoided political propaganda or polemics against Protestantism, government officials began to argue that the Jesuits threatened their authority and destroyed confessional peace. As studies by Mikel Gross (2004), Manuel Borutta (2010), and Lisa Dittrich (2014) have shown, these were the decades of growing anticlericalism and

Protestant anti-Jesuitism, of liberal anti-Catholic hysteria leading up to the culture wars.

3. The culture wars seem to be a third political phase, especially the so-called Prussian-German cultural war (*Preußisch-Deutscher Kulturkampf*), which began about 150 years ago in 1871. Sermons were political because they attacked their enemies, among them the state and liberalism, and because sermons were under observation of the state. In this situation, how did sermons that were expected to be religious manage to convey a hidden political message? In 1873, a priest in Tirol, who was not even affected by the culture war, used Mt. 8:23, in which Jesus and his disciples are in a ship on the stormy sea, to take the ship as a metaphor for the Church and the sea as a metaphor for all its enemies and challenges. The church was the ship in the storm of contemporary times: "Oh, how many enemies have conspired to overthrow the Church!" Satan and many evil persons tried to break the ship of the church:

> Freemasonry has spread widely, and its aims are known to be directed against the Church of God. … Judaism sets out against it with ancestral hatred, especially in the press. Even among the church's own children there are many who raise fist and sword against it. Liberalism, which is spreading mightily, is wreaking great havoc in the Catholic camp. (Skizzierte Predigt 1873: 99–102)

This "great havoc" also referred to the Old Catholic Church, which was established in protest against the dogma of infallibility in June 1870. "The pillars of the kingdom of God begin to totter and Jesus sleeps. But then he got up and saved the ship, as he saves the Church" (Skizzierte Predigt 1873: 99–102).

More than twenty laws mainly directed against the Catholic Church were passed between 1871 and 1878, concerning the expatriation of the Jesuits, school sovereignty, and civil marriage. It is an indicator for the importance of sermons that the very first law of this cultural war was concerned with preachers spreading propaganda for the Catholic party: the so-called pulpit law (*Kanzelparagraph*).

Section 130a of the German Criminal Code provided that a clergyman or a religious minister who, in the exercise of his profession, announced or discussed public matters before a crowd of people or in a church or other place designated for religious assemblies in a manner that endangered the public peace was to be punished by up to two years in prison. The law was passed in November 1871. In fact, it was not often implemented even during the culture war that officially ended in 1887 (Huber 1969: 701, refers to Eberle 1908). And afterward, in the decade between 1894 and 1904, the pulpit law resulted only in four convictions (Kißling 1913: 9; Ross 1998: 96, referring to Scholle 1974). The pulpit law (*Kanzelparagraph*) was quite often applied during the National Socialist period, which could be defined as the next phase of conflict between sermons and politics, while in the First World War there was a great harmony between preachers and the ruling elites.

4. A prominent example of the influence of sermons during Adolf Hitler's regime is Bishop Clemens August Graf von Galen. Already in the early years of the Nazi dictatorship, he warned in a sermon in Coesfeld in 1935 that Christian traditions like Pentecost were being abused by certain nationalist circles that aspired to return to pagan ancestral superstition, worshiping the powers of nature (Sermon by Galen in Löffler 1988: 232–6). Most famous, though, are his sermons against so-called euthanasia, the killing of people with disabilities. These sermons were held in Münster in July and August 1941. While the regime would have liked to sue von Galen for high treason, British bombers flew over Germany and delivered pamphlets of his sermons. They had a significant impact and Hitler stopped the T4 initiative, at least officially (Kuropka 2007; brief introduction: Blaschke 2014: 208–10).

   There were many examples of Catholic and Protestant protest from the pulpit in the period between 1933 and 1945, mainly complaints about church persecution, not against the persecution of communists or Jews. Some pastors were imprisoned in concentration camps, some were murdered. Bernhard Lichtenberg, who dared to pray for the Jews from 1938 onward, was sentenced to prison in 1942—based on the pulpit paragraph of 1871. Lichtenberg died in 1943. The pulpit paragraph was widely used by the National Socialist regime. It was only in 1953 that this law was repealed.

   Other pastors supported National Socialism. In particular, the Protestant ministers of the German Christian movement (*Deutsche Christen*) merged racism with Germanic religion in their sermons (Bergen 1996). However, mainstream sermons were cautious about addressing political issues: In 1935, the general vicar in Munich, Ferdinand Buchwieser, encouraged priests to preach God's word in a manly, thoughtful way and to have a well-prepared manuscript. Political allusions were to be avoided (Forstner 2014: 92).

5. A fifth phase of politicization begins in 1945. Catholic and Protestant bishops and pastors vehemently fought the allied denazification and the charge of collective guilt. The Paderborn Archbishop Lorenz Jaeger is just one example among many (cf. Blaschke and Unterburger 2021). Clemens August Graf von Galen also sharply attacked allied politics in his sermon for Münster pilgrims in Telgte on July 1, 1945: He warned against the vindictiveness of the allies, and against the concept of collective guilt. It was unjust, he said, to present it as if "the whole German people and each one of us had been guilty" (Sermon by Galen in Löffler 1988: 1175). He later had to justify his sermon in front of a British officer.
6. The final phase in the 150-year period under discussion (1800–1950) is the early Federal Republic of Germany, founded in 1949. Catholic clerics supported Chancellor Konrad Adenauer and the Christian Democratic Party (CDU). As in the culture war, their sermons suggested which party a good Catholic ought to vote for in the coming elections (cf. Gauly 1991; Köster 1998: 118). A brief outlook would point toward the year 1989. Sermons in Protestant Churches in East Germany played an enormous role in the first successful German revolution (Pelz 2018).

Hermeneutical Approaches and Their Methodological Problems: Quantification, Representativeness, and Relevance of Sermons

My first scholarly contact with sermons was in 1988, one year before I began my PhD in Bielefeld. In this project led by Lucian Hölscher, we discussed religion and the German bourgeois habitus known as "Bürgerlichkeit." The term "bourgeois values" is close to but not identical with civic values. The question was whether and how bourgeois values, bourgeois gender stereotypes, nationalism, and obedience to the state were reflected in sermons of the nineteenth century or contrasted with them. The results have never been published (unfortunately, Hölscher 1990 barely touches on the results). They lay forgotten in a file until I rediscovered them again for this article. So, I will try here to reconstruct the results of our work, which took place thirty-five years ago, and the methodological problems we identified by then. Our own method was to check selected critical biblical phrases and look up what different Protestant and Catholic preachers said about them during the nineteenth century.

Biblical norms were very often in tension with bourgeois values. A few examples out of many, ranging from poverty over education and gender to politics, might illustrate this.

1. The ideal of disciplined work and the ethos of achieving something in life contrasted strongly with Mt. 6:26 and other passages where the ideal of poverty was held up. The pursuit of prosperity contradicted Lk 6:20-21: "Blessed are you who are poor, for yours is the kingdom of God. Blessed are you who are hungry now, for you will be filled."[3] However, the German Protestant pastors who might choose to preach about this were rather wealthy, at least from the middle of the nineteenth century. Around 1800, a Protestant pastor only earned 70 Taler annually and had to find additional sources of income. A soldier earned 24 Taler, a university professor 600–2,000 Taler (Berger 2020: 301). A century later, a Protestant pastor's income in the countryside was equal to a primary school teacher's and in the urban context to a high school teacher's (Kuhlemann 2002: 245–50). Until the end of the nineteenth century, the system of benefices still applied, so that income varied from parish to parish. Catholic priests on average earned much less than their Protestant colleagues (Götz von Olenhusen 1994: 58).
2. The ideal of higher education, the German *Bildungsideal*, contrasted sharply with, for example, Mt. 5:3: "Blessed are the poor in spirit, for theirs is the kingdom of heaven." This was a true provocation for the German Protestant intellectual elite, among them pastors who belonged to the *Bildungsbürgertum*, the educated classes with a university degree.
3. Another problem was the polarization of gender stereotypes in the nineteenth century. On the one hand, a male self-confidence was established, cultivated, for example, in duels among Protestant students. On the other hand, the Bible demanded humility, peace, and love for others.
4. The German spirit of submission has been widely discussed among historians. Many Germans wanted to be loyal subjects to the authorities, and there was no real successful revolution in Germany until 1989. In contrast, the Bible sets other priorities. God is more important than worldly power. Mt. 22:21: "Give therefore to the emperor the things that are the emperor's, and to God the things that are God's." This sentence could either be taken in order to encourage people to defend God's will or it could be used to discourage them, and thus to evade political conflicts.

5. Other parts of the New Testament evidently suggest submission to authorities: St. Paul's letter to the Rom. 13:1 says, "Let every person be subject to the governing authorities; for there is no authority except from God, and those authorities that exist have been instituted by God."

In 1988, we selected about twenty biblical phrases of this sort and, as far as I can recall, looked closely at 110 relevant sermons, with different denominational backgrounds. The question was: What did preachers do with critical biblical phrases like this? How did they solve conflicts between the normative text of the Bible and the social and political reality they were living in? They had three options:

1. They could subscribe to what the Bible said, presenting an affirmative view.
2. They could be critical of what the Bible said.
3. They could respond evasively.

Our finding was that no sermon was openly critical of the Bible and that often option three was chosen; in particular, Protestant pastors, well-educated state officials, living in decent prosperity, tended to evade the provocations of the Bible. They maneuvered around the problematic issues. Civil values and the Bible found a way to coexist. The tensions between the Bible and civil life were often harmonized.

On the other hand, changes in the course of time and confessional differences could be observed. In 1848, most sermons about the letter to the Romans, chapter 13, concerning obedience to the authorities, defended the ruling aristocracy against democracy. Heinrich L. Heubner (1780–1850), for example, Protestant pastor in Wittenberg and member of the consistorial council, the governing parliament of the Protestant Church in Saxony, argued that St. Paul wrote his letter during the times of cruel and bloodthirsty tyrants who persecuted Christians. And still, Christians at the time had to obey the authorities. Not even under the most inhumane conditions should they revolt against authorities. The evil spirit of outrage came from France in the wake of their revolution in 1789. This spirit aimed to put all the power into the hands of the people. In the context of the failed revolution of 1848, the message could not be any clearer (Heubner 1850: 289–93).

During the culture war in the 1870s, we find diverging interpretations of the same phrase among Catholic priests and Protestant pastors. Catholic priests emphasized that God's rule could not be subordinate to the rule of a state that aspired to be omnipotent despite being only a few years old—in contrast to the church, which was established earlier. Joseph Ehrler in Munich emphasized in 1874 that the church must rule over the souls. Christians were to fight against the evils of the world, including the state if it oppressed the church (Ehrler 1874: 512–13). At the same time, Protestant sermons reinforced worldly authority. Rudolf Kögel, highly ranked preacher in Berlin, emphasized in 1875 that neither papal infallibility nor the people legitimized the authority of the state, but only God. Kögel's sermons were directed against the Pope and the Catholic and socialist masses (Kögel 1891: 295–6).

In Acts 6:13, we read about imputations against Saint Stephen: "They set up false witnesses who said, 'This man never stops saying things against this holy place and the law.'" The Catholic priest C. Sickinger used this phrase in 1885, referring to all those who uttered lies against the truth, against the church, and against infallibility. Because of lies like this, St. Stephen had to die and become the first martyr. Then Sickinger explicitly transferred this story into the realm of contemporary politics:

> Because of these false witnesses, the Church is being persecuted again today in almost all countries and has to go through a severe martyrdom. For everything that is brought forward against the Church in this wretched culture war [*in diesem unseligen Culturkampfe*] is lies and slander, brought forward by those who are declared enemies of God. … Let us learn from St. Stephen that we should rather be persecuted and accused for the truth than live in wealth and opulence with the enemies of Jesus and His Holy Church. Truth opens heaven for us, while lies populate hell. (Sickinger 1885: 66)

What is the value of interpreting sermons? How reliable are they as indicators of social and political transformations, reflecting the limits of hermeneutical approaches? We are confronted with three problems: (1) Quantitative representativeness, (2) Qualitative representativeness, and (3) Relevance and Effects.

1. Quantitative representativeness: The narrow sample of 110 was small in comparison with the millions of sermons produced in the same period. Nevertheless, handling this sample size was already more challenging than an approach that places one hero and a few sermons in the center of the analysis, such as Friedrich Schleiermacher, Adolf Stoecker in Berlin, or Jeremias Gotthelf in Switzerland (cf. Hildmann 2005), or those who were called "machine gun of God," as Pater Johannes Leppich was labeled, echoing the reputation of Billy Graham. These preachers were special rather than representative. They do not reveal general tendencies unless they are compared with ordinary preachers of the time.

We must consider some statistical facts: Around the year 1900, there were about 15,000 Protestant pastors in Germany and about 20,000 Catholic secular clergy (i.e., clergy who were not members of religious orders). This makes the sum of 35,000 pastors (Krose 1909: 258). The numbers for 1928 are 16,244 Protestant pastors and 22,037 Catholic secular clerics (Dahm 1961: 285–6). Assuming they deliver one sermon on a given Sunday, we could follow more than 38,000 sermons on one day alone. If they speak every Sunday, thus fifty-one times in a year, we end up with nearly two million (1,952,331) sermons in 1928 alone. But sermons are not only held on Sundays. If we include other categories of sermons, occasional sermons—for baptism, marriage, funeral, conversion—plus sermons at certain festivities, missionary sermons, and the like (Bendel 1852; Wintzer 1990: 306), we should calculate at least five million sermons in only one year. What did they tell the people? Where have all these sermons gone? How can we measure anything or claim to make valid assertions about them? Was there a difference between village and urban sermons, between charismatic and routine sermons? How typical can 110 sermons be, when selected from millions? This is not a question of complete coverage of all sermons, which no serious historian would attempt, but a question of representativeness: Do selected sermons reveal something not only about themselves, but also about general tendencies?

2. The statistical dilemma leads us to the second question, the question of qualitative representativeness. What did the pastors really say? There are many printed issues of sermons which flooded the Catholic and Protestant markets. Adolf Stoecker's "people's sermons" reached 120,000 readers weekly in their printed version for one penny (Teuteberg 1990: 187). But is there possibly a discrepancy between what the pastors actually preached in a certain situation and what they carefully edited later for their books? It would have been risky to attack the state in a sermon and publish it the way it was said. And the (rare) printed version of a pietist sermon from the early nineteenth century, which didn't follow a manuscript but some sort of inspiration, can hardly capture the emotional situation in the moment it was delivered.

One solution could be to go into the archives. Handwritten manuscripts are much closer to what the pastor might have said or at least planned to say than the polished text for a well-edited volume aimed at a wide readership. I found such notes, for example, in the papers of Lorenz Jaeger in Paderborn (cf. Jaeger 1944: 208/148).

Unfortunately, but often also unavoidably, most scholars use printed sermons. They don't look for the original manuscripts in the archives, even when this is possible. For theologians, sociologists, and anthropologists concerned with contemporary religious practices, work is obviously much easier. They can just visit a religious event and listen to the sermon, even ask people about their responses to it. Research into the last decades is also easier because we have some audiovisual recordings of most prominent preachers, although the outstanding preachers studied might not be representative and could overshadow millions of other "ordinary" preachers, thus leading us in the wrong direction.

Nevertheless, even edited versions of sermons are interesting. They have some value, though they might not reflect the authentic sermon and the atmosphere when they were delivered. Furthermore, printed manuals explaining how to preach also reflect some tendencies of the time. These existed in single volumes by more or less prominent preachers (Kern 1837). They also were published in the form of periodicals. An early and highly influential periodical was *The Preacher and Catechist* (*Der Prediger und Katechet*). The first issue appeared in 1850. This Catholic periodical, which still exists, was directed at priests with little formal education, working in the countryside and small towns. They were to use it to help them prepare their next sermon. Another example is *Voices from the Pulpit* (*Kanzelstimmen*), starting in 1879. Each volume, covering the complete ecclesiastical year, had about 850 pages. In the German-speaking countries, we find thirty different journals, presenting handy blueprints for sermons. We have reports that some priests directly reproduced these sermons on the pulpit, using the manuals as recipe books for their performances. For some, these ready-made sermons covered their homiletic needs for a complete year (Langer 1994: 171).

3. The final methodological issue touches on the relevance and effects of sermons. Did they transport any messages to the audience? How did people's attention differ depending on the type of sermon? Classical distinctions are feast day sermons (sermones de tempore), Sunday sermons (sermones de dominica), sermons about saints (sermones de sanctis), sermons about Mary (sermones Mariales), Lent sermons (sermones de Quadragesima), opportunity sermons (sermones de tempore), and catechetical sermons (cf. Bendel 1852: 648).

   Statistics show that the number of churchgoers declined dramatically in the nineteenth century, down to 20 percent in the wake of the First

> World War, with women always in the majority. In Protestant Hannover around 1900, only 5 percent of Protestants went to Church, in Berlin only 1 percent (Hölscher 1990: 609, 1995, more data in Hölscher 2001). Though the Catholic numbers were much higher, statistics show that the impact radius of sermons was diminishing in the course of the nineteenth century for both Catholics and Protestants. In rural areas and in diaspora situations, the numbers remained higher.

What about those who went to church and attended the sermon? Did what they heard affect their attitudes or their political voting behavior? Were sermons of any social or political relevance?

Many sources show that people were just waiting for the sermon so that they could fall asleep. Catholic services suffered from another problem. It was not the word that was central, but the mass. People knew that the sermon was "no essential element" of the service but was only of "preparatory character" for "the main point and center of the service, the actual mass" (Bendel 1852: 649–50). Thus, male participants left the church during the sermon, which could take an hour, and went into the nearby pub in order to come back for the really important part, the mass. Some of the women hardly behaved better. They took something to read with them in order to get through the sermon. But there were also people who listened. This was the more likely the more vivid or political the sermon was, and the more critical of another denomination (Dietrich 2004: 168–71; Fuchs 2021; Heinz 1978: 228; Lentzen-Deis 2000: 371).

The different approach to sermons between Catholics and Protestants was another opportunity for denominational polemics in the age of fervent confessionalism. Alois Bendel, dean of the Wilhelmstift seminary in Tübingen, emphasized in 1852:

> Among the Protestants, the position of the sermon is shifted [the German word used here, *verrückt,* can mean "shifted" but also translates as "insane"] in that it is an essential and indeed the main component of the service. … In Protestant parishes it also has a positive basis in the Holy Scriptures …, but it takes on a thoroughly subjective character, depending on the opinion of the individual preacher, while Catholic sermons must always bear the stamp of the objective teaching of the Church. In Protestant sermons, objectivity plays second fiddle to subjectivity, just as, conversely, in Catholic sermons, the objectivity of ecclesiastical faith and life must dominate the subjectivity of the preacher. In relation to the mission, too, the Catholic preacher differs significantly from the Protestant. While the former can only be called and qualified for the ministry

through church consecration, the latter only needs a natural qualification. (Bendel 1852: 650)

Like other "sects" (for Bendel, Protestants belonged to sects that split from the mother church; Catholics labeled them "Protestant sects" until the 1960s), Protestant ordination is not comparable to the consecration by the Holy Spirit. Bendel sees an enormous difference between the two: The Catholic preacher speaks in the place of Christ and the church, the Protestant preacher, "on the other hand, preaches either on his own initiative or on behalf of a congregation and preaches only his faith or, in the highest case, the faith of his congregation. … But the true Christian ministry of preaching is only that which was transferred from Christ to the apostles and from them to his successors" (Bendel 1852: 650).

Probably, the relevance and effect of Protestant sermons was higher, though, because of their central position in the service, but this is difficult to verify empirically. On the other hand, we have indications that sermons played a role in the life of people. In a time without radio or television, sermons were often the only change during the week. The pastors, Catholic and Protestant, knew their flock and tried to get as close to their mentality as they could. They tried to appeal to their audiences' interests. The social and intellectual horizon of the parish influenced what the pastor told the people; sermons were the result of a reciprocal process. Thus, they do reflect some historical, social, and political tendencies.

To conclude, there are no ready-made answers to the three methodological questions. But the problems of quantification, representativeness, and relevance ought to make us very careful when interpreting sermons hermeneutically, even if we were to consider 1,000 sermons by 100 pastors. Sermons might—carefully—be used as a mirror for religious, social, and political attitudes at a given moment in history in a given region and situation. The pulpit paragraphs are another indicator that a certain power was attributed to sermons. Bearing in mind the problems of specific, individual sermons and the problems of quantification, representativeness and relevance, studying sermons can be quite fruitful.

Notes

1 Pietism refers to a reformist movement originating in seventeenth century Protestantism. The religious movement puts emphasis on individual piety and aims at renewing faith in the believer and the church.

2 Ultramontanism is a political catholic movement prevalent in the nineteenth and twentieth centuries. Ultramontanes strive for alignment between papal doctrines and local politics. The term was often pejoratively used: Political adversaries claimed ultramontanes lacked strong patriotic feelings as their frame of reference lies beyond the mountains (the Alps) in Rome.

3 This and all following Bible quotations are from the *New Oxford Annotated Bible* (2018).

References

Aubert, Robert (2003), *Catholic Social Teaching: An Historical Perspective*, ed. David A. Boileau, Milwaukee: Marquette University Press.

Bendel, Alois (1852), "Predigt," in Heinrich Joseph Wetzer and Benedikt Welte (eds.), *Kirchenlexikon oder Encyklopädie der katholischen Theologie und ihrer Hilfswissenschaften*, 8, 645–50 Freiburg im Breisgau: Herder.

Bergen, Doris L. (1996), *Twisted Cross: The German Christian Movement in the Third Reich*, Chapel Hill: University of North Carolina Press.

Berger, Frank (2020), *Das Geld der Dichter in Goethezeit und Romantik: 71 biografische Skizzen über Einkommen und Auskommen*, Wiesbaden: Waldemar Kramer.

Blaschke, Olaf (1999), *Katholizismus und Antisemitismus im Deutschen Kaiserreich*, 2nd ed., Göttingen: Vandenhoeck & Ruprecht.

Blaschke, Olaf (2000), "Das 19. Jahrhundert: Ein Zweites Konfessionelles Zeitalter?," *Geschichte und Gesellschaft*, 26: 38–75.

Blaschke, Olaf (ed.) (2002), *Konfessionen im Konflikt: Deutschland zwischen 1800 und 1970: Ein zweites konfessionelles Zeitalter*, Göttingen: Vandenhoeck & Ruprecht.

Blaschke, Olaf (2013), "Anti-Protestantism and Anti-Catholicism in the 19th Century: A Comparison," in Yvonne Maria Werner and Jonas Harvard (eds.), *European Anti-Catholicism in a Comparative and Transnational Perspective*, 115–34, Amsterdam: Brill Academic Pub.

Blaschke, Olaf (2014), *Die Kirchen und der Nationalsozialismus*, Stuttgart: Reclam.

Blaschke, Olaf (2021), "Franz Hitze (1851–1921). Der Sozialreformer als Repräsentant des katholischen Antisemitismus," *Westfälische Forschungen*, 171: 295–321.

Blaschke, Olaf, and Klaus Unterburger (2021), "Lorenz Jaeger, die Entnazifzierung und die 'sogenannten Kriegsverbrecher,'" in Nicole Priesching and Christian Kasprowski (eds.), *Lorenz Jaeger als Kirchenpolitiker*, 117–59, Paderborn: Brill Schöningh.

Borutta, Manuel (2010), *Antikatholizismus: Deutschland und Italien im Zeitalter der europäischen Kulturkämpfe*, Göttingen: Vandenhoeck & Ruprecht.

Braune-Krickau, Tobias, and Christoph Galle (eds.) (2021), *Predigt und Politik: Zur Kulturgeschichte der Predigt von Karl dem Großen bis zur Gegenwart*, Göttingen: Vandenhoeck & Ruprecht.

Dahm, Karl Wilhelm (1961), "Pfarrer, statistisch und soziologisch," in *Religion in Geschichte und Gegenwart*, 5, 3rd ed., 283–9, Tübingen: Mohr Siebeck.

Das Criminal-Gesetz–Buch für das Herzogthum Braunschweig: Nebst Motiven der Herzogl. Landesregierung und Erläuterungen aus ständischen Verhandlungen (1840), Braunschweig: Viehweg.

Dietrich, Tobias (2004), *Konfession im Dorf: Westeuropäische Erfahrungen im 19. Jahrhundert*, Köln: Böhlau.

Dittrich, Lisa (2014), *Antiklerikalismus in Europa: Öffentlichkeit und Säkularisierung in Frankreich, Spanien und Deutschland (1848–1914)*, Göttingen: Vandenhoeck & Ruprecht.

Eberle, Otto (1908), *Der Kanzelparagraph*, Heidelberg: J. Hörning.

Ehrler, Joseph (1873), *Das Kirchenjahr: Eine Reihe von Predigten über die vorzüglichsten Glaubenswahrheiten und Sittenlehren, gehalten an der Metropolitenkirche zu Unserer Lieben Frau in München*, 2nd year, Freiburg im Breisgau: Herder.

Ehrler, Joseph (1874), *Das Kirchenjahr: Eine Reihe von Predigten über die vorzüglichsten Glaubenswahrheiten und Sittenlehren, gehalten an der Metropolitenkirche zu unserer Lieben Frau in München*, Freiburg im Breisgau: Herder.

Forstner, Thomas (2014), *Priester in Zeiten des Umbruchs: Identität und Lebenswelt des katholischen Pfarrklerus in Oberbayern 1918 bis 1945*, Göttingen: Vandenhoeck & Ruprecht.

"Fring's sermons" (2012), in Ulrich Helbach (ed.), *Akten deutscher Bischöfe seit 1945: Westliche Besatzungszonen 1945–1947*, 2, Paderborn: Brill Schöningh.

Fuchs, Guido (2021), *Kleine Geschichte des schlechten Benehmens in der Kirche*, 2nd ed., Regensburg: Pustet.

Gauly, Thomas M. (1991), *Katholiken: Machtanspruch und Machtverlust*, 2nd ed., Bonn: Bouvier.

Götz von Olenhusen, Irmtraud (1994), *Klerus und abweichendes Verhalten: Zur Sozialgeschichte katholischer Priester im 19. Jahrhundert: die Erzdiözese Freiburg*, Göttingen: Vandenhoeck & Ruprecht.

Gross, Michael B. (2004), *The War against Catholics: Liberalism and the Anti-Catholic Imagination in Nineteenth-Century Germany*, Ann Arbor: University of Michigan Press.

Heinz, Andreas (1978), *Die sonn- und feiertägliche Pfarrmesse im Landkapitel Bitburg-Kyllburg der alten Erzdiözese Trier von der Mitte des 18. bis zur Mitte des 19. Jahrhunderts*, Trier: Paulinus.

Heubner, Heinrich Leonhard (1850), *Predigten über die sieben Sendschreiben Jesu Christi in der Offenbarung St. Johannis und das hohepriesterliche Gebet Joh. 17. nebst einigen Reformations- und Gedächtnispredigten*, 2nd ed., Berlin: Albert Gury's Verlag.

Hildmann, Philipp W. (2005), *Schreiben im zweiten konfessionellen Zeitalter: Jeremias Gotthelf (Albert Bitzius) und der Schweizer Katholizismus des 19. Jahrhunderts*, Tübingen: Narr-Franke-Attempto.

Hitze, Franz (1877), *Die sociale Frage und die Bestrebungen zu ihrer Lösung: Drei Vorträge*, Paderborn: Bonifatius Druckerei.

Hofacker, Ludwig (1842), *Predigten für alle Sonn-, Fest- und Feiertage nebst einigen Grabreden*, Stuttgart: Steinkopf.

Hölscher, Lucian (1990), "Die Religion des Bürgers. Bürgerliche Frömmigkeit und protestantische Kirche im 19. Jahrhundert," in *Historische Zeitschrift*, 250: 595–630.

Hölscher, Lucian (1995), "Secularization and Urbanization in the Nineteenth Century: An interpretative model," in Hugh McLeod (ed.), *European Religion in the Age of the Great Cities 1830–1930*, 263–88, London: Taylor and Francis.

Hölscher, Lucian (2001), *Datenatlas zur religiösen Geographie im protestantischen Deutschland von der Mitte des 19. Jahrhunderts bis zum Zweiten Weltkrieg*, Berlin/New York: de Gruyter.

Huber, Ernst Rudolf (1969), *Deutsche Verfassungsgeschichte seit 1789*, 4, Stuttgart: Kohlhammer.

Hufnagel, Carl Friedrich von (ed.) (1839), *Strafgesetzbuch für das Königreich Württemberg vom 1. März 1839 und die damit in Verbindung stehenden Gesetze, nebst erläuternden Bemerkungen*, Stuttgart: Metzler.

Jaeger, Lorenz (1944), "Löschet den Geist nicht aus," in *EBAP, Nachlass Jaeger*, 208/148.

Kern, Christian Gottlob (1837), *Predigten auf alle Sonn- und Festtage des Kirchenjahrs*, Stuttgart: Metzler'sche Buchhandlung.

Ketteler, Willhelm Emmanuel von (1849), *Die großen sozialen Fragen der Gegenwart: Sechs Predigten, gehalten im hohen Dome zu Mainz*, Mainz: Kirchheim und Schott.

Kißling, Johannes (1913), *Geschichte des Kulturkampfes im Deutschen Reiche*, 2, Freiburg im Breisgau: Herder.

Klöckener, Martin (2009), "Homiletik," in *Lexikon für Theologie und Kirche*, 5, 3rd ed., 246–8, Freiburg im Breisgau: Herder.

Kögel, Rudolf (1891), *Der Brief Pauli an die Römer in Predigten dargelegt: Ein homiletischer Versuch [1875]*, 3rd ed., Bremen: hansebooks.

Köster, Markus (1998), "'Betet für einen Guten Ausgang der Wahl!' Kirche und Parteien im Bistum Münster nach 1945," in Damian van Melis and Joachim Köhler (eds.), *Siegerin in Trümmern: Die Rolle der katholischen Kirche in der deutschen Nachkriegsgesellschaft*, 103–24, Stuttgart: Kohlhammer.

Krose, Heinrich A. (1909), *Kirchliches Handbuch für das katholische Deutschland*, 2, Freiburg im Breisgau: Herder.

Kuhlemann, Frank-Michael (2002), *Bürgerlichkeit und Religion: zur Sozial- und Mentalitätsgeschichte der evangelischen Pfarrer in Baden 1860–1914*, Göttingen: Vandenhoeck & Ruprecht.

Kuropka, Joachim (ed.) (2007), *Streitfall Galen: Clemens August Graf von Galen und der Nationalsozialismus: Studien und Dokumente*, Münster: Aschendorff.

Langer, Michael (1994), *Zwischen Vorurteil und Aggression: Zum Judenbild in der deutschsprachigen katholischen Volksbildung des 19. Jahrhunderts*, Freiburg im Breisgau: Herder.

Lentzen-Deis, Wolfgang (2000), "Unterweisung und Unterricht," in Martin Persch and Bernhard Schneider (eds.), *Geschichte des Bistums Trier*, 4, 371–90, Trier: Paulinus.

Meyer, Dietrich (2000), "Das Neben-, Mit- und Gegeneinander verschiedener Konfessionen: Protestantismus und Deutschkatholizismus im 19. Jahrhundert im Raum des Bistums Trier," in Martin Persch and Bernhard Schneider (eds.), *Geschichte des Bistums Trier*, 4, 415–31, Trier: Paulinus.

New Oxford Annotated Bible (2018), New Revised Standard Version, ed. Michael D. Coogan, Marc Z. Bettler, Carol A. Newsom, and Theme Perkins, 5th ed., Oxford: Oxford University Press.

Pelz, Birge-Dorothea (2018), *Revolution auf der Kanzel: Politischer Gehalt und theologische Geschichtsdeutung in evangelischen Predigten während der deutschen Vereinigung 1989/90*, Göttingen: Vandenhoeck & Ruprecht.

"Predigt und Politik: Eine Kulturgeschichte in zwölf Vorträgen von Karl dem Großen bis zur Gegenwart," *H-Soz-Kult*, 08.01.2018. Available online: www.hsozkult.de/event/id/event-85832 (accessed September 12, 2022).

Ross, Donald J. (1998), *The Failure of Bismarck's Kulturkampf: Catholicism and State Power in Imperial Germany, 1871–1887*, Washington, DC: Catholic University of America Press.

Schnabel, Franz (1987 [1937]), *Deutsche Geschichte im neunzehnten Jahrhundert*, 4, München: Deutscher Taschenbuchverlang.

Schneider, Bernhard (1998), *Katholiken auf die Barrikaden? Europäische Revolutionen und deutsche katholische Presse 1815–1848*, Paderborn: Brill Schöningh.

Schneider, Bernhard (2017), "Gottes Ordnung und der Menschen Werk in Zeiten der Massenarmut: Armutsdeutungen und Armenfürsorgepraktiken im katholischen Deutschland zwischen 1800 und 1850," in Andreas Holzem (ed.). *Wenn der Hunger droht: Bewältigung und religiöse Deutung (1400–1980)*, 117–65, Tübingen: Mohr-Siebeck.

Schneyer, Johannes (1969), *Geschichte der katholischen Predigt*, Freiburg im Breisgau: Seelsorge-Verlag.

Scholle, Manfred (1974), *Die preußische Strafjustiz im Kulturkampf 1873–1880*, Marburg: Elwert.

Schorn-Schütte, Luise (2021), *Predigten über Herrschaft: Ordnungsmuster des Politischen in lutherischen Predigten Thüringens/Sachsens im 16. und 17. Jahrhundert*, Stuttgart: Franz Steiner.

"Sermon by Galen, Coesfeld, 10. 6. 1935 (1988)," in Peter Löffler (ed.), *Bischof Clemens August Graf von Galen: Akten, Briefe und Predigten 1933–1946*, 1, 232–6, Mainz: Matthias-Grünewald-Verlag.

"Sermon by Galen, Telgte, 01. 06. 1945 (1988)," in Peter Löffler (ed.), *Bischof Clemens August Graf von Galen: Akten, Briefe und Predigten 1933–1946*, 2, 1172–7, Mainz: Matthias-Grünewald-Verlag.

Sickinger, C. (1885), "Fest des hl. Stephanus: Das falsche Zeugnis gegen die Kirche," in G. M. Schuler (ed.), *Kanzelstimmen: Predigtcyclus auf alle Sonn und Feiertage des Kirchenjahres*, 7, 62–6, Würzburg: Bucher.

"Skizzierte Predigt von einem Priester aus Tirol: Die Fahrt des Herrn auf stürmischem Meere" (1873), in Ludwig Mehler and Johann Evangelist Zollner (eds.), *Der Prediger und Katechet: Eine praktische, katholische Monatsschrift, besonders für Prediger und Katecheten auf dem Lande und in kleineren Städten*, 23, 99–102, Regensburg: G.J. Manz.

Teuteberg, Hans-Jürgen (1990), "Moderne Verstädterung und kirchliches Leben in Berlin: Forschungsergebnisse und Forschungsprobleme," in Kaspar Elm and Hans-Dieter Loock (eds.), *Seelsorge und Diakonie in Berlin: Beiträge zum Verhältnis von Kirche und Großstadt im 19. und 20. Jahrhundert*, 161–200, Berlin/New York: de Gruyter.

Wichern, Johann Hinrich (2014), *Johann Hinrich Wichern, Ausgewählte Predigten*, ed. Volker Herrmann and Gerhard K. Schäfer, Leipzig: Evangelische Verlagsanstalt.

Wintzer, Friedrich (1990), "Evangelische Predigt seit dem ersten Drittel des 19. Jahrhunderts," in Kaspar Elm and Hans-Dietrich Loock (eds.), *Seelsorge und Diakonie in Berlin: Beiträge zum Verhältnis von Kirche und Großstadt im 19. und 20. Jahrhundert*, 293–306, Berlin/New York: de Gruyter.

Wolfes, Matthias (2004), *Öffentlichkeit und Bürgergesellschaft: Friedrich Schleiermachers politische Wirksamkeit*, Berlin/New York: de Gruyter.

Ziegler, Joseph (1873), "II. Fastenpredigt: Verlust der wahren Erkenntnis," in Ludwig Mehler and Johann Evangelist Zollner (eds.), *Der Prediger und Katechet: Eine praktische, katholische Monatsschrift, besonders für Prediger und Katecheten auf dem Lande und in kleineren Städten*, 23, 86–92, Regensburg: G.J. Manz.

2

The Struggle for Hope Continues: The Christmas Sermons of Archbishop Thabo Makgoba, 2009–19

Cas Wepener and Marileen Steyn

Introduction

There are a number of famous Christian pulpits globally, for example, the one in the Riverside Church in New York and Martin Luther's pulpit in Wittenberg. When one shifts the focus to the continent of Africa, there are thriving African Independent and neo-Pentecostal churches such as Action Chapel in Ghana, or Moria, the headquarters of the Zion Christian Church in South Africa. These newer churches are thriving across Africa as well as in South Africa, and the older mainline churches are in serious decline. Nevertheless, we are convinced that to this day the most famous and still very active pulpit in South Africa is the one in St. George's Cathedral in Cape Town.[1]

St. George's Anglican Cathedral is the seat of the Anglican archbishop, and the pulpit was made famous by Emeritus Archbishop Desmond Tutu. To some extent, it has come to be known as a pulpit of struggle, seeking to understand the context of South Africa (and the world) in the light of the good news and the implications thereof for the everyday struggles of South Africans. And even though the Anglican Church in Southern Africa is relatively small compared to the nascent Christian traditions, that pulpit and the sermons of the current archbishop, Thabo Makgoba, exert much influence in the country.

A particularly famous and popular sermon preached annually from that pulpit by Archbishop Makgoba is the Christmas sermon delivered during the Midnight Mass on Christmas Eve. The people attending the service hear it, but in the days that follow, it is also published in full length in newspapers,[2] referred to in columns and articles,[3] uploaded onto the internet,[4] and becomes a centerpiece of many conversations, not just among Anglicans.

On the one hand, it was the popularity and the weight of the homiletical tradition that come with it that served as strong incentives for us to choose the preaching of Makgoba as a subject for this chapter. Despite these factors, there was also something else that struck us and made us curious about the relation between these sermons and the South African and global social contexts.

On December 24, 2019, Archbishop Makgoba acknowledged in his Christmas sermon the feeling of distress and discontent among many South Africans. Regarding 2020, he said: "Here in South Africa we hope it is the year of the orange jump suits, a year of reckoning." These words made a clear allusion to the upcoming trials of people in high positions (including the former president Jacob Zuma) regarding alleged corruption and state capture. The trials have come to form a climax of sorts following a decade of growing unrest, dissatisfaction, and concern among many South Africans, as this article will soon indicate in more detail. Therefore, as we read this in a newspaper, we immediately wondered: What was his message a decade ago and how did this message change during this extremely tumultuous time in South Africa?

Looking at his sermon of 2009, we were first struck by the difference in terms of Archbishop Makgoba's reference to the context within which he was preaching, focusing on global challenges such as the credit crunch and climate change. In this sermon, he encouraged people to use the gift of Jesus toward personal transformation, to communicate Christian values and to change their world. Not only did the content of the two sermons differ vastly, but the 2009 sermon was also written in a completely different tenor than the 2019 sermon. Aside from the different foci and functions of the two sermons, the 2019 sermon (unlike that of 2009) also had a sense of urgency, akin to a latent holy anger undergirding the performance and presentation of the sermon's content.

Thus, the difference between the two sermons were, to our minds, stark. Where the 2019 sermon was deeply rooted in a specific context that could only be preached in Cape Town, the 2009 sermon could fit into any context and could have also been preached in Canberra, Cairo, or Cologne. Where the 2019 sermon made specific calls to action, the 2009 message spoke of general Christian values. This is exactly when the question we address in this chapter arose: What is the relationship between Archbishop Thabo Makgoba's Christmas sermons and the South African social dynamics of the past decade (2009 to 2019)?

In this chapter we thus explore a decade of Christmas sermons preached from the pulpit made famous by Bishop Desmond Tutu, but preached in a completely different context to that of Bishop Tutu. We will do this by looking at the content of the sermons, in addition to (and importantly) connecting it to the performance of these sermons on Christmas Eve. We continue with a word on context, theory, and method.

Context, Theory, and Method

To contextually situate Archbishop Makgoba's sermons, it is necessary to keep a larger transitional period in South Africa in view. During the 1990s and especially after the first democratic elections and democracy that came in 1994, scholars referred to South African society as being in a transitional state and as such in liminality (Burger 1995; Hay 1997; Wepener 2009). Various scholars made use of the insights of Victor Turner, especially his early work, and his theory and field work regarding the so-called Social Drama[5] and rites of passage, in attempts to explain some of the social dynamics of this period.

South Africa as a nation and many institutions in South Africa, such as faith communities, were after 1994 no longer in a state of *societas* characterized by apartheid, but entered a *communitas* period characterized by liminality. South Africa of that era has not yet entered a new *societas* that comes into existence after the Social Drama occurred (cf. Turner 1969, 1972: 390–412, 1996: 511–19, as well as Arbuckle 1991). The fact that a society has experienced the process of a Social Drama means that relationships, social life, and in fact that whole society cannot be the same as they were before the breach (Hay 1997).

The insight that South Africa and South Africans were in liminality was very helpful in 1994 and a decade afterward, but we are not convinced that it is a comprehensive explanation of where the South African society finds itself by 2021. Nor is it helpful in understanding the social dynamics that existed over the past decade in South Africa and in the time of Archbishop Makgoba's Christmas sermons. Liminality entails being betwixt and between and in a space where new identities are acquired in a *communitas* period, a period during which old and fixed positions of the *societas* before 1994 are no longer in place and a new *societas* is awaited. This is not where we will situate the South Africa of the past decade in Turner's scheme.

With reference to Victor Turner's theory, we are of the opinion that South Africa has already begun to enter a new *societas* and is busy figuring out the new roles and structure of positions within this new *societas* (cf. Wepener 2012: 293–307, 2015: 1–8).[6] In biblical terms, and with reference to the Exodus narrative, South Africa is no longer in the slavery of apartheid, nor in the desert of a transitional period, but has crossed the Jordan, entered a promised land and must now actively give shape to something new. However, the first years of a new *societas* are a very challenging time. Therefore, we highlight in this regard a few characteristics of South African society over the past decade which form part of the canvas against which Archbishop Makgoba's sermons should be viewed.

Apartheid belongs to the past. However, according to the South African Reconciliation Barometer (SARB)[7] of the past decade, there have been serious shifts regarding people's attitudes toward reconciliation. During the first polls of the SARB in 2003 and thereafter, the emphasis was on unity and nation-building, whereas the debate shifted in recent years to radical economic transformation and spatial justice. There is also the remaining issue of the nonengagement of many white South Africans in the reconciliation process, a serious decline in trust in leadership, and a persistent view among some that apartheid was not a crime.

According to the SARB, the country was seen as vulnerable in the face of violence, unstable economic circumstances, xenophobic attacks, and violent service delivery protests between the years of 2008 and 2017. The death of Nelson Mandela in 2013 was experienced by many as a call to action regarding reconciliation and justice. In addition, the SARB's findings showed that the only two institutions trusted to facilitate honest dialogue regarding reconciliation in this time are the public media and faith communities (cf. Van der Merwe 2019).[8]

The SARB captured important challenges regarding the South African context of 2009 to 2019. However, we will augment it with aspects that are important in order to situate Archbishop Makgoba's sermons. On an economic level, the country was and is facing many challenges, including inequality, poverty, and unemployment (cf. Pieterse 2001; The South African Economic Reconstruction and Recovery Plan 2020: 5). The news headlines between 2009 and 2019 were dominated by societal issues such as state capture, corruption, crime, mounting anger, and several student movements that included a call for the decolonization of the curriculum at tertiary institutions (cf. Wepener 2015).

This is in brief the social context in which these sermons were preached, a time in which a country was searching for a new *societas* while being plagued by various challenges. In the course of the decade under discussion, certain challenges were more prominent in some years than in others. The details will be highlighted as we discuss the content of the sermons. In summary, the decade saw mounting unhappiness under the leadership of former president Jacob Zuma (in office 2009–18), a surge of hope in 2018 when Cyril Ramaphosa became president, and soon afterward a renewed unhappiness, but with a different emphasis.

For the purpose of this chapter, we find the later work of Victor Turner, in addition to his earlier work, especially helpful, specifically texts in which he revisited liminality and Social Drama (Turner 1979, 1982, 1986). In this phase of his career, he integrated the insights gained from Social Drama and Aesthetic Drama (cf. Schechner 1986: 7), while concepts such as the quotidian, performance, liminoid, public liminality, and plural reflexivity became core to his thinking. We will return to Turner's work in the conclusion and will now briefly focus on method.

After collecting the sermons, we conducted two independent first readings of the Christmas sermons preached from 2009 to 2019. There were thus eleven transcribed sermons in total.[9] In both researchers' preliminary analyses, there were, broadly speaking, three clear lines distinguishable. First, that the sermons were situated in very specific South African, African and global contexts that are described in the sermons and sometimes explicitly named. Second, all the sermons contain what can be described as a theological indicative and third, also an imperative that builds on this indicative. This indicative and imperative entails an incarnational theology in line with the liturgical context of Christmas, the lectionary texts, and the ethical implications of that theology.[10] However, it is important to note that what is not to be found in the transcribed texts, but in the liturgical context and the preaching performance of the sermons, is how Archbishop Makgoba's performance of the sermons in the context of Christmas frames the indicative and imperative in the subjunctive. This is a fourth line to which we will return.

As we read through the sermons, we initially used coding to analyze their content, with the intention of using Grounded Theory, a form of content analysis, as our methodology. However, from our experience in Grounded Theory (Pieterse and Wepener 2018; Steyn 2016, 2019; Steyn, Wepener, and Pieterse 2020), we soon realized that Grounded Theory would not be the appropriate methodology, as it would not indicate the development of the sermons over the course of the decade as desired. The focus in Grounded Theory is on theory generation, rather than on comparing content from individual pieces of content. We thus chose a method through which we could identify themes and compare the themes with the specific context in which they were preached and as such performed by the preacher.

Mayring (2000) points out that content analysis can target two levels of content: it can focus on primary content, the content and themes as they appear in the text (as is the case in Grounded Theory), or on latent content, the context of the text. Content analysis that focuses on latent content applies theories in order to analyze and understand data (Kleinheksel et al. 2020). It is a form of analysis in which the hands of the researchers are more clearly visible as they sift through the text using certain lenses. Following our preliminary analyses, we examined the (latent) content according to the three lines set out above. Keeping in mind the theory of Long (2004: 108–16), we identified the context and formulated the focus and function statement of each sermon and systemized it into a table. We thus first asked what the sermon was about in broad terms, what the core message or theme of the sermon was (focus), and second, what the sermon wanted to do or accomplish in the hearers (function).

It was important to identify the function in addition to the focus, as these sermons are public performances within the context of St. George's cathedral, but also within South African society at large as it is broadcasted and posted on social media. These focus and function statements were used as the basis for a summary of the core themes and intentions of these sermons.

In the next section we turn to the sermons analyzed, which we will present in a chronological and narrative style, spanning the decade. We start each year with a brief description of the main contextual national and international events that are important to keep in mind in order to situate the sermon. Thereafter, we explore only some of the themes that surfaced in the sermon that year in an exemplary manner to show the development that occurred in Archbishop Makgoba's preaching over the course of this decade. The complete sermons are available on the internet.

The Struggle for Hope Continues

Year 2009: A Vague Beginning

At the outset of 2009, Kgalema Motlanthe, who replaced Thabo Mbeki, was the president of the ruling African National Congress (ANC). In April 2009 the ANC won the general elections and in May 2009 Jacob Zuma was appointed president. As was the case before 2009, there were protests in the country pertaining to a variety of issues, but specifically also regarding poor living conditions in townships. Simultaneously, there was mounting national excitement regarding the hosting of the FIFA Soccer World Cup in 2010 in South Africa.

On Christmas Eve in 2009, the focus of Archbishop Makgoba's is as follows: God, as the source of hope, is with the hearers; God steps in amid their darkness and thereby dispels fear and moves them to action. The function of his sermon is to comfort hearers amid challenges and inspire them toward personal and societal transformation. As an example of this, we quote: "Jesus stands with us, and we can put our hands in his. He will be with us, through thick and thin—a listening ear, a shoulder to cry on, a source of strength, a voice of encouragement. This is why we call him Emmanuel—'God with us.'"[11]

Latent in this first sermon is the combination of incarnation and hope, where hearers were called on to display Jesus's presence in their lives and contribute toward solving ecological issues, the prevention of HIV/AIDS, and ethical living. The sermon promoted a link between incarnation and ethical living. When this happens, namely when the hearers start to live from the incarnation, they become agents of hope. This combination of incarnation and ethics remain the basis for all the sermons to follow, but here the implications were still rather vague. In other words, there were not yet many clues regarding what exactly hope as a lived reality entails in the life of the hearers, even though the link between faith and ethical living was suggested. The concluding sentence of this sermon captures the content and atmosphere of the entire sermon well: "So, tonight, come and receive the greatest gift, the most valuable treasure of all—Jesus himself—and let yourselves be transformed by him, to share his treasure with the world."[12]

Year 2010: An Incarnation with Seemingly Few Ethical Implications

In 2010, South Africa hosted the FIFA Soccer World Cup, which created a very vibrant atmosphere, while civil servants staged nation-wide strikes. However, some opine that the year was the best of the decade, with very few issues of significance surfacing (McNamee 2019; Pather 2019).

Despite the overall positive tone of the year, Archbishop Makgoba's sermon of 2010 is one of consolation. The focus is that Jesus is God's greatest gift, which in this sermon means that the hearers do not have to be afraid as they follow God's call to discipleship. The function is to comfort hearers that God would meet them, and encourage them to trust God and move toward discipleship.

The essence of the sermon is roughly the same as the one from the previous year and, compared to the sermons that follow, these first sermons were rather short. One development from the previous year was that the preacher, along with elections in Sudan, named an issue concerning human dignity that is more contextually bound to South Africa. He said: "Jesus will meet the people of Makhaza, as they seek dignity, health, safety through the toilet saga." In his book, Makgoba writes on the topic: "In Makhaza, a flashpoint was created when toilets were installed without any walls or doors giving their users no privacy," and explains how he, because of his activism in this regard, was named "the toilet archbishop" (Makgoba 2017: 136). What is noticeable is that the hearers were not placed between the incarnation and ethics, but Jesus himself is said to meet the people in need. This accent changed in the sermons that followed, and the emphasis on the hearers as agents of hope became all the more prevalent.

Year 2011: The Ethical Implication Becomes Clearer

During 2011, the ANC youth leader Julius Malema was suspended by his party for bringing the ANC into disrepute. During the local elections, the official opposition, the Democratic Alliance (DA), doubled its share of the votes.

The focus of 2011 is that God helps the hearers to grow into a mature faith and full potential by being "God with us" through God's love for the hearers. The function is to encourage hearers toward mature faith that trusts God and that moves beyond worship toward deeds.

Once again, the theme is incarnational theology that impacts ethical living. However, this time, there is a stronger call upon the hearers to act ethically. We quote from this sermon: "It takes guts to commit ourselves to saying the right thing, doing the right thing—especially in a world where it is seen as clever to be bending the rules, cutting corners, telling white lies, jumping the queue—everything short of being found out."[13] Compared to the 2010 sermon, it is noticeable that no specific issues are named, and with regard to ethical living there is a general reference to corruption. However, the hearers themselves are called upon to take a stance. This is a development regarding the theology of hope embedded in all the Christmas sermons we analyzed.

Year 2012: More Contextual, More Direct

In the year 2012, there were several challenging events in the country that Makgoba also references in his sermon. Examples include strikes by Western Cape farm workers, and the Marikana mass shooting in which thirty-four workers at a platinum mine in Marikana, North West Province of South Africa, were killed by police firing on them, leaving seventy-eight more injured and more than two hundred miners arrested. In addition, the Limpopo textbook saga involved the non-delivery of textbooks for the first six months of the school year to schools in the province of Limpopo. Amidst these challenges, Jacob Zuma was once more elected president of the ruling ANC party.

In 2012, the focus is that God "is with us" and therefore Christmas announces a new beginning in the face of a dire need for change in society. The function is to inspire hearers to let God's love be channeled through them and to be agents of change and a new beginning through prayer.

Once again, ethical action is embedded in an incarnational theology. However, the hearers now have a much clearer picture regarding the implications of this theology and their own roles in that regard. The preacher says: "2012 has been a hard year, in many ways—we can look back on the Limpopo textbook fiasco; the Marikana shootings; the Cape farm workers' strikes." The preacher continues to name issues elsewhere on the continent of Africa and the rest of the world and continues: "President Zuma may have been re-elected President of the ANC—but we say to our politicians and all in positions of leadership and influence, it cannot be 'business as usual'. There has to be a greater urgency, a deeper commitment, to doing more and doing it better." Later he continues, "so that we too may be channels of love and peace in God's world."[14]

There is a more articulate naming of where the need is in the country and the world. The preacher is becoming more explicit in naming issues and even persons in his Christmas sermon. This is also the first Christmas sermon under discussion in which the archbishop specifically addresses the country's leadership. The general tone regarding ethical involvement still has a pastoral and comforting tone, as in the previous years. This tone changed in the successive years.

Year 2013: Gaining Momentum

President Jacob Zuma was criticized in 2013 by the anti-corruption ombudsman regarding a 20 million Rand upgrade to his private home in Nkandla, KwaZulu-Natal Province, South Africa. The strikes by Western Cape farm workers continued. In December 2013 former president Nelson Mandela died at the age of ninety-five.

The focus in December 2013 is that God would intervene and is not aloof amid people's plight and fear. The function is to comfort the hearers in times of fear and inspire them to demand justice and living the justice through proclamation, and the asking of questions toward social transformation.

The general Christmas theme based on the lectionary texts continues, but it is more to the point and the urgency is telling. This time, ethical living grounded in incarnation theology sounds as follows:

> God declares, in the company of his heavenly host that he has seen in our world religion being politicised and the persecution of Christians globally escalated; He has smelt the rot and pain of inequality in our midst and the resultant humiliation and exclusion of many from the economic order in his world of plenty; God declares that he has sensed our anxiety and fear, our shame and disgrace when we cannot afford a maternity ward and have to give birth in a shack or a taxi after being sent off home from a local clinic; God puts his feelings on his sleeve and opens up his heart, and his heart is as heavy and broken as are ours by our personal struggles and the global systemic problems of this mortal life. God sends us his heavenly host to call us back from our straying away from what creation was intended to be; to unveil a road back home.[15]

If Archbishop Makgoba's decade of Christmas sermons is to be compared to a race, then here, in 2013, halfway into the decade under discussion, the preacher is gaining momentum. The incarnation theology in his sermons is no longer framed in the language of Jesus as gift, but incarnation entails Jesus's incarnation into the deepest needs of the world. And this incarnation demands solidarity from the hearers with those in need. The implication of incarnation for the ethical living of the hearers is becoming clearer, as is the suggestion that the link between incarnation and ethics entails hope.

Year 2014: A Wider Audience, an Act of Courage

In 2014, the ANC won the South African general elections, thereby introducing President Jacob Zuma's second term in office. In addition, talk about so-called state capture and government corruption became more prevalent in newspapers. The most significant being the final report by Public Protector Thuli Madonsela on the 246 million Rand owed to the South African public following the upgrade to President Zuma's private residence. Eskom introduced "load shedding" (scheduled power outages) for the second time and introduced stage 3 as the highest level of load shedding.

The focus of the archbishop's 2014 sermon is that Christmas brings hope that calls the hearers to see light in the darkness, and confront wrong through courage, knowing that God has already triumphed. The function of this sermon is to motivate hearers to have courage toward a new struggle in order for South Africa to become a "we-society."

Contextually the preacher especially focuses on leadership issues and in particular leadership that brings hope. Hope in this sermon is understood as having a vision and the courage to turn the vision into reality. From this Christmas sermon in 2014, it is also clear that the preacher is by this time very aware of the fact that his hearers are not only the Anglicans sitting in front of him in the pews of St. George's cathedral. He shows awareness that he is concerned with a very public act and that he is also addressing South African politicians.

The thematic analysis of this sermon shows that as the preacher is performing in that pulpit, he is defying the powers and speaking fearlessly against issues of corruption. The analysis and interpretation of these sermons will thus, to our minds, be incomplete if the public performance of the sermons is not also taken into account. During this sermon, he exclaims: "Only light will enable to [sic] us to be repulsed enough by what we see around us to say, 'My children and grandchildren deserve better.' Only by being pro-courage can we really be anti-corruption. We truly begin living when we say, 'Enough is enough and I want more for my family, my community and my country!' "[16] The sermon becomes an act in which what is called for (courage grounded in the hope that comes from the incarnation) is demonstrated in the pulpit by a preacher who engages the powers by means of his sermon.

Year 2015: Pertinent about the Present, Introducing Social Imagery

In 2015 there was once more a spate of xenophobic attacks across South Africa. Government officials also received allegations of bribery to secure the FIFA World Cup bid and criticism for allowing Omar al-Bashir, former president of Sudan, into the country despite a warrant for his arrest by the International Criminal Court. Across South Africa, student movements calling for free education and the decolonization of curricula were in full swing. Thousands marched in protest, asking for the removal of President Jacob Zuma.

The archbishop's sermon of 2015 focuses on the assertion that God comforts hearers with God's presence and rejoices in their responses to the cries of the world. The function is to encourage hearers to hold onto the belief that challenges can be overcome and to get involved in the New Struggle,[17] thereby creating hope through love.

The tendency of the preacher to name issues that should be addressed continues in this sermon, but it now becomes even more articulate. He says, for example: "Growing, deepening discontent is palpable in South Africa, a discontent that is causing even the most beautiful of days to be invaded by the pervasive smell of the rot which is being spread by the moral pollution of our public life." He also states: "The sheer recklessness of the firing of Nhlanhla Nene,[18] the failure to consider the needs of the nation, and particularly the needs of the poor, was staggering."[19]

Theologically, the preacher continues to connect incarnation and ethical living, but in this particular sermon he takes it a step further and begins to provide solutions. So, for example, he says: "We need to build strong systems and institutions which cannot be undermined by one party or person's whim," also later in the sermon, "Join together, organise, lobby and embark on what I call the New Struggle, the struggle to ensure that the sacrifices that so many made for our liberation are not wasted, the struggle against greed, corruption and nepotism, the struggle for true justice, including economic justice, and the peace from God that flows from justice." A final example of the content of this sermon toward its end is: "This Christmas, let us recognise that if we are to be signs of the new dawning Kingdom, it will involve a journey away from all that blinds us to the suffering and misery of others, from inherited forms of privilege and wealth, and from a world view that is comfortable with excluding from the resources of the world the other who is different to us."[20]

In 2015 the preacher not only continues to name the issues in South Africa that hearers must respond to by means of ethical living and action, he also paints the first outlines of what is possible. A kind of social imagery begins to take shape in this sermon. This is a new development in his Christmas sermons.

Year 2016: A Homiletical Crescendo, Explicit Conflict

In 2016, the supreme court ruled that President Jacob Zuma violated the constitution by not repaying public money after improving his private residence. President Zuma told the churches to stay out of politics and pray for the leadership instead. The student movements continued at all universities across the country.

The 2016 sermon's focus is that, amid fear and troubled circumstances, God is still with the hearers, and that God's preferred terrain of work is in the margins and in brokenness. The function is twofold and aimed at two audiences. First, it is directed at the hearers in general to dispel fear and encourage actions promoting God's will, including lamenting injustice and being in solidarity with those suffering. Second, the function is to inform President Zuma that his call for the church to stay out of politics in the course of 2016 would be ignored. Noticeably, this is the first Christmas sermon in which there is explicit conflict with the leadership of the nation.

Christmas Eve of 2016 in St. George's Cathedral in Cape Town was no silent night where everything was calm and bright, in the words of the famous Christmas carol "Silent Night." Although the preacher calmly began by connecting the brokenness of the incarnation with the miracles that often happen amid brokenness, he swiftly moved from the brokenness of the stable in Bethlehem to a broken South African society, exclaiming that South African communities yearn for hope and courage from leaders. The incarnation, according to the 2016 sermon, compels all hearers to live in solidarity with those on the periphery of society and those who are suffering most. This sermon is significantly longer than the first sermons from this decade and the preacher also asks questions such as, "People of faith need to begin asking: At what stage do we, as churches, as mosques, as synagogues, withdraw our moral support for a democratically-elected government?"[21] and "When do we name the gluttony, the inability to control the pursuit of excess? When do we name the fraudsters, who are unable to control their insatiable appetite for obscene wealth, accumulated at the expense of the poorest of the poor?"[22]

There is a homiletical crescendo that can be detected in the foci and functions of the sermons from 2009 to 2016 in which the implications of the theology of incarnation for ethical living are more and more fleshed out in the sermons. Incarnation flows over into ethics concretely in the behavior and conduct of the hearers so that ethical living makes hope concrete in the South African society. The indicative in the sermons thus remains the incarnation, but the imperative that is elicited by the specific indicative becomes more apparent. The possibility for hope is thus created through the sermons in the twofold way of naming the issues, but also imagining the possibilities of addressing them. The new line of imagining that started in 2015 is thus continued in concrete ways in the preaching of 2016.

Year 2017: Rising Conflict, Clearer Vision

Controversially, President Jacob Zuma dismissed finance minister Pravin Gordhan, and the credit rating of the country was cut to so-called junk status. The pressure of state capture and corruption by the president and several government officials also mounted. The president survived his eighth motion of no confidence while marches asking for his removal resurged.

In the Christmas sermon of 2017, the focus is again that God is with those suffering in the margins, conquering oppression and injustice, and bringing hope to the personal and social lives of hearers. Once more, the function is for two audiences, namely, to motivate hearers to dream, name, and get involved in the fight against injustice, and to ask Cyril Ramaphosa to take action and cut the umbilical cord with President Jacob Zuma.

A similar line to that of the 2016 sermon is followed in this sermon. The call to care for marginalized people continues, but there is also a demand that President Zuma should be replaced as president of South Africa and that a cabinet reshuffle is needed. The preacher calls for a new vision, namely that hearers and leaders should dare to see their country through the eyes of the poor, and, unlike the three wise men, to look for God in places of power. He calls on all hearers to dream, but also to realize their dreams. We quote from the sermon:

> After our liberation, too many of us folded our arms and waited for the government to fulfil our dreams. We didn't take lessons from other democracies; we didn't realise that good governments are there to create the environment in which we are guaranteed equality of opportunity, guaranteed the space in which we can get our hands dirty, do things for ourselves.[23]

The theological line of combining incarnation and ethics, in which the preacher hermeneutically links the lectionary texts and the changing South African context, is continued, but what is needed, the dream or social imagery and how it can be accomplished, is made much more concrete in this sermon.

Year 2018: A Sigh of Relief

The Zondo commission inquiring into allegations of corruption and state capture was formed. Jacob Zuma resigned under pressure over corruption charges and Cyril Ramaphosa was chosen as his successor. Gender-based violence was also an ongoing issue in the country.

That God's vision of hope lies with the marginalized and the spirituality of Christmas empowers believers; this is the twofold focus of the sermon of Christmas 2018. The function is to motivate hearers to help root out corruption and examine their own behavior, especially regarding the levels of aggression in the country.

Even though the theology and theme of the sermon is in direct continuity with the previous Christmas sermons, the tone is completely different in 2018. The preacher says that he senses "a renewed energy in our country." In the light of the change in presidency, the preacher continues: "This Christmas, I believe we're about to re-enter a new age, an era where we define the new South Africa. So tonight, thankfully, I don't feel compelled to spend as much time as at past Christmases speaking about the need for our leaders to become more enlightened, more illuminated and more conscious about our country's social and economic crises."[24]

Archbishop Makgoba continues to encourage hearers, specifically to work toward achieving outcomes not by means of violence. The tone of the sermon is captured in these words: "Tonight I want to focus on the biblical themes of hope and light facing us, and somewhat less on the challenges of darkness and sin. It's a time for us as South Africans to speak about finding our cultural confidence, a time for us to remember our national values and mostly, a time to begin trusting again." Violence is named as a problem, but now there is a much stronger focus on possibility. The homiletical crescendo that has been mentioned before was interrupted in 2018 with a sermon in a completely different register that to a certain extent sounded like a sigh of relief.

Year 2019: Disappointment, yet Hope

Cyril Ramaphosa was president of South Africa and the Zondo Commission of Inquiry looked at cases of state capture and corruption that occurred. Xenophobic riots resurged. Large-scale protests against gender-based violence took place. South Africa won the Rugby World Cup. Eskom power outages were escalated to level 6—a first in the history in South Africa.

The focus of the last of the eleven sermons to be discussed here is that challenges are recognized, but not accepted, and that naming problems and differences and mobilizing people to overcome them are acts of hope. The function is to inspire leaders and hearers to take matters into their own hands and reflect God's hope in their personal and communal lives by demanding justice.

The sermon of 2018 makes it sound as if the tide was turning, with a new dawn inaugurated by the change in political leadership in South Africa. However, in 2019 the theological-ethical line from before 2018 is continued. In general, the Christmas sermon of 2019 exudes disappointment. The preacher starts out by calling 2019 "a difficult year for South Africans," and stating that "a dark cloud is hanging over us."[25] He then continues, adding that there is still hope, but that hope has to do with naming, with mobilizing, and with acting in order to overcome challenges. In this last sermon of the decade, the preacher is critical of the leaders of government who, according to him, have not gotten their act together in the two years they were given.

The following expression from this sermon has since become quite famous in South Africa and we quote it again, this time more extensively: "Here in South Africa, we hope it is 'the year of the orange jump-suit', a year of reckoning for those whose greed has driven the country to the brink of disaster. On this night, of all nights, I don't want to appear vindictive. Nor do I want to join the ranks of those who would put undue pressure on prosecutors to rush their work." He goes on to say:

> Botched prosecutions and widespread acquittals would be a disaster, sending the wrong signals to the corrupt and plunging the country into despair. But there must be consequences for corruption, both for those in the private sector who facilitate it and those in the public sector who take advantage of it. The justice, the peace, the reconciliation and the abundant life which a flourishing democracy promises will be achieved only if those who threaten to subvert it are held accountable. So I pray that our hope is not misplaced.[26]

After these relatively harsh words, he continues to sketch possibilities, such as having courageous conversations in South Africa and creating new global economic frameworks that could transform the market economy to become more equitable and less exploitative. At this point, Archbishop Makgoba's Christmas sermons reach a certain theological maturity. This may also be the homiletical line that will continue in the years to come, namely that the ethical conduct of all his hearers, from those in the pews to those in parliament, should be grounded in the incarnation, which entails that God is in solidarity with the poor and marginalized, and which requires a combination of continuously naming what is wrong and imagining what is possible. According to the sermons we analyzed, lives that embody this are hope incarnated.

Conclusion

In the course of just over a decade, Archbishop Makgoba developed a theology of hope in his Christmas sermons. This development can be seen most clearly when looking at excerpts from 2009, 2014, and 2019, each of which work with the themes of darkness versus light, hope, and the ethical implications for people.

Year 2009: Hope Incarnated: God Who Struggles

> Where is there darkness in this world? ... Jesus ... is the light who shines in every darkness; and no darkness can ever extinguish it ... Where is there no peace? Where is there injustice? Where is there a lack of righteousness—where is there dishonesty, malice, and downright evil? Jesus will step in—if we invite him, if we make space for him ... Yes, Jesus is the source of all hope—real, concrete hope. His zeal will see to that.[27]

Year 2014: Hope Emboldened: A Nation Which Struggles

> To say as Christians that we must live in hope does not imply that we should sit by passively and indulge in wishful thinking for that which has no prospect of being realised to come about ... Hope confronts wrong and the abuse of power; it is risky and requires patience and endurance... But there is another characteristic they shared that is particularly powerful in converting hope to reality, and that is courage ... So this Christmas let us commit ourselves to a new struggle ... The good news is, as Christians we struggle with a firm hope, that Christ our light and our hope, has already triumphed and broken all barriers.[28]

Year 2019: Hope Embodied: A People Who Struggle

> God is a god of all, not just for Christians, and the Incarnation calls us to witness to God in almost everything; to bring God's light to where there is darkness, and to witness to the light wherever we are ... No, I am hopeful because to hope is to be determined to name our problems and highlight our differences, precisely in order to mobilise people to overcome them. As Denise adds: "To live out my hope is to try to make that which I hope for come about—sooner rather than later."[29]

As already pointed out, there is a growing tension between the theme of darkness and encroaching threat, and the response by the hearers as a result of the coming of the Light of the world. Whereas Archbishop Makgoba initially situated hope within the acts of Jesus alone, he came to expand hope to include the struggle of a nation and eventually Christians in general (while continuing to emphasize that Christ struggled and triumphed). It is a hope that is rooted within the incarnation, but that drives people forward through calls toward ethical action.

Ultimately, Archbishop Makgoba simultaneously named the demons and inspired social imagination. This is needed to give direction to those who are building a new *societas*. In the search for, and also the struggle for, a new *societas*, the preacher kept hope alive as a means of fostering a social imagination in the hearers. In a new *societas*, all citizens have their role, comparable to the structure of roles in an old *societas*, but different to it as well as to the time of liminality and *communitas*. The content of the theology of hope is embedded in the indicative and imperative identifiable in all the sermons. However, the ritual performative frame of the public liminality of Midnight Mass, and the performance of the sermons by the preacher, add the subjunctive to the indicative and imperative, which connects with the social imagination fostered by the sermons.

In a religious and strongly Christian country such as South Africa, the preacher legitimizes his calls and claims theologically by means of the incarnation. In *Faith and Courage*, Makgoba (2017: 27) writes: "We must stand in the gaps between feeling hopeless and hopeful, between hurting and being healed." What is telling about Makgoba's Christmas sermons is how they build up as if the archbishop is more inspired by a kind of holy anger that is akin to lament every year. The sermons themselves can be seen as expressions of anger and cries of lament, embodying what Emmanuel Katongole calls a "theology of hope" (cf. Katongole 2017). However, there is also a frustration in the sermons; the expression of anger does not remain at the level of expression and a cry of lament, but later, a longing becomes perceptible that the anger should also be heard by those who should hear it (see also Wepener and Van der Merwe 2021).

In the light of Victor Turner's later work regarding ritual and performance, the Christmas sermons of Makgoba can be viewed as public meta-social rites, in which Midnight Mass in St. George's Cathedral, which is also broadcasted on national television, with a Twitter feed and Facebook posts, becomes a kind of public square.[30] The performance of these Christmas sermons sets up a frame in which a momentary public liminality occurs, during which *communitas* appraises the power structure (Turner 1979: 468). This public ritual performance dramatizes, to a certain extent, secular, legal, and political relationships in which lampooning can occur and the powers are challenged (Turner 1979: 474, as well as Campbell and Cilliers 2012). Turner (1979: 476) calls this kind of public liminality the "eye and eyestalk which society bends round upon its own condition." This type of performance as part of public liminality elicits plural reflexivity on the side of participants. It is thus noteworthy that not only the content of the sermons preached but also their annual performance was important as this engaged the social dynamics of a new *societas* in South Africa.

Makgoba thus utilized public liminality created by the frame of Midnight Mass and the performance of his Christmas sermon. This public liminality is, in the words of Turner (1979: 465–6; see also 1986: 25) "full of potency and potentiality," and is "similar to the subjunctive mood" and the "reflexive voice." Both the content and the performance of the sermons act as mirrors of society and as agents of change as the performative reflexivity that it fosters enables a society to reflect back on itself and scrutinize the quotidian world of South Africa (cf. Turner 1986: 24–7). Archbishop Makgoba furthermore also utilized the playful mood and mode of Christmas Eve to actively encourage public reflexivity that, according to Turner (1979: 466), is the reason why public liminality is dangerous to the powers that be. "Public liminality can never be tranquilly regarded as a safety valve, mere catharsis, 'letting off steam'. Rather it is communitas weighing structure, sometimes finding it wanting, and proposing in however extravagant a form new paradigms and models which invert or subvert the old."

In summary, Archbishop Makgoba's Christmas sermons are theological texts containing a specific theology of hope, but hope that is augmented by the meaning implicit in the public performance of the content and as such engaging the social dynamics of a young democracy.

Notes

1 Many of Thabo Makgoba's predecessors at St. George's Cathedral, such as Joost de Blank, were outspoken critics of apartheid (cf. Makgoba 2017: 114–15).
2 For some of his Christmas sermons, see the South African newspaper *Daily Maverick*: "Christmas Sermons in the Daily Maverick: Makgoba,Thabo," (Makgoba n.d.).
3 See, e.g., Alec Hogg (2020).
4 See Manelisi Dubase (2019). Article includes a video of the sermon; see also the website of the Anglican Church of Southern Africa: https://archbishop.anglicanchurchsa.org/ (accessed June 27, 2023).
5 At the beginning of the Social Drama, existing social relationships in a society, also called *societas*, are broken down and the group moves to a time of looser and more informal relationships called *communitas*.
6 Of course, it is not possible to generalize in this regard, and various groups and individuals will find themselves in different spaces with regard to a transitional period.
7 See latest surveys of the SARB (Potgieter 2019).
8 For a summary and discussion of the findings of the SARB between 2003 and 2019, see Van der Merwe (2020: chapter 3), as well as Van der Merwe, Wepener, and Barnard (2019). In this time, South African homileticians focused on a variety of these challenges in their publications. Pieterse (2013) explored preaching in a

context of poverty; Nell (2009) looked at preaching and xenophobia; Kruger (2019) at preaching and corruption; Wepener and Pieterse (2018) at preaching and anger; Wessels (2020) at postcolonial preaching; Müller and Wepener (2019) at preaching and social capital formation, and several homileticians, such as Laubscher (2017), explored the theme of prophetic preaching in a changing South African context.

9 All sermons are accessible via this link to the website of the Anglican Church of Southern Africa: https://archbishop.anglicanchurchsa.org/2019/12/archbishops-sermon-for-midnight-mass.html.

10 It should be noted that Archbishop Makgoba consistently worked with the lectionary texts, so, every year, he is preaching on very similar readings from Scripture, just twelve months apart. In some cases, instead of Luke chapter 2, John chapter 1 is used. Thus, even though the texts differ, thematically the biblical texts deal with similar themes and theology, such as incarnation.

11 "Mary Treasured These Words, and Pondered Them in Her Heart" (Makgoba 2009).

12 "Mary Treasured These Words, and Pondered Them in Her Heart" (Makgoba 2009).

13 "Sermon at Midnight Mass" (Makgoba 2011).

14 "Christmas Sermon" (Makgoba 2012).

15 "Sermon at Midnight Mass" (Makgoba 2011).

16 "Welcome the Season of Light by Becoming a Society of Long Spoons," (Makgoba 2014).

17 This refers to new issues in a postcolonial context, thus a new struggle after the struggle against apartheid and colonialism.

18 Nene was the finance minister controversially removed by President Zuma on December 9, 2015, to be briefly replaced by Des Van Rooyen, succeeded by Pravin Gordhan.

19 "Glad Tidings of Peace Demand Courage and Action" (Makgoba 2015).

20 "Glad Tidings of Peace Demand Courage and Action" (Makgoba 2015).

21 Makgoba (2017: 183–4) himself refers to this sermon in *Faith and Courage.*

22 "Sermon for Midnight Mass"(Makgoba 2016).

23 "Archbishop's Christmas Sermon, 2017" (Makgoba 2017).

24 "Archbishop Thabo's Christmas Sermon, 2018" (Makgoba 2018).

25 "Archbishop's Sermon for Midnight Mass, Christmas 2019" (Makgoba 2019).

26 Makgoba (2019).

27 Makgoba (2009).

28 Makgoba (2014).

29 Makgoba (2019).

30 See in this regard also the work of Mirella Klomp (2020) and her book *Playing On: Re-staging the Passion after the Death of God.*

References

Arbuckle, Gerald (1991), *Grieving for Change. A Spirituality for Refounding Gospel Communities*, Homebush: St. Paul Publications.

Burger, Coenie (1995), *Gemeentes in transito. Vernuwingsgeleenthede in 'n oorgangstyd*, Cape Town: Lux Verbi.

Campbell, Charles, and Johan Cilliers (2012), *Preaching Fools: The Gospel as a Rhetoric of Folly*, Waco, TX: Baylor University Press.

Hay, Mark (1997), "*Ukubuyisana*. Reconciliation in South Africa," PhD dissertation, Chicago.

Katongole, Emmanuel (2017), *Born from Lament. The Theology and Politics of Hope in Africa*, Grand Rapids, MI: Eerdmans.

Kleinheksel, A. J. and Nicole Rockich-Winston, Huda Tawfik, Tasha R. Wyatt (2020), "Demystifying Content Analysis," *Am J Pharm Educ*, 84 (1): 127–37, January 2020. Available online: 7113. doi: 10.5688/ajpe711 (accessed June 27, 2023).

Klomp, Mirella (2020), *Playing On. Re-staging the Passion after the Death of God*, Leiden: Brill.

Kruger, Ferdi (2019), "Homiletic Contours for Preaching to Listeners Who Fear the Disastrous Consequences of Corruption, with an Emphasis on Cognitive Distortions," *Acta Theologica*, 39 (2): 70–89.

Laubscher, Martin (2017), " 'As if Nothing Happened'? Karl Barth and the Study of Prophetic Preaching in South Africa today," *Acta Theologica*, 37 (2): 51–68.

Long, Thomas (2004), *The Witness of Preaching*, Louisville, KY: Westminster John Knox.

Makgoba, Thabo (2017), *Faith & Courage. Praying with Mandela*, Cape Town: Tafelberg.

Mayring, Philipp (2000), "Qualitative Content Analysis," *Forum Qualitative Sozialforschung: Qualitative Social Research*, 1 (2) Art. 20, June 2000. Available online: https://doi.org/10.17169/fqs-1.2.1089 (accessed June 27, 2023).

Müller, Bethel, and Cas Wepener (2019), "Belief, Behaviour and Belonging: The Changing Ritual of Preaching and Worship," in Cas Wepener, Ignatius Swart, Gerrie ter Haar, and Marcel Barnard (eds.), *Bonding in Worship. A Ritual Lens on Social Capital Formation in African Independent Churches in South Africa*, 209–28, Leuven: Peeters Press.

Nell, Ian (2009), "The Tears of Xenophobia: Preaching and Violence from a South African Perspective," *Practical Theology in South Africa*, 24 (2): 229–47.

Pieterse, Hendrik (2001), *Preaching in a Context of Poverty*, Pretoria: University of South Africa Press.

Pieterse, Hendrik (2013), "An Emerging Grounded Theory for Preaching on Poverty in South Africa with Matthew 25:31–46 as sermon Text," *Acta Theologica*, 33 (1): 175–95.

Schechner, Richard (1986), "Victor Turner's Last Adventure," in Victor Turner (ed.), *The Anthropology of Performance*, 7–20, New York: PAJ Publications.

Steyn, Marileen (2016), "A Grounded Theory Analysis of a Selection of Sermons on Racism," MDiv dissertation, University of Pretoria, Pretoria.

Steyn, Marileen (2019), "*Gebedspraktyke en geloofsoortuigings van kerklos millennial Christene. 'n Ritueel-liturgiese verkenning*"," MA dissertation, University of Pretoria, Pretoria.

Steyn, Marileen, Cas Wepener, and Hendrik Pieterse (2020), "Preaching during the COVID-19 Pandemic in South Africa: A Grounded Theoretical Exploration" / "Prediking ten tyde van die COVID-19-pandemie: 'n Gegronde Teoretiese verkenning"," *International Journal of Homiletics*, 4: 1–21.

Turner, Victor (1969), *The Ritual Process. Structure and Anti-Structure*, London: Routledge & Kegan Paul.

Turner, Victor (1972), "Passages, Margins and Poverty: Religious Symbols of Communitas," *Worship*, 46 (7): 390–412.

Turner, Victor (1979), "Frame, Flow and Reflection: Ritual and Drama in Public Liminality," *Japanese Journal of Religious Studies*, 6 (4): 465–99.

Turner, Victor (1982), *From Ritual to Theatre. The Human Seriousness of Play*, New York: PAJ Publications.

Turner, Victor (1986), *The Anthropology of Performance*, New York: PAJ Publications.

Turner, Victor (1996), "Liminality and Communitas," in Ronald Grimes (ed.), *Readings in Ritual Studies*, 511–19, Upper Saddle River, NJ: Prentice Hall.

Van der Merwe, Suzanne (2020), "*Liturgie en versoening in die Nederduitse Gereformeerde Kerk: 'n Liturgies-rituele benadering*," PhD dissertation, University of Pretoria, Pretoria.

Van der Merwe, Suzanne, Cas Wepener, and Marcel Barnard (2019), "n Liturgiese praxisteorie vir 'n teologie van versoening en geregtigheid," *LitNet Akademies*, 16 (3): 345–72.

Wepener, Cas (2009), *From Fast to Feast. A Ritual-Liturgical Exploration of Reconciliation in South African Cultural Contexts*, Leuven: Peeters Pers.

Wepener, Cas (2012), "Liminality: Recent Avatars of This Notion in a South African Context," *Scriptura*, 110 (1): 293–307.

Wepener, Cas (2015), "'Bliksem!' / Damn it!: Ritual-Liturgical Appreciation of a Deadly Sin," *Verbum et Ecclesia*, 36 (3): 1–8.

Wepener, Cas, and Hendrik Pieterse (2018), "Angry Preaching," *International Journal of Public Theology*, 12 (3–4): 396–410.

Wepener, Cas, and Suzanne van der Merwe (2021), "Angry Listening and a Listening God. Liturgical-Theological Reflections," *Stellenbosch Theological Journal*, 7 (1): 1–19.

Wessels, Wessel (2020), "Postcolonial Homiletics? A Practical Theological Engagement with Postcolonial Thought," PhD dissertation, University of Pretoria, Pretoria.

Internet References

Dubase, Manelisi (2019), "Makgoba Hopes 2020 Will Be a Year of 'Orange Jumpsuits' for the Corrupt," *SABC News*, December 25. Available online: https://www.sabcnews.com/sabcnews/makgoba-hopes-2020-will-be-a-year-of-orange-jumpsuits-for-the-corrupt/ (accessed May 17, 2023).

Hogg, Alec (2020), "2020 Unlikely to Be Year of the Orange Overalls—Paul Hoffman. #Corruption," *BizNews*, February 14. Available online: https://www.biznews.com/leadership/2020/02/14/unlikely-year-orange-overalls-paul-hoffman-corruption (accessed May 17, 2023).

Makgoba, Thabo (n.d.), "Christmas Sermons in the Daily Maverick: Makgoba, Thabo," *Daily Maverick*. Available online: https://www.dailymaverick.co.za/author/thabo-makgoba/ (accessed May 17, 2023).

Makgoba, Thabo (2009), "Mary Treasured These Words, and Pondered Them in Her Heart," *Archbishop Thabo Makgoba*, December 25. Available online: https://archbishop.anglicanchurchsa.org/2009/12/sermon-at-midnight-mass-st-georges.html/ (accessed May 17, 2023).

Makgoba, Thabo (2011), "Sermon at Midnight Mass," *Archbishop Thabo Makgoba*, December 26. Available online: https://archbishop.anglicanchurchsa.org/2011/12/sermon-at-midnight-mass.html (accessed May 17, 2023).

Makgoba, Thabo (2012), "Christmas Sermon," *Archbishop Thabo Makgoba*, December 25. Available online: https://archbishop.anglicanchurchsa.org/2012/12/christmas-sermon.html (accessed May 17, 2023).

Makgoba, Thabo (2013), "Sermon at Midnight Mass," *Archbishop Thabo Makgoba*, December 25. Available online: https://archbishop.anglicanchurchsa.org/2013/12/updated-sermon-at-midnight-mass-georges.html (accessed May 17, 2023).

Makgoba, Thabo (2014), "Welcome the Season of Light by Becoming a Society of Long Spoons," *Archbishop Thabo Makgoba*, December 25. Available online: https://archbishop.anglicanchurchsa.org/2014/12/welcome-season-of-light-by-becoming.html (accessed May 17, 2023).

Makgoba, Thabo (2015), "Glad Tidings of Peace Demand Courage and Action," *Archbishop Thabo Makgoba*, December 24. Available online: https://archbishop.anglicanchurchsa.org/2015/12/glad-tidings-of-peace-demand-courage.html (accessed May 17, 2023).

Makgoba, Thabo (2016), "Sermon for Midnight Mass," *Archbishop Thabo Makgoba*, December 24. Available online: https://archbishop.anglicanchurchsa.org/2016/12/sermon-for-midnight-mass-at-st-georges.html (accessed May 17, 2023).

Makgoba, Thabo (2017), "Archbishop's Christmas Sermon, 2017," *Archbishop Thabo Makgoba*, December 24. Available online: https://archbishop.anglicanchurchsa.org/2017/12/archbishops-christmas-sermon-2017.html (accessed May 17, 2023).

Makgoba, Thabo (2018), "Archbishop Thabo's Christmas Sermon, 2018," *Archbishop Thabo Makgoba*, December 24. Available online: https://archbishop.anglicanchurchsa.org/2018/12/archbishop-thabos-christmas-sermon-2018.html (accessed May 17, 2023).

Makgoba, Thabo (2019), "Archbishop's Sermon for Midnight Mass, Christmas 2019," *Archbishop Thabo Makgoba*, December 24. Available online: https://archbishop.anglicanchurchsa.org/2019/12/archbishops-sermon-for-midnight-mass.html (accessed May 17, 2023).

McNamee, Terence (2019), "Ten years in South Africa: An unreliable guide to the decade that was," *Daily Maverick*, December 18. Available online: https://www.dailymaverick.co.za/article/2019-12-18-ten-years-in-south-africa-an-unreliable-guide-to-the-decade-that-was/ (accessed June 27, 2023).

Pather, Dennis (2019), "The 2010s Were a Truly Turbulent Decade for South Africa," *IOL*, December 28. Available online: https://www.iol.co.za/news/opinion/the-2010s-were-a-truly-turbulent-decade-for-south-africa-39781647 (accessed November 10, 2022).

Potgieter, Elnari (2019), "SA Reconciliation Barometer 2019," *Institute for Justice and Reconciliation*. Available online: https://www.ijr.org.za/portfolio-items/sa-reconciliation-barometer-2019/ (accessed May 17, 2023).

"The South African Economic Reconstruction and Recovery Plan" (2020). Available online: https://www.gov.za/sites/default/files/gcis_document/202010/south-african-economic-reconstruction-and-recovery-plan.pdf (accessed November 10, 2022).

Website of the Anglican Church of Southern Africa. Available online: https://archbishop.anglicanchurchsa.org/ (accessed May 17, 2023).

3

Moral Exhortation in Islamic Discourse: Performance and Ethics in Islamic Sermons

Abdulkader Tayob

Introduction

Ayatollah Khomeini's 1989 *khuṭbah* condemning Salman Rushdie for *The Satanic Verses* has created a lasting image of the danger of Islam's preachers (Azm 2005; Kepel 2002: 9; Mozaffari 1998). Twenty-five years later, another *khuṭbah* became notorious when it announced the establishment of the Islamic State of Iraq and Syria (ISIS). Abu Bakr al-Baghdadi's first sermon in 2014 symbolized ISIS's bid for power in Iraq, and the trail of death and destruction that it left in the aftermath of the American invasion. These prominent and iconic images of the *khuṭbah* seem to inspire studies of more prosaic Muslim preaching. Against a global image of the *khuṭbah* advocating violence and rejection of Western values, the general scholarly response is to emphasize the diversity of most Muslim exhortations in mosques and new media. When a preacher is associated with controversial groups such as the Salafis and Islamists in the public sphere contemporary scholarship seems to be particularly at pains to show the benign and everyday nature of most Muslim preaching (Hanafi 2019; Janson 2006; Olsson 2020; Sounaye 2017; Stjernholm 2020; Stjernholm and Özdalga 2020).

This chapter takes the *khuṭbah* and related moral exhortations beyond the global and Western public spheres and media images. It argues that the *khuṭbah* and pre-*khuṭbah* addresses are part of the discourse of Islam, which is both local and global. As creative interventions in the discourse of Islam, they neither sacrifice their link with the past nor their engagement with the present. This chapter offers a close study of a pre-*khuṭbah* talk in a prominent mosque in Cape Town in February 2021, which discussed the closing and opening of mosques during the Covid-19 pandemic. Given after some restrictions were lifted, the pre-*khuṭbah* talk criticized the decision of some Muslims to evade government measures imposed on social gatherings. At the same time, it presented a vivid account of the significance of mosque practices. I argue that the pre-*khuṭbah* talk demonstrates Islamic discourse engaging with an ethical decision, weighing an established mosque performance against the demands of the pandemic. The ethical decision is not made by stepping outside the discourse, but by engaging with it.

Islamic Sermons between Monolithic Civilization and Modernization

Recent scholarship on the *khuṭbah* and other public talks have emphasized the diversity of moral exhortations in Muslim societies in the past and present. This diversity seems to undermine the dominant public perception of the uniformity of Islam as a civilization and culture (Aydin 2017; Eaton 1990). And yet, I would like to argue that most studies continue to struggle with the long shadow of classical Islamic Studies and modern social sciences. The former seems unable to move beyond an essentialist representation of Islam, while the latter reveals a deep-seated modernization theory and its construction of religion *for* a modern world. These frameworks are useful for showing aspects of Islamic moral exhortations in historical and contemporary contexts, but they also reveal a predilection for essentialist models for understanding Islam in the past and present.

The *khuṭbah* is part of the formal religious service on Fridays, on the two major festivals (*ʿīds*), and at the formalization of a marriage contract. When appropriate, it may be given on other occasions as well. The word *khuṭbah* is derived from the triliteral verb form *kh-ṭ-b*, which is closely associated with oratory (*balāghah*) (Qutbuddin 2008). In addition to *khuṭbah*, other words are used to refer to moral exhortations in Muslim societies. These are called *waʿẓ* or *mawʿiẓah* (moral exhortation), *dars* (lesson), *dhikr* or *tadhkīr* (remembrance or reminder), or *qirāʾah* (recitation) (Jones 2006: 33; Qutbuddin 2008: 203). Most *khuṭbah* studies recognize these differences but devote themselves to the study of moral exhortations in Muslim societies in general. The word commonly used for this activity is preaching, but sometimes, the Christian word homily is used (Berkey 2001: 42; Jones 2006; Khalidi 1994: 201; Stjernholm and Özdalga

2020: 9). I will refer to the growing body of literature as *khuṭbah* studies but keep in mind the distinctions used by Muslims.

The most prominent studies of the *khuṭbah* in premodern times have emphasized the problem of leadership in Islam. Johannes Pedersen's seminal study identified preaching as a symbol of authority contested by different claimants. He identified a group of preachers (*quṣṣāṣ*) who were part of Islam in the beginning, and with "the necessary limitation," doing the "work of the Prophet" (Pedersen 1955: 215). But a scholarly class (*'ulamā'*) later emerged who "feared an activity that was not controlled" and launched a sustained attack on these preachers (Pedersen 1955: 230). Pedersen's work prepared the ground for Berkey's lengthier study of popular preachers between 1000 CE and 1500 CE (Berkey 2001, 2020). Like Pedersen, he too found a sustained criticism of "popular" preachers among the *'ulamā'* (Berkey 2020: 75, 77, 78). Berkey tries to identify in controversial preaching a distinctive popular culture in Islam. But his analysis reveals that the lines between popular preaching and scholarly activity were not as clearly delineated as he had anticipated (Berkey 2001: 50).

Pedersen and Berkey's analyses merit some reflection on the theoretical framework used to identify essentialized features of the *khuṭbah* (Ahmed 2017). Berkey opens his study by reflecting briefly on the question of the Orientalist gaze, with its "monolithic" understanding of Islam (Berkey 2001: 3). In spite of this cautionary note, however, Berkey follows Pedersen by declaring that popular preaching reveals a deep problem of authority in medieval Islam. Authority in Islam was "*inherently* problematic, and the tension over it was productive of much of the intellectual and social dynamism of pre-modern Islamic societies" (Berkey 2020: 68; emphasis mine). Moreover, Berkey identifies this problematic area as an indication of something missing in Islam: "There was nothing resembling an organized church, no formal institutional network of schools, no distinctive clerical class" (Berkey 2020: 68). This analysis compares Islam with Christianity and discovers an enduring gap in Islam, which it interprets as an explanation for the *khutbah.* There are no doubt valuable insights in Pedersen and Berkey's studies of preaching and preachers, but this totalizing framework betrays the continuing universalizing gaze of an Orientalism in which Christianity serves as a model of religious institutionalization.

Linda Jones's contextual studies of individual preachers pay homage to the general framework of Pedersen and Berkey. But her work yields better insights into the *khuṭbah* as hermeneutical strategies employed by preachers. Her study of the preacher Ibn ʿAbbād of Ronda (d. 1390) does not conclude that authority is inherently problematic in Islam. It shows the preacher navigating between different scholarly trends in his *khuṭbah*, showing an "ability to tap into and direct a spirituality that appealed to Maliki religious experts, Sufis and a laity not necessarily affiliated to any Sufi order" (Jones 2006: 49). Her more recent study comparing medieval and modern preachers on the rights of women also addresses the hermeneutical strategies found in sermons (Jones 2020). Jones's analyses show that preachers navigate a rich and complex discourse of Islam, and not only an inherent problem of authority.

Khuṭbah studies in modern Muslim societies seem to depart from the monolithic understanding of the *khuṭbah* by celebrating the diversity of moral exhortations, their content, delivery, and mediatization. Despite this, however, they reveal a dominant modernization framework best seen in Clifford Geertz's framing of religion and ritual for the modern world. Geertz argued against Émile Durkheim and Bronisław Malinowski that rituals were not a reflection of society or a source of harmony or solace. Rejecting these static frames of culture, he proposed a model for symbolic action that focused on the tension between a meaning system and the social structure in which it was articulated: "Sacred symbols function to synthesize a people's ethos … and their world view" (Geertz 1966: 3). In rituals, Geertz argued, "men attain their faith as they portray it" (Geertz 1966: 29). To understand how this becomes a model *for* religion, one needs to turn to Geertz's essay on a Javanese funeral in the 1950s, which describes what happens when a symbol or practice is out of sync with a new social reality (Geertz 1957: 34). The social reality at the time was transformed through what Geertz calls the intrusion of ideologies such as Marxism, Nationalism, and Islamization (Geertz 1957: 36). Geertz hardly says anything about the colonial Dutch regime that had radically transformed Javanese societies during the past hundred years or more. Nevertheless, he shows how symbols and rituals are ineffective when they fail to adapt to the new social structure. In this way, his theoretical model becomes more than a representation of reality. It shows how his model expects the social structure to be confirmed and consecrated by ritual. Rather than a neutral model that posits the tension between a symbolic system and social reality, Geertz's model shows how religion must adapt to an inevitable new reality. This essay provides a good example of how social theories of religion are more than representations. Rather, as Talal Asad has argued, they are models for religion (Asad 2003).

I suggest that this model of disruption and desired synthesis may be seen in modern studies of the *khuṭbah*. They are not only representations for how *khuṭbah* were delivered, but models for how they might bring about change in the presence of new social realities. A short review will show how modern *khuṭbah* studies seemed to be guided by this deep modernizing model of religion for society.

Bruce Borthwick's 1967 study of Egyptian sermons argued that the ritual is ideally suited to communicating a modernizing message in the Middle East. The sermon and its symbols represented the society's symbolic system, which was out of sync with the modern world. Postcolonial leaders took the lead in delivering appropriate sermons for their nationalist projects, and their example was then followed by preachers (Borthwick 1967). Richard Antoun's anthropological study of a Muslim preacher approaches the Islamic sermon in a Jordanian village from a similar perspective. Mediating between the Great and Little traditions of Islam, the preacher shows how modernization could be justified in religious terms. The study demonstrates how the *khuṭbah* as ritual stitched together the disjuncture between an inherited symbolic system (Islam) and a new reality (modernization) (Antoun 1989). In his study of Egyptian *khuṭbah*, Patrick Gaffney found that sermons either consecrated modern Egyptian society or opposed it by transporting Muslims to a different world. Sermons that were successful at integrating religious values with modernity were contrasted with those that defined Islam as a nation or a politics, not a religion (Gaffney 1988, 1994). For Geertz, the symbolic system that did not adapt to the new social reality failed. For Gaffney, it became an unacceptable political outlook.

More recent approaches to *khuṭbah* and other moral exhortations have turned to their aesthetic dimensions or their offline and online mediatizations. Dorothea Schulz's study of female preachers in Mali asks how women's preaching mediates between the inherited meanings of Islam and new media technologies. She argues that the latter facilitates women's preaching against strong resistance from Islamic conceptions of women and their voices in public life (Schulz 2012). Abdoulaye Sounaye approaches the aesthetics of young Salafi preachers who employ "jokes, mimicry, and theatrics" to keep new audiences ("urbanites") entertained and wooed (Sounaye 2017: 10). The online space offers opportunities for multi-modal preaching, as discussed in some recent studies on online preaching and their effects in societies (Makboul 2020; Stjernholm 2020). The shadow of Geertz is evident in these studies too. A worldview meets social and technological change, which then demands some accommodation from the worldview through Islamic ritual.

Charles Hirschkind's studies of sermons in modern Egypt offer a different approach that brings us back to the work of moral admonishment in the *khuṭbah*. He focuses particularly on preaching in Egypt that does not consecrate modernity. Paying attention to the soundscape created by popular preachers, Hirschkind argues that they employ an aesthetic of audition that stands against modernity's visual hegemony. The soundscape of the preachers fostered a counter-public in Egypt, one that could not be easily located in its public sphere of rational deliberation (Hirschkind 2001). Moreover, the aesthetic of sound was designed to cultivate pious subjects through a repertoire of Prophetic advice, narratives of the early Muslims (*salaf*), and deep introspection (Hirschkind 2006). Hirschkind's discursive approach breaks out of the Geertz model by focusing on the ethical work done through preaching.

This review of *khuṭbah* scholarship shows that, with some exceptions, the totalizing gaze of Orientalism or the demands of modernization provide its framework. The Orientalist gaze defines medieval Muslim society by a lack (institutionalized authority). This attention to authority is replaced in more recent studies with a focus on the demands of modernization. This time, modernization transforms the social structure and leaves behind supposedly traditional cultures such as Islam. The preacher's task seems to be successful when he or she brings Islam up to date with new developments. All the while, fundamental questions raised in the moral exhortations about the new social structure and its values are ignored. Following Geertz's model for understanding the relation between an inherited worldview and a new social structure, the work of symbols and rituals is directed at the former. Modernity is represented by apparently neutral technological developments and necessary social transformations that force themselves on resistant Muslim societies and their worldview. Mostly, the analysis concentrates on how ritual apparently affects an inherited worldview, rather than what it does to the social structures imposed by colonialism, technology, and associated values.

The *Khuṭbah* in Islamic Discourse

Instead of a totalizing Orientalist gaze or modernist framework, *khuṭbah* studies may benefit from appreciating its location within a complex and changing discourse of Islam. Since the seminal arguments put forward by Talal Asad, scholarship has been deeply divided on the nature of Islamic discourse. Some argue that an Islamic discourse is constituted by embodied performances acquired over a long period of learning, engagement, and transformation. This idea of discourse has drawn insights from a revival of Aristotelian ethics and its medieval Islamic translation to identify Islamic discourse as a lifelong commitment to religious texts, values, and sentiments (Hirschkind 2001; Mahmood 2001; Mittermaier 2014). Another group, which I would associate with the Geertzian model presented above, challenges this characterization of Islamic discourse by showing that Muslims in contemporary society are faced with alternative worldviews and frameworks such as modernization, nationalism, and the like. Islamic discourse is by its very nature impossible or difficult to implement and adopt in contemporary times (Abenante and Cantini 2014; Schielke 2014). Both groups assume that Islamic discourse is complete and bounded, the one focusing on its successful embodiment and the other on its alienation from the contemporary world. It is my contention that Islamic discourse is connected and linked to the past, through which it meets modern challenges with resistance, creativity, and internal debate. Islamic discourse sometimes presents itself as coherent and committed to devotion. At other times, it exhibits dissent and creativity.

Studying the *khuṭbah* means paying attention to how the Qur'an and hadith are articulated and refracted through a textual tradition built over centuries. This textual tradition is vast and voluminous, accumulated through commentaries and amendments. It includes some clearly defined disciplines like jurisprudence (*fiqh*), dialectical theology (*kalām*), Sufism, and philosophy. The discourse has been produced across the globe by intellectuals, teachers, commentators, and students. Preachers have differing access to this corpus. Some may only know one prophetic hadith for a moral exhortation, while others are adept at working in the larger archive. In moral exhortations, the tropes and questions from this library are interwoven in expected and unexpected ways.

The discourse of Islam is characterized by intense debate and deliberation. It is, by definition and in practice, determined by an addressability. Interlocutors engage in the discourse in the conviction that others understand, agree, or disagree. Debate and deliberation have produced a rich and sometimes apparently confusing diversity of views and positions. The plurality of voices that constitutes Islamic discourse has been part of Islam from the very beginning. It is evident in the major theological divisions of Islam (Sunni and Shi'a), and in minor jurisprudential issues such as when and whether one needs to perform the Friday prayer. The diversity of the discourse of Islam has remained in motion, through students in search of teachers, pilgrimage, migrations, movements of reform, and the flow of manuscripts, pamphlets, and *fatwas*. This diversity is multiplied when the discourse takes shape in local contexts, informed by history, politics, and economy. But the local manifestation is always identifiable in its connection to a nonlocal shared discourse. The *khuṭbah* as moral exhortation may emphasize one position, while suppressing the unsettled nature of the discourse on a particular point.

Given the unsettled nature of the discourse, we should not be surprised to find dramatic and subtle changes in Islamic discourse over time. Major changes in the history of Islam have brought about significant shifts in the discourse. These can be characterized as political and epistemological transformations that include but are not limited to the formation of empires and sultanates and the encounter with Hellenistic thought through Eastern Christianity, with Persian statecraft through translations and conversions, and with Buddhist contemplation in Central Asia. These changes are reflected in the development of distinctive hermeneutical strategies in jurisprudence, theology, and Sufism. But changes in the discourse have also come about more subtly through what Ludwig Wittgenstein calls the practical application of a language game. Wittgenstein puts forward this possibility in his typical rhetorical fashion: "Is there not also the case where we play [the language game of Islam] and—make up the rules as we go along?" (Wittgenstein 1958, §83). *Khuṭbah* moral exhortations, even while appealing to Muslims to hold onto practices and values from the past, are transformed through new articulations. *Khuṭbah* exhortations are ideal for appreciating how Islamic discourse mediates, resists, and legitimates changes.

The discourse is focused on what must be done in a particular time and place. Asad has paid close attention to performances as the primary objective of Islamic discourse, setting it apart deliberately from the model of Protestant Reformism that sublimates the inner constitution of belief and conviction. For Asad, "meanings are embodied in practice" (Asad 2020, 404). Jones and Hirschkind have illustrated this dimension of *khuṭbah* in their studies, showing how preachers focus on the formation of ethical subjects (Hirschkind 2006; Jones 2006). But practices related to the *khuṭbah* should not be limited to ethical formation. My analysis of preaching in South Africa is concerned with the performances that have constituted mosques and Imams over the political and social history of the country. Certain practices were developed regarding how to build, manage, and maintain mosques. Similarly, practices regarding how to become an Imam, teacher, and preacher emerged over time. These practices were derived from prophetic statements and jurisprudence, given specific shape in a legal and political history of colonialism, apartheid, anti-apartheid activism, and racism. Furthermore, they were reflected and promoted in the pre-*khuṭbah* talks delivered in mosques (Tayob 1999: 12–13).

The *khuṭbah* and other moral exhortations, then, are part of the discourse of Islam, which is characterized by plurality, contestation and deliberation, performance, and critique. It defies easy generalization as culture or civilization that have been used in Islamic Studies. It may be subjected to the modeling of religion in modernity (Geertz), but it would be better served by paying close attention to its engagement in global and local dimensions. The *khuṭbah* and other moral exhortations offer a unique perspective on the invocation of Islamic discourse in local contexts.

Sermons in South Africa

Shortly after midday on Friday, the streets around mosques in major cities can become difficult to navigate as drivers look for parking and other Muslims stream into the mosques on foot. Following an injunction in Islamic jurisprudence that worship may not be missed without justification for three consecutive Fridays, Muslim men generally go to great lengths to attend Friday prayer.[1] This is one practice that cannot be left out of the weekly routine. In recent decades, women in the Western Cape have also attended in increasing numbers, but there remains strong resistance among some men and women, who see this as a male obligation in Islamic jurisprudence. Friday worship is central to a gendered Muslim performance in South Africa.

A *khuṭbah* is an essential part of the Friday worship, which also includes individual and communal postures of prayer called *rakaʿāt*. The formal *khuṭbah* address is usually given in Arabic, read from a prepared book, and presented in a formulaic manner from a raised pulpit (*minbar*) facing the congregation. There have been some attempts in South Africa to deliver the address in English, but this has been vehemently resisted by most religious scholars and communities. In South Africa, as elsewhere, another address is given in the vernacular before the formal service. This is the address which I am calling a pre-*khuṭbah* following local usage. It is an opportunity for delivering a weekly message to the congregation that demonstrates knowledge and rhetorical skills. In 1994, the Claremont Main Road Mosque in Cape Town broke with tradition by inviting Professor Amina Wadud to deliver the pre-*khuṭbah* talk. Like the practice of adopting English for the formal *khuṭbah*, the practice of a woman presenting the pre-*khuṭbah* talk was also resisted by most religious leaders and their communities in the city.

The Covid-19 pandemic that spread across the globe in 2020 placed a strain on religious gatherings and practices in mosques, churches, and temples. Government decisions to impose restrictions on public gatherings opened a significant debate among religious leaders in general, and Muslims in particular. Most Muslim leaders agreed to conform to government measures and encouraged others to do so. However, a vociferous group resisted the closure of mosques and other preventative measures. They campaigned vigorously against making any changes to the form of worship. The following is one example of this rejection:

> When the government decides to somewhat "ease" its oppression by granting permission for the Musaajid [*sic*] to open, it will obviously attach a host of haraam [prohibited] conditions. One such condition is the shaitaani [devilish] "social distancing" which the Munaafiqeen [hypocrites] had introduced in Musjids under their illegitimate control. ("Taraas-Soo!" 2020)

This statement rejects all measures taken to prevent the spread of the virus. Following this argument, a temporary coalition of Muslim organizations and individuals unsuccessfully contested the government's measures in court.[2] As a result of this ongoing debate, some mosques disregarded government regulations such as the wearing of masks or social distancing. Some mosques were divided into two sections, one for those who wear masks and practice social distancing, and another that ignores these restrictions.

Many mosques and groups of people in Cape Town took their Friday worship online. Some of the online *khuṭbah* were broadcast simultaneously on YouTube and Facebook. When mosques were reopened, these online practices continued for those who could not be accommodated in the mosques, and for those who preferred to follow the service online. I take a closer look at a Friday pre-*khuṭbah* talk delivered on February 5, 2021, to a physically distanced congregation in a prominent mosque in Cape Town. The sermon went live on a YouTube channel, which I listened to a few weeks later.[3] I chose this from a number of similar sermons that I listened to over the course of 2020 and 2021. The Imam's pre-*khuṭbah* talk on mosques provides an excellent reflection of a mosque performance threatened by disruption through closure.

Moral Exhortation in Cape Town

The Imam was born in 1960 in District 6, one among many places that became iconic for resisting forced removals under apartheid legislation. His family was relocated to a working-class neighborhood of Bonteheuvel, set aside by the apartheid regime exclusively for a designated racial group called coloureds. After completing high school, the Imam went to study for two years in Newcastle, in the UK, at a Deobandi seminary. He then went to the city of Durban, where he joined the popular Ahmad Deedat as a trainee preacher. In the 1980s, Deedat became famous for his debates with Christian ministers and pastors, first in Durban and then globally (Vahed 2009). The Imam regarded his stay with Deedat as a major stage in his training for his religious and personal development. Deedat gave him the confidence to express himself in public, a skill that he continues to use in his present position.

After a short period as an imam in a small town in another province of South Africa (Polokwane), the imam returned to Cape Town to continue his studies at the Islamic College of South Africa. The college was founded as an initiative to introduce prospective Muslim leaders to both Islamic and modern social sciences. After graduating from the college, which entitled him to be called a Shaykh in Muslim society, the imam was appointed to the Bridgetown Mosque in a working-class neighborhood. He became a popular teacher, leading prayers in the mosque and offering additional lectures to a growing following. The period of service to the Muslims in Bridgetown consolidated his position as a religious leader in the city.

In 2009, he was offered a position as chief imam at one of the largest and most imposing mosques in the city in an affluent neighborhood. It is very likely that his reputation as a popular preacher and teacher endeared him to the mosque committee of the Masjidul Quds. Named in honor of the mosque in Jerusalem, this mosque was founded by traders in 1989 in an apartheid-defined Indian area. For its twenty-fifth anniversary, the board of the mosque produced a full-color coffee-table book documenting its history and special features (Parker 2018). It describes the founding of the mosque in the context of forced removals and the relocation of businesses and places of worship during apartheid and celebrates the design and development of the mosque for its uniqueness in the city and country. More recently, the mosque board has ventured into several revenue-generating projects to become self-sufficient. These include silver- and gold coin collections for marriage gifts, the sale of DVDs showing prominent speakers at the mosque, the sale of food on Fridays, and the organization of international religious tours. The businessmen on the mosque board seem to be using their skills to turn the mosque into a revenue-generating enterprise.

The commemorative volume prides itself on the distinction of the Masjidul Quds in two respects. First, the mosque not only consists of a space for prayer and worship, but it also includes a religious school (*madrasah*), a library, a gift shop, and a soup kitchen. The commemorative volume takes pride in the multifunctional character of the mosque. In addition, it praises the "open policy" in relation to the speakers and ideas presented at the mosque. The imam referred to this distinction in his pre-*khuṭbah* talk and emphasized it in an interview.[4] It was the first mosque in South Africa, he said, that decided that the preservation of life (*ḥifẓ al-nafs*) demanded that the mosque be closed during the pandemic. He explicitly referred to the *maqāṣid al-sharīʿah* (the general purposes of the Shariah) to justify his decision. The decision was taken while his colleagues in the Muslim Judicial Council were still deliberating on the matter. For this and other reasons, the imam identifies the mosque as "progressive."

This claim to distinction has been part of the history of mosques in the Western Cape. From the time when these mosques were founded toward the end of slavery, imams competed against each other on their educational credentials, the religious schooling they offered for children and adults, and their attendance to the central rites of passage. They vied with each other for leadership of the mosques, and often reminded their followers of their distinctiveness (Davids 1980: 5; Shell 1984; Tayob 1999: 27). Such claims do not go unchallenged, and the imam's time at the Masjidul Quds has not been without controversy. When the mosque extended an invitation to popular American preacher Nouman Ali Khan for the Ramadan of 2019, a petition was begun to demand that the invitation be reversed. Khan was accused of sexual impropriety with some of his students and admirers.[5] The imam and the mosque maintained that the charges against Khan were not proven in a court of law. Besides, Khan had eventually declared to have made his *tawbah* (repentence) with Allah, the imam told me in an interview. The controversy did not deter worshippers from attending Khan's lectures. Like other prominent and popular speakers and Qur'an reciters invited before him, he attracted hundreds to the mosque with his nightly lectures.

The Pre-*khuṭbah* Talk

The pre-*khuṭbah* talk revolves around the challenge of closing mosques during a large part of 2020 (see "The Flow of the Pre-khuṭbah Talk"). Given when the state relaxed lockdown regulations in early 2021, the pre-*khuṭbah* talk celebrates the opening of the mosques, with most of the talk focusing on the significance of mosques in Islam. It emphasizes a narrative of primordial mosques associated with Adam, Abraham, and Muhammad, and links this narrative to mosques in the city. But this celebration stands in contrast with the imam's ethical argument and decision to close the mosque. The Imam criticizes the abuse of the Qur'an in the responses of some religious leaders to the Covid-19 lockdown measures. The pre-*khuṭbah* talk moves between these two points. The one underlines a performance that binds mosques together, while the other justifies the ethical decision to close the mosque. By connecting these two points, the pre-*khuṭbah* talk demonstrates how commitment, ethics, and creativity meet in an Islamic discourse.

I have identified three features of the pre-*khuṭbah* talk that show the imam's ability to represent and engage Islamic discourse. The first was a recitation of verses from Qur'an and the use of Arabic phrases that establishes a connection between the talk and Islamic discourse. Second, the talk uses metaphors to connect the mosque, other mosques in the neighborhood, and the great mosques of Islam. These metaphors play an important role in linking local traditions and performances to the general discourse of Islam. Third, the Imam's talk includes creative and ethical pronouncements that stand in tension with an established mosque practice.

The Flow of the Pre-*khuṭbah* Talk

- Masjid now open again
- Opening verses from Quran: Surat al-Shams for Muslims to "nurture [an] angelic quality"
- Major Mosques in Islam: Adam, Abraham, Muhammad
    - Cape Town Mosques connected to these
- Mosques in Covid-19 Times
    - Masjidul Quds first to close mosque to avoid becoming a super-spreader
    - An argument against those who do not want to close mosques
- Imam's illness
    - Personal visit to the mosque during lockdown
    - Mosque inhabited by angels and *jinns*
- Mosques and the Ka'ba in Mecca
    - Qur'an verse: *shajaratun tayyiba*
    - Prophetic hadith: mosques as the garden of paradise
- Conclusion
    - Go to the mosque wherever you may be
    - Contribute to the expenses (water and electricity)
    - Prayer for the sick, and those who have recovered from Covid-19

The Meaning of Arabic

The imam is adept at quoting from the Quran and prophetic hadith, and other Arabic terms and phrases. He recites the Qur'an beautifully, in a slow and measured manner. The imam told to me that he had not memorized the whole Qur'an, but his talk shows him quoting effortlessly without relying on notes or memory cards. I will present some examples from the pre-*khuṭbah* talk on his citation of the Qur'an and conclude this section with a reflection on the significance of Arabic that emerged in the pre-*khuṭbah* talk given by the chairperson of the Mosque Board on June 4, 2021.[6]

As is customary, the pre-*khuṭbah* talk opens with a verse from the Qur'an. In this case, the verses from the *Surah al-Shams* (The Sun) do not seem directly relevant to the main theme of the talk. But the imam uses them to remind listeners "to nurture … [an] angelic quality and to nurture the divine in man." While somewhat off topic, the commentary on the verse falls in line with moral exhortation in Islam. More substantially than the first quotation from the Qur'an, three other quotations hold the theme of the talk together. They are directly relevant to mosques and the challenge of Covid-19. The imam cites the verses and translates them for the audience.

The first Qur'anic citation sets up a primordial base for mosques:

> *Inna awwala bayt wuḍiʿa lilladhī bibakkata mubārakan wa hudan li ʾl-ʿālimīn.* (Qur'an 3:96)
>
> The first place and masjid of worship on this earth was the Kaʿba, the first building to be built by the first man, the first building to be built, by the first man was Adam, Nabi Adam (*alayh al-salam*), *huda li al-ʿālamīn*, as a guidance, for the entire humanity and so we can see that the Kaʿba as it stands there in all its glory and Majesty is the symbol of *tawhid* [oneness of God].

The translation of the verses is blended with a free commentary by the preacher. The next citation from the Qur'an is a criticism of those who were hesitant or refused to close mosques during the Covid-19 epidemic:

> *Wa man aẓlam mimman manaʿa masājid allah an yudhkara fīhā 'smuhu wa saʿā fī kharābihā.* (Qur'an 2:114)
>
> Who can be more unjust than those who prevent others from the *masājid*, where the name of Allah is remembered?

The third citation does not refer directly to mosques in the Qur'an. But the imam interprets it creatively to evoke a global image of mosques aligned to the Kaʿba in Mecca:

> … *kalimatan ṭayyibatan ka shajaratin ṭayyibatin aṣluhā thabit wa farʿūhā fī 'l-samāʾ.* (Qur'an 14:24)

> That a good word and good *du'ā'* like a giant strong tree, the roots is [*sic*] firmly entrenched in and its branches are stretching in every direction. So, the Ka'ba, in the context of our discussion, can be seen as that giant tree with thousands and thousands of branches stretching throughout the world and every masjid is a branch of that Ka'ba.

The Qur'anic references anchor the talk. Some are used to support his theme, while some are used to support his criticism of others.

The pre-*khuṭbah* talk employs many Arabic terms and words that do not require translation: *du'ā'* (supplication), *ṣalāt*, *masjid* and *masajid* (mosques), *jinn* and *malā'ikah* (angels). Here is one good example from the talk that shows the frequent use of Arabic in an English sentence:

> I felt there was presence in this *Masjid* whether it was the presence of the *malā'ikah*, whether it was the presence of the good *jinn* [who] also make *ṣalāt* here with us and they worship Allah.

This statement brings together several Islamic terms in Arabic directly related to a mosque (*masjid*). The Arabic used in the pre-*khuṭbah* talk is part of the discourse of Islam, which is centered in Arabic through the Qu'ran, prophetic hadith, and other literatures.

The significance of Arabic became a subject of reflection in the pre-*khuṭbah* talk given by the chairperson of the mosque board on June 4, 2021. The talk was dedicated to the practice of *jumu'ah* (Friday worship), the day itself and the special devotions assigned for it. The preacher singles out the Arabic *khuṭbah* for special consideration in his talk:

> When the imam climbs the *mimbar* [raised pulpit] we are supposed to be absolutely quiet and listen to the *khuṭbah*. Someone feels that this is Arabic and I don't understand, and believe you me, and this is an experience that I [too] have found. Although you do not understand it, it is miraculous that you know what is going on and you really do understand. You pick up some of the words and you pick up the essence of the Arabic *khuṭbah*.

This statement is important for at least two reasons. First, the value of Arabic supersedes cognitive understanding. Arabic in the pre-*khuṭbah* draws on the power of Arabic as a universally shared sound, whose essence can be "picked up" by those present. Without cognitive control, different meanings (essences) may be sensed through this inaccessibility. But the statements reveal some disquiet about listening to an address (*khuṭbah*) in a language that most of those present do not understand. The chairperson is aware of this anomaly, which he attributes to a miracle. This awareness reveals a moment of self-reflection, perhaps even a doubt, that a moral exhortation would normally be cognitively accessible.

This dimension of the pre-*khutbah* talk, then, is a profusion of verses from the Qur'an, which are beautifully recited but economically translated by an imam. The auditory sound is an important part of the performance that is skillfully used by the preacher to direct his presentation. But the cognitive dimension of the interpretation may be limited or expanded by the experience of a miracle through Arabic, the sound of which is central to Islamic discourse.

The Work of Metaphor

Recent scholarship has pointed to the close connection between preaching (*khiṭābah*) and oratory (*balāghah*) (Qutbuddin 2008). This pre-*khuṭbah* talk employs metaphorical tropes that connect the present with a significant past (Ricœur 1978). The Imam connects his mosque with the prophets of Islam (Adam, Abraham, and Muhammad), and with the sacred house in Mecca. He also uses the history of a neighboring mosque to make a connection to a local practice. In general, he uses metaphor to connect his mosque and all other mosques in the world to the Kaʿba in Mecca. These metaphors assign significance to the everyday mosque practices in the city in general, and in this mosque in particular.

The metaphorical process is evident in the Imam's narrative of the founding moment of the Prophet's mosque in Medina, and the first mosque in this part of the city. Their respective locations were marked by animals which their riders (the Prophet Muhammad and Soofie Saheb, respectively) allowed to stop where they wished:

> When he reached Medina the very first thing that the Prophet (saw) did when he arrived in Medina, he said where my camel Qaswa stops, there will I build my Masjid.
>
> … when Mawlana Abd al-Karim (*raḥmat allah alayh*), that great *Walī* of Allah that is buried there in the Habibyya complex [mosque nearby], when he arrived under the instruction of his teacher, his spiritual mentor Hazrat Soofie Saheb (*rahmat allah alayh*), he said also wherever my horse is going to stop there I am going to build a Masjid.

In Medina and Cape Town, the exact location of the mosques was left to the will of God working through the camel and horse, respectively. After demonstrating this similarity, the imam asserts that there is a universal pattern of founding mosques: "And so you can see the sunnah of all the Prophets have become the inherent sunnah of every Muslim community." The founding of mosques is everywhere divinely determined in meticulous detail. It is a *sunnah*, a normative practice, that never changes.

In another example, the imam reinforces the local mosque tradition and its practices. Using a prophetic tradition this time, he connects all mosques to an eschatology:

> And so the Prophet (saw) encourages us by saying *wa idhā marartum bi riyāḍ al-janna, fa arta'u* whenever you walk past the gardens of paradise, *farta'ū* take from the fruit of that *jannah*.
>
> Listen to this, whenever you walk past the gardens of *jannah*, enjoy from the fruits of that *Jannah*. And so that *Saḥāba* asked, '*wa mā riyad al-janna ya rasūl allah?* What are the gardens of Paradise? And the Prophets (saw) said: *al-masajid.*

This citation comes at the end of the talk when the imam is encouraging those present to support the mosque by visiting it and by supporting it financially. Using this hadith, he encourages greater participation in the activities of the mosque. This participation is placed in a grand eschatological scheme in which all mosques take part.

These examples of metaphors used in the pre-*khuṭbah* talk illustrate how local practices are connected to primordial and global practices. Historically, mosques are connected to an imaginary canvas of Adam, Abraham, and Mecca. Everyday practices are also consecrated through this inclusive image. While most of these metaphors may easily be shared by different preachers, the imam also demonstrates some creativity in his representation of the discourse. For example, his use of *sunnah* for a historical event is unusual. Used in jurisprudence and hadith, the *sunnah* is well known to his audience for prophetic practices that they adopt or ought to adopt. The imam uses the term to articulate a normative social model.

Covid-19 Disruption

While the imam devotes most attention to the significance of mosque practices, he cannot ignore the threat posed by Covid-19 and related government measures. He addresses this threat by criticizing those who refused to close mosques. He also shares his personal experience of Covid-19, which demonstrates his personal attachment to the mosque. The tensions between mosque practices and the ethical decision to close the mosques are not fully resolved. The discourse emphasizes the central role of mosques, while an ethical decision demands their closure.

After a short introduction, the imam celebrates the reopening of the mosque:

> *Al-ḥamdu lillah*, the *masjid* is once again open, praise be to Allah, and this is the sign and expression of relief that you hear from so many people, *Al hamdlu lillah*, we can go to the masjid.

This is then followed by extensive quotations from the Qur'an and hadith on the significance of the mosque in Islam. At the same time, the imam celebrates the mosque's closure to save lives: "Masjidul Quds was the first masjid that was to close down in South Africa." The decision was taken, he argues, so that the mosque did not become a "super-spreader." Despite the closure, he adds, the "blessings of Allah and *raḥmah* [mercy] of Allah will always descend on the Masjid."

The imam then turns to those who did not close the mosques immediately, or at all. He does not dwell on the juridical debate raging in South Africa among Muslim leaders. He argues instead that they built their objection on a misunderstanding of the Qur'an:

> They quoted the Quranic ayah totally out of context *Wa man aẓlama mimman manaʿa masajid allah wa saʿā fi kharābihā*. "Who can be more unjust than those who prevent others from the *masājid* in which the name of Allah is remembered." This *ayah* [verse] was originally sent by Allah against the *kuffār* [disbelievers] who went out of their way to prevent the prophet and the Muslims from praying in the *Masjid al-Ḥarām* [the sacred mosque in Mecca]. It does not refer to us who had the fear of the virus being spread here.

The imam criticizes the decision of those who "quoted the Quranic *ayah* totally out of context." His criticism is based on the value of contextual interpretation, which he most likely learnt in his training with Deedat or the Islamic College of South Africa. The idea of contextual interpretation became dominant among some Muslims in the 1980s, derived essentially from the work of the Pakistani scholar and intellectual Fazlur Rahman (Esack 1988).

However, the imam does not stop there, but continues to a deeper challenge posed by the pandemic to the fundamental dispositions of Muslims during times of crisis:

> And it is proven throughout the country that people who came to the Masjid and they had *imān* [faith], they had *tawakkul* [trust] in Allah, but they contracted

> the virus. Because Islam does not teach you irresponsibility; Islam does not teach you to be reckless.

The imam reminds his listeners that those who insisted on going to the mosque with faith and trust in God were not protected against the virus. Faith and trust in God are central dispositions of a Muslim's relation with God. In this case, these dispositions did not prevent the rapid spread of the pandemic. While the imam argues against his opponents on misquoting a verse, he opens an important theological question. He concludes this line of thinking with a statement that appears to offer an answer: "Islam does not teach you to be reckless."

The imam then devotes considerable time in sharing his personal experience of Covid-19, which further accentuates the significance of mosques and the decision to close them. He indirectly mentions his illness and his recovery at a hospital. But more extensively, he dwells on how he came to the mosque when it was locked down for everyone else:

> I felt there was presence in this *Masjid* whether it was the presence of the *malā'ikah*, whether it was the presence of the good *jinn* [who] also make *ṣalāt* here with us and they worship Allah.

This personal touch confirms his commitment to the tradition of visiting the mosque, and how it ought to continue.

> So it is not easy for us to keep the Masjid closed. But if the situation demands ... [then] we have to do it. But now that the Masjid is open let us take maximum use of this opportunity. Let us once again link our hearts to this Masjid.

He seems to be telling any detractors that he is committed to this practice despite closing the mosque at the start of the pandemic. He continued to visit the mosque and can confirm that the angels were also there while humans could not enter.

In the context of closing mosques for a long period of time, the imam seems to recognize the threat posed by Covid-19 to the mosque practice. On the one hand, he uses the opportunity to show the ethical response of the mosque to the lockdown measures. He dismisses those who refused to close mosques or were hesitant to do so. He and his mosque demonstrated their leadership role in Covid-19 times. But the imam may also be concerned about the threat that a long-term closure poses to mosque performances. He fills the mosques with spirits when the humans are no longer there. And he urges humans to come as soon as they are able to do so.

Conclusion

I have presented a close analysis of one sermon given during the Covid-19 pandemic in Cape Town. It offers a vivid example of how a pre-*khuṭbah* moral exhortation takes part in Islamic discourse. It does this through the employment of quotations and terms from the long history of this discourse. It also employs metaphors that connect the general discourse of Islam to a local history and practice. Recalling key Qur'anic verses, the talk puts together a narrative of mosques founded by God's messengers from Adam to Muhammad. The imam's talk establishes the fundamental value of the mosque in Islam, interwoven with the history of a local mosque. He consecrates a practice and authority of mosques shaped in the history of Muslims in the country.

This general significance of mosques stands in tension with the demands of the Covid-19 pandemic. The government of South Africa forced mosques and other public spaces to close, which challenged the practices of imams and Muslims. While most of his talk was directed at highlighting the significance of the mosques in Islamic discourse, the imam insists that he did the right thing by closing the mosque. The ethical choice made stands in contrast to mosque performances in general and in South Africa in particular. The imam's articulation of this ethical decision, however, is drawn from resources in the discourse. He offers a "correct" reading of the Qur'an, and a rejection of those who do not take context into consideration. His decision shows that a discourse is not limited to committed performance but includes self-reflexive and creative engagements with it.

Islamic discourse is a complex phenomenon that mediates the past, the global, and the local. The pre-*khuṭbah* talk celebrates and further extends a recognizable mosque performance with creative and idiosyncratic engagement. At the same time, it does not avoid taking a critical, ethical stand. The challenge comes from the world out there, but the ethical response is woven from a rereading and appraisal of resources in the discourse. The pre-*khuṭbah* talk may be a temporal event that passes, but it is part of a discourse whose past is known but whose future is difficult to predict.

Islamic discourse should not be characterized as a bounded code or performance that is either represented by obedient and intense performance or unsettled by the challenges of modernity. It is both. Moral exhortations confirm a performance shaped by the teachings of Islam in local history and politics. They do this by recalling and retelling significant events and texts. But they are not blind to the complexity and depth of the discourse that can be employed as part of this performance. Moral exhortations do not offer a definitive account of how Muslims in general or the imam in particular respond to threats and challenges. However, in their consideration of these threats and challenges, they offer some insight into how the discourse may be reshaped and extended.

Notes

1 Cf. a juridical opinion (*fatwā*) on missing the Friday service: https://darulifta-deoband.com/home/en/jumuah-eid-prayers/36922 (accessed May 17, 2023).
2 Mohamed and Others versus President of the Republic of South Africa and Others (21402/20) [2020] ZAGPPHC 120; [2020] 2 All SA 844 (GP); 2020 (7) BCLR 865 (GP); 2020 (5) SA 553 (GP) (April 30, 2020).
3 The sermon can be found here: https://www.youtube.com/watch?v=LccFmh9l7oE (accessed May 17, 2023).
4 The interview was conducted in person on March 8, 2021 between the imam and Abdulkader Tayob.
5 Hannah Allam (2017) and Shabnam Palesa Mohamed (2019).
6 The talk can be found here: https://www.youtube.com/watch?v=TLx6Vpb2uBw (accessed May 17, 2023).

References

Abenante, Paola, and Daniele Cantini (2014), "Introduction," in Paola Abenante and Daniele Cantini (eds.), *Life-Worlds and Religious Commitment: Ethnographic Perspectives on Subjectivity and Islam*, 3–19, Venice: La Ricerca Folklorica.

Ahmed, Shahab (2017), *What Is Islam? The Importance of Being Islamic*, Princeton, NJ: Princeton University Press.

Antoun, Richard (1989), *Muslim Preacher in the Modern World*, Princeton, NJ: Princeton University Press.

Asad, Talal (2003), *Formations of the Secular: Christianity, Islam, Modernity*, Stanford: Stanford University Press.

Asad, Talal (2020), "Thinking About Religion through Wittgenstein," *Critical Times*, 3 (3): 403–42.

Aydin, Cemil (2017), *The Idea of the Muslim World: A Global Intellectual History*, Cambridge, MA: Harvard University Press.

Azm, Sadik (2005), "Islam, Terrorism, and the West," *Comparative Studies of South Asia*, 25 (1): 6–14.

Berkey, Jonathan (2001), *Popular Preaching and Religious Authority in the Medieval Islamic Near East*, Seattle: University of Washington Press.

Berkey, Jonathan (2020), "Preaching and the Problem of Religious Authority in Medieval Islam," in Elisabeth Özdalga and Simon Stjernholm (eds.), *Muslim Preaching in the Middle East and Beyond: Historical and Contemporary Case Studies*, 67–82, Edinburgh: Edinburgh University Press.

Borthwick, Bruce (1967), "The Islamic Sermon as a Channel of Political Communication," *Middle East Journal*, 21 (3): 299–313.

Davids, Achmat (1980), *The Mosques of Bo-Kaap: A Social History of Islam at the Cape*, Cape Town: The S. A. Institute of Arabic and Islamic Research.

Eaton, Richard (1990), *Islamic History as Global History*, Washington, DC: American Historical Association.

Esack, Farid (1988), "Three Islamic Strands in the South Africa Struggle for Justice," *Third World Quarterly*, 10 (2): 473–98.

Gaffney, Patrick (1988), "Magic, Miracle and the Politics of Narration in the Contemporary Islamic Sermon," *Religion and Literature*, 20 (1): 111–37.

Gaffney, Patrick (1994), *The Prophet's Pulpit: Islamic Preaching in Contemporary Egypt*, Berkeley: University of California Press.

Geertz, Clifford (1957), "Ritual and Social Change: A Javanese Example," *American Anthropologist*, 59 (1): 32–54.

Geertz, Clifford (1966), "Religion as a Cultural System," in Michael Banton (ed.), *Anthropological Approaches to the Study of Religion*, 1–45, London: Tavistock Publications.

Hanafi, Sari (2019), "'We Speak the Truth!': Knowledge and Politics in Friday's Sermons in Lebanon," *Contemporary Arab Affairs*, 12 (2): 53–80.

Hirschkind, Charles (2001), "Civic Virtue and Religious Reason: An Islamic Counterpublic," *Cultural Anthropology*, 16 (1): 3–34.

Hirschkind, Charles (2006), *The Ethical Soundscape: Cassette Sermons and Islamic Counterpublics*, New York: Columbia University Press.

Janson, Marloes (2006), "'We Are All the Same, Because We All Worship God.' The Controversial Case of a Female Saint in the Gambia," *Africa*, 76 (4): 502–25.

Jones, Linda (2006), "Ibn 'Abbad of Ronda's Sermon on the Prophet's Birthday Celebration: Preaching the Sufi and Sunni Paths of Islam," *Medieval Sermon Studies*, 50 (1): 31–49.

Jones, Linda (2020), "Discourses on Marriage, Religious Identity and Gender in Medieval and Contemporary Islamic Preaching: Continuities and Adaptations," in Elisabeth Özdalga and Simon Stjernholm (eds.), *Muslim Preaching in the Middle East and Beyond: Historical and Contemporary Case Studies*, 173–200, Edinburgh: Edinburgh University Press.

Kepel, Gilles (2002), *Jihad, the Trail of Political Islam*, Cambridge: Belknapp Press.

Khalidi, Tarif (1994), *Arabic Historical Thought in the Classical Period*, Cambridge: Cambridge University Press.

Mahmood, Saba (2001), "Rehearsed Spontaneity and the Conventionality of Ritual: Disciplines of Ṣalāt," *American Ethnologist*, 28 (4): 827–53.

Makboul, Laila (2020), "Going Online: Saudi Female Intellectual Preachers in the New Media," in Elisabeth Özdalga and Simon Stjernholm (eds.), *Muslim Preaching in the Middle East and Beyond: Historical and Contemporary Case Studies*, 107–31, Edinburgh: Edinburgh University Press.

Mittermaier, Amira (2014), "Beyond Compassion: Islamic Voluntarism in Egypt," *American Ethnologist*, 41 (3): 518–31.

Mozaffari, Mehdi (1998), *Fatwa: Violence and Discourtesy*, Aarhus: Aarhus University Press.

Olsson, Susanne (2020), "Advising and Warning the People: Swedish Salafis on Violence, Renunciation and Life in the Suburbs," in Elisabeth Özdalga and Simon Stjernholm (eds.), *Muslim Preaching in the Middle East and Beyond: Historical and Contemporary Case Studies*, 155–72, Edinburgh: Edinburgh University Press.

Parker, Abdus Sataar (2018), *A History of Masjid Al-Quds, Celebrating 25 Years of Devotion and Inpsiration*, Cape Town: Masjid a-Quds Institute.

Pedersen, Johannes (1955), "The Criticism of the Islamic Preacher," *Die Welt des Islams*, 2 (4): 215–31.

Qutbuddin, Tahera (2008), "*Khuṭba:* The Evolution of Early Arabic Oration," in Beatrice Gruendler and Michael Cooperson (eds.), *Classical Arab Humanities in Their Own Terms: Festschrift for Wolfhart Heinrichs*, 176–273, Leiden: Brill.

Ricoeur, Paul (1978), "The Metaphorical Process as Cognition, Imagination, and Feeling," *Critical inquiry*, 5 (1): 143–59.

Schielke, Samuli (2014), "I Want to Be Committed: Short-Lived Trajectories of Salafi Activism in Egypt," *La Ricerca Folklorica*, 69: 21–37.

Schulz, Dorothea (2012), "Dis/embodying Authority: Female Radio 'Preachers' and the Ambivalences of Mass-Mediated Speech in Mali," *International Journal of Middle East Studies*, 44 (1): 23–43.

Shell, Robert (1984), "Rites and Rebellion: Islamic Conversion at the Cape, 1808 to 1915," *Studies in the History of Cape Town*, 5: 51–46.

Sounaye, Abdoulaye (2017), "Salafi Aesthetics: Preaching among the Sunnance in Niamey, Niger," *Journal of Religion in Africa*, 47 (1): 9–41.

Stjernholm, Simon (2020), "Brief Reminders: Muslim Preachers, Mediation and Time," in Elisabeth Özdalga and Simon Stjernholm (eds.), *Muslim Preaching in the Middle East and Beyond: Historical and Contemporary Case Studies*, 132–52, Edinburgh: Edinburgh University Press.

Stjernholm, Simon and Elisabeth Özdalga (2020), "Introduction," in Elisabeth Özdalga and Simon Stjernholm (eds.), *Muslim Preaching in the Middle East and Beyond: Historical and Contemporary Case Studies*, 1–16, Edinburgh: Edinburgh University Press.

Tayob, Abdulkader I. (1999), *Islam in South Africa: Mosques, Imams and Sermons*, Gainesville: University of South Florida Press.

"'Taraas-Soo!' (Shoulder to Shoulder—Like a Solid Steel Wall) (Hadith)" (2020), *The Majlis*, May 28, 46.

Vahed, Goolam (2009), "Ahmed Deedat and Muslim-Christian Relations at the Cape, C. 1960–1980," *Journal for Islamic Studies*, 29 (1): 2–32.

Wittgenstein, Ludwig (1958), *Philosophical Investigations*, Oxford: Basil Blackwell.

Internet References

"Fatwā on Missing the Friday Service." Available online: https://darulifta-deoband.com/home/en/jumuah-eid-prayers/36922 (accessed May 17, 2023).

Alexander, Abdurahman (2021), "Jumah Lecture," *YouTube*, February 5, 2021. Available online: https://www.youtube.com/watch?v=LccFmh9l7oE (accessed May 17, 2023).

Allam, Hannah (2017), "Payoffs, Threats, and Secret Marriages: How an Accused Preacher Is Fighting to Save His Empire," *BuzzFeed.News*, December 21, 2017. Available online: https://www.buzzfeednews.com/article/hannahallam/payoffs-threats-and-sham-marriages-women-say-a-celebrity (accessed May 17, 2023).

Mohamed, Shabnam Palesa (2019), "Nouman Ali Khan Does Not Deserve Public Platforms in South Africa," *Al-Qalam*, April 29, 2019. Available online: https://alqalam.co.za/nouman-ali-khan-does-not-deserve-public-platforms-in-south-africa/ (accessed May 17, 2023).

Parker, Hajie Abdussattaar (2021), "Jumah Lecture," *YouTube*, June 4, 2021. Available online: https://www.youtube.com/watch?v=TLx6Vpb2uBw (accessed May 17, 2023).

Part 2

Popularity and Normativity in Sermons

4

Unity and Justice and Freedom: Preached Religious Staging of Political Values in the Public Sermons on the Day of German Unity (*Tag der Deutschen Einheit*)

Jan Hermelink

Potsdam Day (Der Tag von Potsdam, March 21, 1933): Ambivalences of Popular Preaching in Protestant Germany

Popularity and preaching—these are not easy to combine in Germany, at least not in the twenty-first century, and not in the Protestant state churches. But these churches, their programs, and their practices are my field of research. So I had to look for a current form of preaching that is—or at least tries to be—popular while giving normative orientation.[1]

In Christian churches, there is at least one kind of popular sermon that is also highly normative, namely political preaching (*Politische Predigt*): affirming or criticizing political decisions, the balance of political power, and the dominant values of society (Grözinger 2004: 183–213; Keller 2017). This kind of preaching has a long tradition, perhaps beginning with the prophets of the Hebrew Bible, and in the Protestant churches with Luther's sermons for the magistrates and kings (Braune-Krickau and Galle 2021). And political preaching remains popular now—at least in some religious milieus, where criticizing political decisions is a safe way to get approval and support.

But what about a political preaching that tries to transcend the familiar milieus of the religiously engaged? Is there a place for political preaching that really tries to become popular, in a broader sense? In answering this question, my attention has been drawn to popular, even national events, where a sermon may reach politics and the people. However, this path is quite ambivalent, especially in Germany. This is illustrated by an event that took place some ninety years ago, on March 21, 1933, in three churches in Potsdam.

The so-called Potsdam Day was a propaganda event arranged by the recently installed government of Adolf Hitler (Kopke and Treß 2013). After the National Socialist Party had won the national election, on March 5, 1933, Hitler's gang planned a public reconciliation of old and new power, an act of state at which Paul Hindenburg, war hero and president of the Reich, welcomed Hitler as the hero of the nation's future. Whereas this ceremony, carefully staged, took place at the Garrison Church (*Garnisonkirche*), it was prefaced by two services in other churches, for the Catholic and for the Protestant members of the new parliament. At the Protestant service at St. Nicholas Church (*Nikolaikirche*), the general superintendent and later bishop of Berlin, Otto Dibelius, preached the sermon. Here are just some sentences of that sermon:

> In the Peasants War, Martin Luther openly encouraged the authorities to act ruthlessly to establish order again in Germany. But with the same sternness, Luther admonished the authorities not to falsify their [divine] office by revengefulness and conceit. Luther demanded justice and mercy, as soon as order was restored, and we as Protestant church must say this with Luther's frankness: No confounding of political office and personal despotism! Justice and love must reign so that every honest man can be in favor of his nation again. (Brechenmacher 2013: 95; Fritz 1988: 399–400; transl. JH)

Dibelius's sermon oscillated between nationalist populism and restrictive admonition (Schieder 2021: 287–9); and reactions were also highly ambivalent. Hermann Göring named it "the best sermon I ever heard," while another National Socialist official sharply rebuked Dibelius's "assault against our movement" (Koch 1988: 8). In these contrasting comments, the twofold tradition of political preaching in Germany is condensed paradigmatically. On the one hand, there is a long tradition, especially in the Lutheran churches, of affirming the political system and strengthening the sovereign's power: "Throne and altar" were placed close to each other. On the other hand, there is a long tradition of criticizing the ruler's decisions or performance—without contesting the system of political power.

In today's Germany, with a democratic constitutional order and mostly democratic institutions, this balancing act of political preaching is nevertheless essential: How to balance political affirmation, especially for a democratic system, with criticism of political failure and misconduct? This ambivalence is the heritage of every public preaching, aiming at popular and normative effects at the same time. And there are some events in every democratic society where this complex mission becomes especially delicate, for example, at the opening of a new parliament's session, or at the day celebrating the constitution. In contemporary Germany, there is a further occasion for preaching politically, which is even more popular, namely the celebration of German reunification, the Day of German Unity (*Tag der Deutschen Einheit*), which since the 1990s has become a kind of civic fair.

The Day of German Unity (October 3): Popular Event, Normative Claims, Political Preaching

In Germany, the Day of German Unity (*Tag der Deutschen Einheit*) is a public holiday that commemorates the reunification of East and West Germany, on October 3, 1990. Since then, national festivities have taken place in one of the federal states, changing every year.[2] Before the opening of the state ceremony—with speeches by the Federal President and other political representatives—a service, usually ecumenical, is celebrated; most of the official guests participate in it.

Some political speeches given on that day have gained popularity. In 2010, in Bremen, Federal President Christian Wulff said: "Christianity and Judaism belong to Germany. And meanwhile, Islam also belongs to Germany."[3] This sentence was debated fiercely—because it was heard (and meant) as a clear normative statement, affirming religious plurality in German society.[4]

At the Christian services opening the Day of German Unity, the sermons are mainly preached by local bishops. Up to half a million people watch the events on television. Many other church services are held on that day in most federal state capitals, at some former border crossings, and at national monuments. All the sermons delivered on that occasion are addressed to the public—not only to people worshiping regularly; and at any rate, the sermons at the national festivities can be seen as paradigms of political preaching. For a chapter on popularity and normativity in religious speech, it should be instructive to investigate some of these sermons: How do they use religious tradition and religious language to validate the dominant values of society, to affirm some political norms, and to criticize others?

For this research, I used the manuscripts of about twenty sermons delivered at the national festivities of the Day of German Unity since 1990; I also read many further sermons given on that occasion by bishops, deans, and other church leaders.[5] For this chapter, I'll focus on three sermons that I consider not only as representative, but also as high-quality examples of public preaching.[6] It may be by coincidence that two of these sermons were preached in Potsdam—or it may be the prejudice of the researcher.

In the following sections, I offer an insight into the process of empirical research that is common in the social sciences, including practical theology: Starting with a few initial questions about the material, there is a detailed reading, gradually identifying typical rhetorical traits, familiar content, and paradigmatic strategies of preaching. At the same time, the categories become clearer, more differentiated. It is a process of permanent oscillation between theory, methodology, and empirical material. To present my findings here, I will begin by explaining some basic criteria; then apply these perspectives to a sermon, which results in the criteria being extended; they are applied to two further sermons. Some brief conclusions can be drawn at the end.

Criteria of Sermon Analysis I: Religious Rhetoric and Political Designation

Sermon analysis is a complex business, because sermons are a very special form of communication. They are not written documents, as we are reminded in this volume; they are not interviews, not stories, and nor are they ordinary public speeches, but a very specific sort of religious utterance. So, for sermon analysis it is important not only to focus on the content of the speech, but also not to pay too much attention to the biography or religious background of the preacher. As the Swiss homiletics researcher Albrecht Grözinger says, "a sermon is a sermon is a sermon" (Grözinger 2004: 15)—it is, in many ways, an autonomous piece of art that must be analyzed as a singular performance and with specific criteria. In the context of this article, I'll concentrate on the sermons' rhetorical, their aesthetical dimensions that—in a homiletical perspective—constitute the framework of their normative claims and also of their (intended) popularity (Grözinger 2008: 177–203).

Three sets of criteria seem adequate for my research question. First, we must examine the religious rhetoric of the respective sermon: Which forms of religious language are used here, by which means does the sermon refer to the Christian tradition, in which ways is religious direction given? And what is the perspective on the congregation: Are they sinners or redeemed, subject to God's wrath or living by divine grace (Burbach 1990: 140–4, 167–8)?

A second set of analytical questions pertains to the political field: Which structures of power are named and challenged? Which dominant values of society are affirmed or criticized—and again: Which rhetorical means are used for that? Are any political conflicts mentioned, and in which light do they appear (Hermelink 2017)? Are there specific forms of political speech that are adopted in the sermon, and even may be varied?

Third, how does the sermon strive to be popular? Is there a shared aesthetic program that would aim at capturing the audience's attention? What are the "mechanisms of exclusion and inclusion" used by the sermons to popularize their claim (Conrad et al. in this volume: 3)? Especially for the sermons on German unity, one should ask: How are people integrated into the nation's community, and, also, how does the sermon handle the difference between believers and nonbelievers, between religious people and those sitting in the pews for other reasons?

Wolfgang Huber in Potsdam (2005): Preaching for Politicians

In 2005, the national Day of German Unity was celebrated in Potsdam, the capital of Brandenburg. The service took place in the St. Nicholas Church, again, and the preacher was Wolfgang Huber, bishop of the Protestant Church of Berlin and Brandenburg. Huber, who was strongly influenced by Dietrich Bonhoeffer, had been a professor of theological ethics from 1980 in Marburg, then Heidelberg, and was active in public Protestantism, for example, as president of the German Evangelical Church Assembly (*Deutscher Evangelischer Kirchentag*). In 1994, he was elected as bishop in Berlin-Brandenburg; from 2003, he also was chairman of the council of the Protestant church in Germany (EKD) (Gessler 2012). In these positions, he initiated fundamental reforms in church structure and communication, and he was a well-known public intellectual in the fields of social ethics.

The sermon Huber gave at St. Nicholas Church presents itself as a religious speech from the very beginning: "We pause before God to give thanks to him and ask him to show us the way. … We are united in the word of Jesus: *whoever wishes to become great among you must be your servant, and whoever wishes to be first among you must be slave of all* [Mk. 10:43-44]."

In many of its sections, especially sections 7–10, the sermon is interpreting the biblical passage from Mark's Gospel. In other passages, Huber refers to the cross, as a sign that "stands for a life path which did not end in the palaces of the mighty" (section 5), but was aligned "to serve, and to give his life a ransom for many." Jesus took "the sting out of death" and was resurrected to life. It may be noted that many other sermons preached on the Day of German Unity also refer to Jesus's cross, to His solidarity with the ones in pain and His "reevaluation of all values."

Another important religious motif in this sermon is the image of the believers (section 8) "bowing only to God, and to nobody else in this world. They stand up straight and refuse to bend. They put themselves in the service of a message in which the love of God is connected with love for their neighbors." This is a posture the preacher also recommends for politicians (section 10) "who bow to God, but otherwise stand straight and remain unbending. We need responsible people who are willing to extend their hand to those in need so that the strong and the weak can achieve their goals together."

There is much more religious rhetoric in this sermon, including many allusions to biblical, hymnal, and theological texts. But let us turn to the rhetoric of politics. This rhetoric dominates the first sections of the sermon (2–4) and also its last passages, from section 10. Whereas the motifs in section 2 are common to many sermons at the Day of German Unity—giving thanks for fulfilled hopes, and then disappointments, even laments over the trials and tribulations of life—the next section (3) is quite unique. It sounds like a political speech to initiate fundamental reforms in economy and society. Also, sections 11 and 12 could easily have come from a politician, maybe a Federal President. Huber was even suggested by some for this position in 2010.[7]

These passages must be understood in the contemporary political context (cf. Brettschneider, Niedermayer, and Weßels 2007).[8] After Chancellor Gerhard Schröder had initiated a fundamental reform of the welfare system in 2003 and 2004, his Social Democratic Party lost some state elections and also the federal election in September 2005. As both Christian and Social Democrats (CDU and SPD) had won nearly the same amounts of mandates, there was a bitter dispute over which party could nominate the chancellor; the negotiations were persisting when this sermon was preached. So the hint at the elections (section 9) and the phrases in section 11—"Political tasks are more important than the combinations of political colors. The topics that move people weigh heavier than the names that concern them"—can be read as a commentary on these political quarrels.

In this context, the preacher unfolds the rhetorically impressive image of "the three domes which shape the image of Potsdam" (section 4). He underlines the political burden Atlas must shoulder, depicts Fortuna as "the goddess of globalization," and portrays the church dome with the cross as a symbol of service until death—and also as an architectural "story of a small resurrection" (section 6). By the way, this reference to the local history of the respective churches and towns is usual for many sermons on the Day of German Unity.

By unfolding this local perspective and extending it into a general orientation, the sermon tries to become popular, for both the religious and the political audience. This dual public is also addressed by naming Jesus's "direction" at the sermon's beginning and end, which is substantiated in the admonition "to give a hand to those in need" and to work hard for "common tasks" (sections 10, 11)—these again are usual topoi in most unification sermons.

But the main line of this sermon is not popular in a general sense. This sermon clearly does not address all citizens, or even every believer—instead, it is directed at the establishment: the elite in church and state. In respect to the ecclesial leadership, the preacher reflects—section 8—on "the responsibility of the churches" and on the topic of power, using intricate wording that reveals much academic skill. To the expert's ear, there are also some hints at the Theological Declaration of Barmen (1934) (*Barmer Theologische Erklärung*): Its fourth thesis is headed by the same biblical quotation as this sermon, and the church's responsibilities are described here in similar words as in section 8.

At the beginning of the sermon, the celebration's congregation (*Festgemeinde*) is addressed, and the "we" of this congregation—pausing before and thanking God—is discerned from the expressed delight over "so many guests [that] have chosen to join us." But in fact, these guests, leading persons in state and society—are the main addressees of this sermon. This preacher is preaching to politicians, he is—in the words of the Barmen Declaration—"calling to mind God's commandment and righteousness, and thereby the responsibility both of rulers and of the ruled" (thesis V). Huber speaks as a church leader and uses the biblical tradition to establish ethical values that are common to the rulers in both spheres (Huber 1990).

Criteria of Sermon Analysis II: Theological Reflection and Popular Scenario

Having explored this example of political preaching, the criteria for analyzing further sermons should be expanded, at least slightly. Just three aspects may be named here.

At first, there is a remarkable amount of theological reflection in this sermon. The task of the church, or the nature of power are reflected here; and also a lot of implicit theological work can be identified: by the preacher's citing ethical key concepts and presenting a complex argumentation. This rhetoric of reflection may not be important directly for popularity, but it enhances the persuasive power of the normative claims. It obviously promotes the communication of basic values, especially to this elite audience.

Second, we can see a constant double coding,[9] a kind of bilingualism in the sermon. The words of admonition, of orientation and encouragement, can be understood in a religious way, but—quite easily—also in a political sense. This double coding can be seen here also in respect to the guiding images, the central metaphors and some other rhetoric means.

One specific double coding seems of particular interest: the image, or the constellation of the three domes in the city of Potsdam, and the view of Atlas, standing on the town hall, seeking orientation with a glance to Fortuna and a glance at the Cross. This may be a religious perspective, but it is also a visualization of the political task. So the central scene, shaping the sermon's imagination until its end, is double coded.

To generalize that observation, it can be assumed that the basic scenario of a sermon, its dramaturgical model, not only supports its "vividness and perspicuity" (Conrad et al. in this volume), but may also be an important rhetorical means for integrating different audiences in popular preaching (Grözinger 2008: 301–2; Nicol and Deeg 2005: 21–4). So the sermon's respective basic scenario will be explored also in the following sermons.

Johannes Hempel at Berlin (1990): From Demonstration to Worship

The very first central church service following German reunification, in 1990, took place at Berlin's medieval St. Mary's Church, situated nearby Alexanderplatz and the Berlin town hall—the traditional preaching site of the Protestant bishop.[10]

In 1990, the sermon was given by a prominent east German theologian, Bishop Johannes Hempel (Hahn 1996). From 1959, he was a lecturer at the St. Paul's Church seminar in Leipzig, and then students' pastor in the same city. In 1972 he was elected bishop of the Protestant Lutheran Church of Saxony, retiring in 1994. From 1990, Hempel was also deputy chairman of the council of the Protestant Church in Germany (EKD). He was active in the World Council of Churches, and was a prominent church spokesperson in the conflicts between many Christians and the Socialist state authorities, which escalated in the late 1980s.

Hempel's sermon is characteristic for a rather traditional style of preaching in Germany. The biblical text is interpreted diligently, and the sermon is clearly divided into three parts, each with a short headline, taken from the biblical motto (Meyer-Blanck 2011: 478–85). There is a lot of religious vocabulary, including most of the verbal phrases in part one and part three: "testifying," "trusting," "turning to God." Other biblical texts are cited also, such as the watchword in section 9. And every part ends with solemn religious speech acts: a thankful turn to God (6), a firm assurance of divine guidance (8), a biblical benediction at the very end (13).

In this sermon, the density of theological language is also remarkable. The acceptance by Christ is explained, or better it is condensed in a tight abbreviation (section 2): "Who he is: supremely independent and sometimes mysteriously hidden." We hear the same density in section 6, on the "riddle of [God's] different leadership," and in section 9: "Christ is not simply, constantly here 'for us' and 'with us' "—this is an allusion to the religious affirmation of political power as well as to Germany's military aggression; and it is also a shortcut of complex Christological reflection (Kühn 2003: 184–213)—double coding again.

Much more political rhetoric can be found in this sermon. At first, most issues named by the preacher refer to the problems arising around the unification process (and these issues can be found in most of the successive sermons at that occasion—Pelz 2019): remembering those "who protested on the streets of the cities in the fall of 1989" (section 4), economic problems and societal frictions after unification (section 7), the call for individual engagement (section 8), and the perspective on "the poor and those without rights in this world" (section 10). Furthermore, many verbal phrases have a political sound: "remembering," "dismay" (section 7), "urgent decisions," and "crisis talks" (section 9).

But does this sermon even try to be popular? Or is the preacher confining himself to "hear and contemplate the word of God" (section 1), and to lamenting over political worries and anxieties? Let's first observe the "we" of that sermon, the specific group the preacher aims to represent at that worship. Is it really only a Christian assembly that he's speaking to? There are some hints that Hempel is not speaking only for Christians. In section 5 he says: "We thank the federal government … And we thank our outgoing government for being active and staying active under difficult conditions." This is clearly an East German perspective; and this eastern "we" can also be found in many other phrases—for example, when "our way of living and thinking" is named (end of section 7), "which emerged in and despite the GDR." This preacher is speaking in the name of the East German people, addressing their (often presented as superior) western counterparts, that "many also fear" (section 7 also).

By which means does the sermon try to make East Germans' sensitivities plausible, or—in a sense—to popularize this perspective, these worries and hopes? What is the guiding scenario here? In my view, the key to that question is again section 7, with its many compact phrases, each addressing a new issue. Which situation is evoked by this way of speaking? Which scenes can be associated with that rhetoric? At first, I thought of a kind of political manifesto, perhaps also a religious manifesto: not ninety-five, but fifteen theses, issued at the city church of Berlin.

But consider the scenes the preacher has evoked some minutes before: "the prayers for peace in a lot of churches"—the ones "who protested on the streets of the cities in the fall of 1989." These are references to the huge processions in Berlin, in Rostock, in Leipzig: starting at churches, with candles, and moving through the city centers, getting larger every week (Timmer 2000).[11] I imagine these phrases—"we think about the spidery fingers of the State Security," "We do also have worries today," the preoccupation with "West German superiority"—being spoken in a peace prayer, and at a political demonstration, perhaps in Alexanderplatz.

So the imagination of this sermon, I think, is double-coded again. It is citing the religious prayer and the political protest, it recalls demonstrations with candles and banners. The East German people are marching here again, in front of their West German counterparts.

But this sermon does not only stage a protest march. As we have seen, each part of the sermon ends with a religious speech act, with solemn intercessions or a final benediction. So in the scenario of this sermon, the protest march is guided from the streets back into the church. All the people whose worries are expressed here, in well-known phrases, are brought to a service at the end; they are encouraged by Christ's critical presence and by God's benediction. Is this popular? At any rate, it is highly normative.

Christian Stäblein at Potsdam (2020): Opening a Popular Banquet

Recently, in October 2020, the state of Brandenburg again hosted the national celebration of German unity; the festivities took place in Potsdam. The opening service was held in the Catholic Church of Saints Peter and Paul, and the sermon was preached by Bishop Christian Stäblein. Stäblein has been principal of the preachers' seminary of the Hanover church in Loccum; in 2014, he became provost of the Protestant Church of Berlin-Brandenburg, leading the theological affairs of its consistory. In 2019, he was elected bishop of that church. He is committed to Jewish-Christian dialogue; and he is a passionate and—in my view—highly gifted preacher.

There is quite another atmosphere in this sermon, much more emotional—with courage, joy, and happy confusion—with rather colloquial wording, with constant wordplay, with images, and with hashtags. Nonetheless, this is a religious speech too, using religious vocabulary—"good news," "handing out the bread" (section 6), "giving thanks in God's name" (section 11)—and interpreting a biblical text, the story of the feeding of the five thousand. The imagery of this story is used in manifold ways: the people being nourished by bread and words, the motif of not being overlooked by Jesus (sections 2 and 10), and the image of the full baskets coming back after the meal. And there is a clear theological structure to this sermon, starting with the Gospel (sections 1–4), moving on to annoyance and doubt (sections 5 and 6), treated exegetically, and then flowing into encouraging appeals.

Almost every one of the sermon's phrases and motives is double-coded. The baskets are filled with good stories, from the Bible and from unification history. The small town of Staaken is unified politically, and its church's picture shows Catholics and Protestants in "'Reconciled Unity'" (section 4).[12] Even most emotions—trust, thanks, joy, and freedom—can be heard both in religious and in secular terms.

The scenario of the biblical feeding of the five thousand is also deployed in some clear political causes, for example, mocking the hoarding toilet paper and food in the pandemic (section 6 at the end), and the several allusions to the refugee issue, such as the hashtag in section 2: "#wehavespaceandevenmore," or—in section 9—the mention of the burning refugee camp in Greece.[13]

As we have seen, this sermon is not averse to being popular: in wording, in posting, in telling some stories from Brandenburg (section 7). But the most popular aspect of this sermon, I think, is its imaginative structure, its underlying scenario. How can this be described? Let us discuss its use of metaphor.

The sermon makes use of food metaphors throughout: being hungry and being sated, breaking bread and sharing basic food, full baskets and even rubbing one's belly. There is a sharing of stories, of courage, of life, a mutual trust that there will be enough of all necessary supplies. And there is movement in this sermon: looking around and filling a gap, bringing in something new and going out to share it. In my mind, the scene of a banquet begins to appear—a large crowd at the tables, meeting friends and sharing stories, enjoying a variety of food and some surprising images—and maybe donating for some good cause.

If this sermon can be heard with the imagination of a popular banquet, then its function is clear: Using religious resources and double-coded hashtags, this sermon is opening the festival that will take place at the Day of German Unity; the sermon gives a theological framework to the celebrations as well as a religious basis.

Conclusion: Crossfading Religious and Popular Scenarios

Just a few concluding remarks. It is worth analyzing the double coding of public preaching: a multilayered naming of issues, the postures recommended for religious as well as for ordinary people, the practices of thanking and of lamenting that occur on the streets and in church. So, research into sermons could make an important contribution to the discussion of "bilingualism" (*Zweisprachigkeit*) within Public Theology (Bedford-Strohm 2015; Van Oorschot and Ziermann 2019): In many communicative situations, also in the public sphere, there are not two distinguished language systems, for example, "the" religious and "the" political language. But in fact, there is—not only in sermons—a kind of interference, or semantic oscillation between different rhetorical codes that enrich and intensify each other.

This oscillation between different codes of communication also pertains to the guiding scenarios. The domes can be glimpsed from the town hall and from the church; a procession may lead through the streets and start at a church, and a banquet can take place at a religious jubilee and at a folk festival. Obviously, the central rhetoric device of this popular preaching consists in blending different scenes, in crossfading (*überblenden*) diverse images. And it's important, I think, that this crossfading goes back and forth: from church to town hall, from the streets to a church service.

Finally: What about normativity? While working on these sermons, a dissertation on ethical preaching came to my mind (Fritz 2011). Regina Fritz analyzed some preaching in Leipzig and East Berlin churches in the fall of 1989. And she also argues that the ethical impact of these sermons is established mainly by concise scenarios, by imagining basic scenes of ethical action. So I think that the sermons on the Day of German Unity are also normative, as they enfold those scenarios: They imagine the values of integration and responsibility, they stage inclusion and encouragement.

And in fact, the sermons that were presented here also stage, in quite a normative way, the relevance of preaching itself: A society in unity, justice, and freedom (*Einigkeit und Recht und Freiheit*—the words of the German national anthem) needs public preaching—it needs worship ceremonies that give these values a horizon of religion. This normative claim is stated by these sermons, by their thematic diligence, by their rhetorical quality, by their careful staging of complex religious visions of political life. And it is homiletical research—I only gave a short example—that demonstrates that claim may gain popularity.

Notes

1 For this text, I kept most of the formulations that were used in the oral presentation.

2 Cf. Text: Landeszentrale für Politische Bildung Baden-Württemberg (2022), "Tag der Deutschen Einheit—3. Oktober 2022," *LPB*, September. Available online: https://www.lpb-bw.de/tag-der-deutschen-einheit (accessed June 26, 2023).

3 Speech by Christian Wulff (2010).

4 Cf. "Zehn Jahre nach Christian Wulffs Rede: Der Islam in Deutschland ist bunter geworden" (Agai 2020).

5 Warm thanks to Lea-Katharina Müller, Göttingen, who made great efforts to collect the sermons—not only on the internet and in books, but also by writing friendly requests to the offices of many churches and bishops.

6 The sermons may be found in the appendices of this volume. They were translated by Amelie Bulitta, Göttingen, and Lucy Duggan. The numeration of the paragraphs is mine, for the use of the analysis given here.

7 Cf. "Die Favoriten" (Heithecker and Sturm 2010) and "Auf Gott vertrauen, den Nächsten lieben und auch mit sich selbst sorgfältig umgehen" (Huber 2014).

8 Cf. also "Bundestagswahl 2015," *Wikipedia*.

9 This term was criticized when I presented an earlier version of this chapter as a talk, as it often seems to refer to a differentiation between a public and a hidden layer of speaking, especially in totalitarian contexts. My use of the phrase "double coding" is meant more technically, in a semiotic context.

10 Cf. Homepage Marienkirche: Eric Haußmann, Alexander Arno Heck, Gregor Hohberg, Antje Lorenz, Roland Stolte, and Corinna Zisselsberger: "Evangelische Kirchengemeinde St. Marien-Friedrichswerder." Available online: https://marienkirche-berlin.de/ (accessed June 27, 2023).

11 Cf. also "Montagsdemonstrationen 1989/1990 in der DDR," *Wikipedia: Die freie Enzyklopädie*.

12 This may be an allusion to the ecumenical phrase of "reconciled diversity"—cf. Meyer (1975).

13 See also the reference to people in jail in Hongkong and Belarus. "Barmer Theologische Erklärung," *Evangelische Kirche Deutschland.* Available online: https://www.ekd.de/en/The-Barmen-Declaration-303.htm (accessed June 27, 2023).

References

Bedford-Strohm, Heinrich (2015), "Öffentliche Theologie in der Zivilgesellschaft," in Florian Höhne and Frederike van Oorschot (eds.), *Grundtexte öffentlicher Theologie*, 211–25, Leipzig: Evangelische Verlagsanstalt.

Braune-Krickau, Tobias, and Christoph Galle (eds.) (2021), *Predigt und Politik: Zur Kulturgeschichte der Predigt von Karl dem Großen bis zur Gegenwart*, Göttingen: v&r unipress.

Brechenmacher, Thomas (2013), "Zwischen Nikolai- und Garnisonkirche: Die Festpredigt des Generalsuperintendenten Otto Dibelius in der Potsdamer Nikolaikirche," in Christoph Kopke and Werner Treß (eds.), *Der Tag von Potsdam: Der 21. März 1933 und die Errichtung der nationalsozialistischen Dikatatur*, 87–99, Berlin/Boston: De Gruyter.

Brettschneider, Frank, Oskar Niedermayer, and Bernhard Weßels (eds.) (2007), *Die Bundestagswahl 2005: Analysen des Wahlkampfes und der Wahlergebnisse*, Wiesbaden: VS-Verlag für Sozialwissenschaften.

Burbach, Christiane (1990), *Argumentation in der "Politischen Predigt": Untersuchungen zur Kommunikationskultur in theologischem Interesse*, Schriften zur Praktischen Theologie, 17, Frankfurt/M.: Peter Lang.

Fritz, Hartmut (1988), *Otto Dibelius: Ein Kirchenmann in der Zeit zwischen Monarchie und Diktatur*, Göttingen: Vandenhoeck & Ruprecht.

Fritz, Regina (2011), *Ethos und Predigt: Eine ethisch-homiletische Studie zu Konstitution und Kommunikation sittlichen Urteilens*, Tübingen: Mohr Siebeck.

Gessler, Philipp (2012), *Wolfgang Huber: Ein Leben für Protestantismus und Politik*, Freiburg im Breisgau: Kreuz Verlag.

Grözinger, Albrecht (2004), *Toleranz und Leidenschaft: Über das Predigen in einer pluralistischen Gesellschaft*, Gütersloh: Gütersloher Verlagshaus.

Grözinger, Albrecht (2008), *Homiletik*, Gütersloh: Gütersloher Verlagshaus.

Hahn, Udo (1996), *Annehmen und frei bleiben: Landesbischof i.R. Johannes Hempel im Gespräch*, Hannover: Lutherisches Verlagshaus.

Hermelink, Jan (2017), "Öffentliche Inszenierung des Individuellen: Praktisch-theologische Beobachtungen zu den politischen Implikationen der Praxis evangelischer Predigt in der Gegenwart," in Sonja Keller (ed.), *Parteiische*

Predigt: Politik, Gesellschaft und Öffentlichkeit als Horizonte der Predigt, 105–24, Leipzig: Evangelische Verlagsanstalt.

Huber, Wolfgang (1990), *Konflikt und Konsens: Studien zur Ethik der Verantwortung*, München: Kaiser.

Keller, Sonja (ed.) (2017), *Parteiische Predigt: Politik, Gesellschaft und Öffentlichkeit als Horizonte der Predigt*, Leipzig: Evangelische Verlagsanstalt.

Koch, Werner (1988), *Der Kampf der Bekennenden Kirche im Dritten Reich: Beiträge zum Widerstand 1933–1945*, Berlin: Gedenkstätte Deutscher Widerstand.

Kopke, Christoph, and Werner Treß (eds.) (2013), *Der Tag von Potsdam: Der 21. März 1933 und die Errichtung der nationalsozialistischen Diktatur*, Berlin/Boston: De Gruyter.

Kühn, Ulrich (2003), *Christologie*, Göttingen: Vandenhoeck & Ruprecht.

Kusmierz, Katrin, and David Plüss (eds.) (2013), *Politischer Gottesdienst?!*, Zürich: Theologischer Verlag Zürich.

Meyer-Blanck, Michael (2011), *Gottesdienstlehre*, Tübingen: Mohr Siebeck.

Meyer, Harding (1975), "'Versöhnte Verschiedenheit'—Korrekturen am Konzept der 'konziliaren Gemeinschaft'," *Lutherische Monatshefte* 14: 675–9.

Nicol, Martin, and Alexander Deeg (2005), *Im Wechselschritt zur Kanzel: Werkbuch Dramaturgische Homiletik*, Göttingen: Vandenhoeck & Ruprecht.

Oorschot, Frederike, and Simone van Ziermann (eds.) (2019), *Theologie in Übersetzung? Religiöse Sprache und Kommunikation in heterogenen Kontexten*, Leipzig: Evangelische Verlagsanstalt.

Pelz, Birge-Dorothea (2019), *Revolution auf der Kanzel: Politischer Gehalt und theologische Geschichtsdeutung in evangelischen Predigten während der deutschen Vereinigung 1989/90*, Göttingen: Vandenhoeck & Ruprecht.

Schieder, Rolf (2021), "1914–1945: Metamorphosen eines Predigers," in Tobias Braune-Krickau and Christoph Galle (eds.), *Predigt und Politik*, 277–95, Göttingen: v&r unipress.

Schwier, Helmut (ed.) (2015), *Ethische und politische Predigt: Beiträge zu einer homiletischen Herausforderung*, Leipzig: Evangelische Verlagsanstalt.

Timmer, Karsten (2000), *Vom Aufbruch zum Umbruch—die Bürgerbewegung in der DDR 1989*, Göttingen: Vandenhoeck und Ruprecht.

Internet References

Agai, Bekim (2020), "Zehn Jahre nach Christian Wulffs Rede: Der Islam in Deutschland ist bunter geworden," *Tagesspiegel*, September 27. Available online: https://www.tagesspiegel.de/politik/zehn-jahre-nach-christian-wulffs-rede-der-islam-in-deutschland-ist-bunter-geworden/26219282.html (accessed September 5, 2022).

"Auf Gott vertrauen, den Nächsten lieben und auch mit sich selbst sorgfältig umgehen," Wolfgang Huber im Gespräch mit Birgit Wenzien, *Deutschlandfunk*, March 13, 2014. Available online: https://www.deutschlandfunk.de/wolfgang-huber-auf-gott-vertrauen-den-naechsten-lieben-und-100.html (accessed September 5, 2022).

"Bundestagswahl 2005," *Wikipedia: Die freie Enzyklopädie*. Available online: https://de.wikipedia.org/wiki/Bundestagswahl_2005#Nach_der_Wahl_%E2%80%93_Probleme_der_Regierungsbildung (accessed September 5, 2022).

Heithecker, Marcus, and Daniel F. Sturm (2010), "Die Favoriten: Wer könnte Bundespräsident werden? Und was muss er können? Acht Kandidaten im Kurzprofil," *Welt*, June 20. Available online: https://www.welt.de/welt_print/politik/article7879313/Die-Favoriten.html (accessed September 22, 2022).

Landeszentrale für politische Bildung Baden-Württemberg (2022), *Tag der Deutschen Einheit—3. Oktober 2022: 32 Jahre Deutsche Einheit*, September. Available online: https://www.lpb-bw.de/tag-der-deutschen-einheit (accessed September 5, 2022).

"Montagsdemonstrationen 1989/1990 in der DDR," *Wikipedia: Die freie Enzyklopädie*. Available online: https://de.wikipedia.org/wiki/Montagsdemonstrationen_1989/1990_in_der_DDR (accessed September 5, 2022).

"Tag der Deutschen Einheit," *Wikipedia: Die freie Enzyklopädie*. Available online: https://de.wikipedia.org/wiki/Tag_der_Deutschen_Einheit (accessed September 5, 2022).

"The Barmen Declaration" (1934), *Evangelische Kirche Deutschland*. Available online: https://www.ekd.de/en/The-Barmen-Declaration-303.htm (accessed June 27, 2023).

Wulff, Christian (2010), "Vielfalt schätzen—Zusammenhalt fördern: Rede zum 20. Jahrestag der Deutschen Einheit," *Der Bundespräsident*. Available online: https://www.bundespraesident.de/SharedDocs/Reden/DE/Christian-Wulff/Reden/2010/10/20101003_Rede.html (accessed September 22, 2022).

5

Joel Osteen's Prosperity Gospel and the Enduring Popularity of America's "Smiling Preacher"

Maren Freudenberg

Introduction

This chapter focuses on the extent to which religious speakers make claims of collective validity and the linguistic and rhetorical devices they use to substantiate these claims, and examines a case study from contemporary American Christianity, more precisely the neo-Pentecostal tradition. Lakewood Church in Houston, Texas, is America's largest megachurch (Sinitiere 2011; Carney 2012), and its senior pastor Joel Osteen has been dubbed the "smiling preacher" (Lee and Sinitiere 2009; Romano 2005) for his charismatic leadership, media affinity, and message of hope and prosperity for all. Below, I analyze a sermon Osteen preached on January 31, 2021,[1] called "Trouble Is Temporary." It can be considered representative for most other sermons by Osteen because they are typically very similar in style, structure, and message.

Before delving into the analysis, I provide a brief introduction to the American megachurch and a more detailed introduction to Lakewood Church. Lakewood can be characterized as a charismatic, pastor-focused church (Hunt 2020b) under Osteen's leadership and stands out due to its professionalized television ministry, developed by Joel Osteen starting in the 1980s, that reaches millions of viewers each week (Einstein 2008). The church has all but perfected its marketing strategy via various channels, inevitably including the internet, and is a prime example of how religion is commodified in our neoliberal age (Gauthier and Martikainen 2013). After introducing Lakewood, I turn to neo-Pentecostalism as an experiential strain in contemporary Christianity that differs from classical Pentecostalism in its general emphasis on the all-encompassing power of the Holy Spirit as opposed to the manifestation of spiritual "gifts" such as glossolalia, healing, or prophecy. Osteen combines neo-Pentecostal theology with psychological approaches to self-development and self-actualization in his version of the Prosperity Gospel, which promises personal health and individual wealth to faithful believers.

The analysis of the sermon "Trouble Is Temporary" is divided into two parts. First, using theoretical coding in Grounded Theory (Thornberg and Charmaz 2014), it investigates Osteen's claims to collective validity, understood here as norms, values, and worldviews that the speaker posits as mandatory and true for his followers. Osteen's validity claims, as we will see in more detail below, are that positive thinking and articulating one's positive thoughts verbally, paired with faithful adherence to the Bible and unwavering trust in the Holy Spirit, will lead to God changing believers' lives for the better. In making this claim, Osteen draws a discursive boundary between "successful" believers (the in-group, as I call it) and the rest of the world (the out-group), thus activating mechanisms of inclusion and exclusion on the basis of both biblical and his own authority[2] and by using examples from the Bible and everyday life. The second part of the analysis focused on Osteen's rhetorical,[3] linguistic and performative style by drawing from literary theory (e.g., Fludernik 1996) and deductive categorizing in qualitative content analysis (Julien 2008). It reveals that Osteen strategically employs humor, repetition, simple sentence structures, and frequent imperative clauses to strengthen identification with Lakewood, thus consolidating in-group ties, and works with what has been called narrative experientiality (Fludernik 1996) in literary theory, rendering his message easily intelligible and immediately relevant to his listeners. The fact that Osteen performatively embodies his validity claims and offers a highly scripted yet seemingly genuine performance to his broad public further helps to popularize the message. The main results of the analysis are summarized and contextualized in a brief conclusion.

A disclaimer is necessary at this point: This chapter adopts a sociological, not a theological, perspective in its investigation of Osteen's message and style. It is concerned with understanding how he constructs his claims as valid, not with offering a normative assessment of his claims.

Lakewood Church and the Prosperity Gospel

The megachurch landscape in the United States is both diverse and dynamic. Because most megachurches are focused on membership growth, unique institutional logics and structures have evolved to attain these goals (e.g., Pruisken et al. 2022; von der Ruhr 2020; Wellman Jr., Corcoran, and Stockly 2020). The formal, basic definition of a megachurch is an average weekly attendance of around two thousand people (Hunt 2020b). With a pre-pandemic weekly attendance of over fifty thousand people[4] (Carney 2012; Sinitiere 2011), Lakewood Church in Houston, Texas, is America's largest megachurch. According to a typology of megachurches by the Hartfort Institute of Religious Research (see Hunt 2020b), it can be characterized as a charismatic, pastor-focused church.[5] The concept of charismatic authority goes back to Max Weber and is a relational one, in which charisma is an "extraordinary" personal quality, either "of divine origin" or at least "exemplary," which followers attribute to a leader (Weber 1978 [1922]: 241). Charisma, as a social relationship, is thus always dependent on the legitimation of the leader in the eyes of his or her followers.[6] In the present example, Joel Osteen's charismatic authority at Lakewood Church is continuously legitimized through his claims to collective validity as well as his rhetorical, linguistic, and performative style.

Lakewood Church

Joel Osteen is a media celebrity and one of today's most famous proponents of the Prosperity Gospel, also called the Health and Wealth Gospel. His father, John Osteen, founded Lakewood Church in 1959 and expanded the congregation to five thousand members in two decades (Sinitiere 2011). When John Osteen died in 1999, his youngest son, Joel, succeeded him and turned Lakewood into what it is today: the country's largest megachurch, highly professionalized and steeped in the Prosperity Gospel. Because Joel Osteen's weekly sermons are televised and made available online, and he and his co-pastors additionally write blogs and publish prayers and other contributions on the internet, Lakewood reaches tens of millions of people every week, according to the *Christian Post* (Kumar 2018)—while Lakewood itself claims to reach over two hundred million households in the United States and abroad (Lakewood Church undated). Osteen's followers are heterogeneous in terms of race, economic background,[7] education level, and age (Lee and Sinitiere 2009; Sødal 2010), and their numbers have increased continuously. The church is housed in a former sports stadium in the heart of the city, the Compaq Center, which seats sixteen thousand people (though in-person worshippers were limited to a quarter of the total capacity during the Covid-19 pandemic). Carney (2012) notes that "Lakewood's self-contained and self-sustaining environment creates a utopian experience for its congregants" (61) and that, like other megachurches, "by using Prosperity Gospel theology and by crafting an ornate and multi-functional church space, [it] attempt[s] to create a 'heaven on earth'" (66) for its members. Various facilities are available, including a book shop, a childcare center, and conference rooms. Because the analysis to follow is concerned with Osteen's preaching in the sanctuary, we will briefly concentrate on its layout. The sanctuary is oval, with seats extending upward far beyond the level of the stage. A console area for the church's technical crew, responsible for the sanctuary's light, sound, camera, and screen projection systems, is located at the opposite end of the floor to the stage. The stage itself is framed by theatrical scenery: Images of blue skies and white clouds float above imitation rock landscaping, which is sometimes replaced with waterfalls. Three screens, two smaller and one large, show live footage of the pastors so that they are visible to the entire audience. Elevated at the back center of the stage stands the large, slowly rotating globe, continents cast in gold, which has become a Lakewood trademark. At the front center stands an elegant wooden lectern sporting the Lakewood logo.

With its focus on the Prosperity Gospel and the transformative power of the Holy Spirit, Lakewood Church can be considered a neo-Pentecostal megachurch (Carney 2012; Sinitiere 2015). Neo-Pentecostalism differs from classical Pentecostalism in that manifestations of spiritual "gifts," the Biblical charismata, including prophecy, discerning the spirits, glossolalia, and healing (as listed in 1 Cor. 12:7-11 NIV) are typically rare. According to Lee and Sinitiere (2009),

> It is ... accurate to distinguish Osteen as a Charismatic or neo-Pentecostal preacher because he places less emphasis on speaking in tongues than traditional Pentecostals, and more focus on the power of God's spirit to transform every aspect of the believer's life. Joel Osteen tells members to trust in God's supernatural intervention and yet focuses on personal agency by exhorting members to have positive thoughts and to speak positively in order to shun negativity from all aspects of their lives. (Lee and Sinitiere 2009: 32)

We will return to Osteen's claim regarding positive thinking and positive declarations immediately below. First, however, it is important to point out that neo-Pentecostals are less sectarian and world-rejecting than many of their Pentecostal brethren, instead increasingly affirming middle-class values such as self-development and self-actualization, but also a consumer ethos and entrepreneurial spirit in religion (Hunt 2002). Hunt (2002) calls neo-Pentecostalism "a major carrier of the North American capitalist ideology" and identifies "the principal carrier of this new ethos" as "the so-called 'health and wealth gospel'" (16). He highlights the inherently materialistic focus of the Prosperity Gospel as "a kind of consumer 'instantism' evident in the Faith teaching that prosperity and health is the automatic divine right of all bible-believing Christians" (16). Regarding Joel Osteen's version of the Prosperity Gospel specifically, Lee and Sinitiere (2009) note that "he constructs a vision of happy living that blends well with our consumerist self-indulgent culture and offers a narrative of hope grounded in the discourses of religious and bourgeois American middle-class sensibilities" (39) while at the same time crafting "his redemptive message in the discourses of cognitive psychology, self-help, and individual betterment" (50).[8]

Health and Wealth: Joel Osteen's Prosperity Gospel

The term "Prosperity Gospel" is misleading in that it suggests a unified theology, when it is in fact far from such, being interpreted and preached in vastly different ways by its proponents. Coleman (2016) suggests understanding it as "a set of ethical practices that can be combined and reconstituted in very different cultural contexts, and which may in fact work through ambiguity and play as much as through the expression of apparently firm and exclusive religious convictions" (276–7). He also calls it a "tricksterish" cultural form that evokes "feelings of unease as well as delight, ambivalence as well as inspiration" (277). Adherents of the Prosperity Gospel strive for health—physical, mental, and emotional as well as in the sense of nurturing harmonious relationships—, various kinds of material wealth as evidence of divine grace and depth of faith as a source of power to transform people's lives for the better (Porterfield, Corrigan, and Grem 2017).

The tricksterish nature of the Prosperity Gospel is somewhat similar to predestination theology in that adherents are constantly searching for evidence of being favored by God. As long as they enjoy good health and a secure financial situation, all is well, but what if they fall ill or into debt? Does this indicate divine neglect? And how to keep up one's spirits and maintain optimism in such dire situations? As we will see in the analysis below, Osteen has become an expert at discursively focusing on feelings of delight and inspiration instead of on unease and ambivalence, to use Coleman's terms quoted above. Bowler (2013) calls this strategy "soft prosperity," which, instead of judging "people's faith by their immediate circumstances ..., appraises believers with a gentler, more roundabout, assessment" (7–8). Making a similar point, Lee and Sinitiere (2009) point out:

> Unlike some evangelicals who continue to preach fire-and-brimstone messages, Osteen never preaches about hell, judgment day, or sin. Similarly, Osteen's biblical exhortations have a pragmatic rather than didactic function: they guide people toward healthy and happy living, rather than moralize about a holy, sinless existence. (Lee and Sinitiere 2009: 44)

According to Bowler (2013), the roots of the Prosperity Gospel as it developed in the United States can be traced back to "three distinct though intersecting streams: Pentecostalism; New Thought (an amalgam of metaphysics and Protestantism …; and an American gospel of pragmatism, individualism, and upward mobility" (11). Contemporary versions were also shaped by twentieth-century revivalism in the style of Oral Roberts and Kenneth Hagin: Coleman (2016) notes that the influence these prominent speakers have on the way the Prosperity Gospel has developed reflects "the Pentecostal transition from the more marked denominationalism of the first part of the twentieth century to the freer, entrepreneurial, theologically looser, 'neo-Pentecostal' and charismatic developments of the century's last decades" (280). Joel Osteen is a prime example of a "theologically loose" preacher in the sense that he never completed a seminary education or comparable theological training. Instead, he learned his craft on the job, once noting that he does not understand himself as a Bible scholar or theologian but "a minister equipped to offer people hope and to teach individuals how to become better people, find God's purpose, and live a better, happier life" (Lee and Sinitiere 2009: 46).

According to Sinitiere (2015), Osteen's interpretation of the Prosperity Gospel is made up of four parts: positive thinking, positive confession, providence of positive outcomes, and the promotion of the Christian body as a site of improvement. Osteen's central validity claim, which we will return to in the analysis below, is that formulating positive thoughts and expressing them verbally will activate the power of God to change one's life for the better because, he argues, God has promised to provide if the faithful ask for blessings. Divine blessings include, first and foremost, a healthy body and mind as well as material wealth. In this way, Osteen "combines psychological tactics like positive thinking and self-actualization with neo-Pentecostal theology about the blessings of the Holy Spirit" (Carney 2012: 67), simultaneously emphasizing divine omnipotence and individual agency. Bowler (2013) argues that the Prosperity Gospel must be understood as

> a special form of Christian power to reach into God's treasure trove and pull out a miracle. It represent[s] the triumph of American optimism over the realities of a fickle economy, entrenched racism, pervasive poverty, and theological pessimism that foretold the future as dangling by a thread. (Bowler 2013: 7)

In this context, faith is "an activator, a power that unleashes spiritual forces and turns the spoken word into reality" (Bowler 2013: 7). If the faithful adopt a mindset of overcoming present burdens, of optimistically believing that life will improve, and if they verbally articulate these convictions, God will intervene on their behalf and turn them into victors, so Osteen's claim. The terms "victor" and "victory" appear frequently in his rhetoric; Sødal (2010) notes that "he speaks more about the human potential for victory than … for sin" (39). It is important to highlight that Osteen communicates victory as normative, as a direct result of strong faith, by presenting himself as healthy in body and mind, as successful and materially well-off. In so doing, he combines optimism as a psychological asset with the neo-Pentecostal conception of an all-powerful Holy Spirit. At the same time, he uses his personal popularity and wide outreach to implicitly convey the standards constituting the ideal embodiment of health and wealth:

> Joel Osteen specializes in providing what Americans want: the possibility to remake oneself, the ability to find hope in hopeless circumstances, and the fortitude to achieve certainty in the midst of chaos. A major part of his success is an uncanny ability to be winsome, attractive, energetic, and relevant. His boyish charm and friendly demeanor are at the center of his appeal. The "smiling preacher"[9] excels at offering a positive message, one that uplifts the self rather than denigrating the other person. Osteen's focus is not on past regrets but on the future of possibility. It is on the relevance of the here and now, and the material and spiritual return God offers for the right kinds of investment. (Lee and Sinitiere 2009: 49)

The strategic use of marketing and media at Lakewood is critical to get Osteen's message across. Osteen dropped out of Oral Roberts University in 1983 to start a television ministry for what was then still his father's church, and he has honed and perfected his marketing skills ever since (Sinitiere 2015). Einstein (2008) highlights Lakewood's marketing pattern as adopted from the secular world of capitalism and adapted to the religious sphere:

> Prospects are "brought into the tent" with messages they want to hear but are not presented with their responsibilities until later. If you just heard the positive message of Joel, you would assume that following his faith simply means being positive all the time—certainly a difficult task in and of itself. But Joel's message is

> not only about this. Beyond the smile and the upbeat words, it is about accepting Jesus as your Lord and Savior and accepting the Bible as the inerrant word of God. It is about joining a good Bible-based church. (Einstein 2008: 125–6)

The message of positive thinking and positive declarations[10] in combination with living by the Bible and accepting Jesus into your heart is disseminated across a broad range of channels. At the time of writing, still in the midst of the Covid-19 pandemic, Lakewood offers two in-person services that are also accessible for online viewers and two online-only services per weekend. There is an additional online service on Wednesday nights, and all services are broadcast via television and made available on the internet. Each service is followed by advertisements for special events and Osteen's bestselling books. Furthermore, a host of other resources is accessible to anyone interested, including the Lakewood website, Joel Osteen's website, daily "e-votionals" circulated via email, blogs, podcasts, and the like. This makes it possible to reach a huge audience, one that has likely only increased during the pandemic, and the focus is always on Osteen's message of optimism and hope. The fact that he adheres to a literalist hermeneutic of the Bible (Sinitiere 2015) and is opposed to abortion and homosexuality (Einstein 2008) is not a topic he discusses publicly.

"Trouble Is Temporary": Joel Osteen's Validity Claim and His Rhetorical, Linguistic and Performative Style

This section will analyze a typical sermon by Joel Osteen to investigate, on the level of content, his specific claim to collective validity and, on the level of style, the rhetorical, linguistic, and performative strategies he employs to get this message across. The sermon "Trouble Is Temporary" of January 31, 2021, can be considered typical in the sense that all of Osteen's sermons are scripted in similar ways, as we will see below. Here as in other sermons of his, his characteristic narrative of life changing for the better is carefully constructed, on the level of content, as a claim to collective validity not only through biblical references but also and mainly through frequent references to everyday life to render Osteen's version of the Prosperity Gospel immediately relevant for believers. On the level of style, he uses the rhetorical devices of repetition and humor and the linguistic device of simple sentences and imperative clauses, but also performatively display emotion and thus switches from narrating self—as the person telling the story—to experiencing self—as the subject of the story—to render his message intelligible to his audience. The worship service of January 31, 2021, whose roughly thirty-four minutes consist mainly of the twenty-five-minute sermon "Trouble Is Temporary," was analyzed using theoretical coding in Grounded Theory (Thornberg and Charmaz 2014) to show how Osteen substantiates the claim that God favors those who cultivate a mindset of positivity, optimism, and a hopeful outlook. The transcript and video of the sermon were additionally analyzed from the perspective of literary studies (Fludernik 1996, 2003) and with deductive content analysis (Julien 2008) to reveal Osteen's rhetorical, linguistic, and performative strategies.

The service begins, as it always does, with Osteen welcoming the physically present attendees and greeting the virtually tuned-in audience. He emphasizes that "we are together in spirit" and "one big family," repeating "we love you" several times here and at the end of the service. Next, he goes toward the lectern to speak a blessing, but then seemingly spontaneously changes his mind—this is all scripted, however, because every service begins this way—and reverts to telling a secular joke instead. This week's customary kick-off joke is about a Hindu priest, a Jewish rabbi, and a televangelist, with the joke ultimately (and good-humoredly) on the televangelist. The joke is followed by the Lakewood Bible pledge, recited communally at the beginning of every service (see also Einstein 2008: 127):

> This is my Bible. I am who it says I am. I have what it says I have. I can do what it says I can do. Today I will be taught the Word of God. I boldly confess: My mind is alert; my heart is receptive; I will never be the same. I am about to receive the incorruptible, indestructible, ever-living seed of the Word of God. I'll never be the same. Never, never, never. I'll never be the same in Jesus' name. Amen.

Already, we see the rhetorical device of repetition, the linguistic device of simple, single clauses, and the central claim that following the Bible as the Word of God is fundamentally life-changing in the most positive sense. Once the roughly four thousand attendees have taken their seats, Osteen dives into the sermon, arguing throughout that a negative outlook on life will lead to circumstances staying negative, while a positive outlook, optimism, and hope will lead to God changing things for the better "soon." As we will see, the word "soon" is central here: God, Osteen argues, will not only change believers' circumstances at some point in the future, but he will do so in the *near* future—*if* they embrace an optimistic and hopeful outlook and claim, by positive thinking and positive confession, what God has to offer.

Claims of Collective Validity

Following the framework of the present volume, this chapter understands "claims of collective validity" as encompassing norms, values, and worldviews that speakers hold as being mandatory and true for their followers. Osteen constructs his validity claims of optimism and hope as fulfilled through positive thinking and positive confession by tapping into affect rather than cognition, and by discursively drawing clear boundaries between what I call the in-group and the out-group (i.e., those who have accepted his message of optimism and hope vs. those who have not).

Focusing on the level of content, the analysis reveals that Osteen references several biblical passages and especially the story of Job throughout the sermon to reinforce his claim, emphasizing Job's harsh trials and desolate situation. He argues that while at first Job was discouraged and developed what Osteen calls a "forever mentality"[11]—that is, the mentality that his situation would always remain difficult—Job then "switched over to faith" and was rewarded by God with a long life and "twice as much" health and wealth as he'd had before. Osteen uses this story make the point that "it's okay to have times when you feel discouraged, … but don't finish there." He makes the claim that the act of declaring that things will soon take a turn for the better defies "the enemy," by which, of course, he means Satan and his evil forces. The reference to defying the devil by praying out loud reveals the practice of spiritual warfare that is central in the lives of neo-Pentecostal and other charismatic Christians, who believe themselves to be "locked in an epic end-times battle with the demonic" (Marshall 2016: 93). The framework of spiritual warfare understands evil as taking manifold forms, sinful behavior in the broadest sense, from lust (premarital sex, adultery) and gluttony (addictions of various sorts) to sloth (failing to contribute to God's work on earth).

In this context, Osteen gives an example from Lakewood's history to illustrate the claim that positive prayer, particularly when spoken out loud, can conquer evil in miraculous ways. He tells his audience that when Lakewood Church won a city council vote to move into the Compaq Center, the large former sports arena the church now calls home, a federal lawsuit was filed that prevented the congregation from moving in. Osteen emphasizes that such lawsuits can take years and that he was very worried about losing it, especially after he had sold the idea of moving into the Compaq Center to the church and members had already donated substantial sums of money to make the move possible. Miraculously, a few months later, the lawsuit was dropped, and Lakewood was able to move into the Compaq Center. Osteen attributes this success to his faith in God and the fact that he remained optimistic and confident, praying regularly that God would intervene on the church's behalf. Using an example right out of the lives of church members to develop this claim, Osteen makes it immediately relevant to his listeners, thereby arguably driving home his message more effectively.

Highlighting that people tend to think their troubles will go on forever, Osteen then returns to the story of Job, noting that what seems like a process that took years in the biblical story was only a few months of difficulties in the life of Job, who then lived to the age of 140. Osteen comes back to this point several times throughout the sermon: Job's suffering seems long, he says, because the forty-two chapters of the Book of Job exclusively focus on this and talk about nothing else, but the final sentence states how happy Job became and how long he lived. Incidentally, this example is a favorite of his and one that he uses in his bestselling publication *Your Best Life Now: Seven Steps to Living at Your Full Potential* (2014). The fact that Osteen refuses to focus on the suffering so very prominent in the Book of Job, instead concentrating on the final sentences and on Job's rewards and compensations after his tribulations, is a striking instance of his version of the Prosperity Gospel and stands in stark contrast to historical-critical biblical interpretation (Sødal 2010).

Osteen tells his listeners that it is easy to live with a "forever" mindset—in the sense of despairing and believing that difficulties will last forever—but that the task given by God is to switch over to a "soon" mentality:

> Switch over to a "Soon" mentality—I know some things take time, but God promises us in this verse [no verse referred to, MF] that the trouble will soon be over. He's about to do something out of a normal time frame, something unusual, sooner than you think. "What if I believe this and it doesn't happen?" What if you believe it and it does happen? It probably won't happen if you've already accepted it's going to be a long time to get out of this trouble, a long time to get well, to meet the right person, to accomplish your dream—that's limiting what God will do. I'm asking you to believe for sooner than later.

In this passage, Osteen undergirds his claim that God will change people's lives for the better if they accept not only the possibility but the likelihood that he will. What is especially interesting is that the juxtaposition between a "forever mindset" and a "soon mentality" suggests that agency is somehow granted to God only through the latter: only if one embraces and declares the idea that God will bring about changes soon will changes occur, while if you are stuck in a "forever mindset," Osteen claims, God might not intervene on your behalf. Here,

Osteen seems to indirectly contradict God's omnipotence by implicitly limiting his agency to those cases in which individuals actively and vocally confirm his omnipotence. More importantly for our context is the fact that Osteen is drawing clear in-group/out-group boundaries by framing the "soon mentality" as normative for belonging to the circle of the prosperous, healthy, and wealthy, while the "forever mindset" is negatively sanctioned and will lead to exclusion from the same.

Underscoring the centrality of positive declarations in his version of the Prosperity Gospel and of actively claiming one's dues from God, Osteen then goes on to give what could be considered a prep talk, a motivational speech to his audience, listing the things God has in store for believers who declare their faith in Him:

> God was showing us [in the story of Job, MF]: the trouble is temporary, the trouble is not going to last forever. You may be in a difficult time, but that is not how your story ends. That loss is not going to define you, that sickness is not going to ruin the rest of your life. That person that walked away, the bad break, the unfair situation is not going to stop your destiny. God has an "After this" for you: After the trouble there's going to be great joy in your life, after the loss, after the sickness, after the legal battle you're going to see new friendships, new opportunities, new growth. Don't be discouraged by the trouble, it's not stopping anything God has for you. God is storing up all the joy, all the good breaks, the favor, the resources that have been put on hold because of the temporary trouble.

As he recites this and continues in the same vein, Osteen becomes emotional, tearing up, and even turning his back on the audience at one point to wipe his eyes. He seems overwhelmed by God's power and benevolence. Soon, however, he is his cheerful and smiling self again, bringing another example from everyday life to further underpin his claim that positive thinking and positive confession lead to fundamental change in people's lives: He was once on an airplane to India with his father, he says, and the plane experienced a short phase of extreme turbulence, with everyone on board afraid of crashing. After ten minutes, it was back to smooth flying, and Osteen compares this experience to other difficult situations in life which seem never to end but which, he claims, will be over sooner than you think. Comparing larger trials and suffering to airborne turbulence may seem like a mundane example, but Osteen arguably uses it very consciously to connect to the everyday experiences of his listeners in order to render his message more intelligible and relevant to them.

Rhetoric, Linguistics, and Performance

Osteen is able to construct his claims of collective validity regarding optimism and hope not only through the content he draws from—both biblical and everyday life examples— but also and crucially through his rhetorical, linguistic, and performative style. He strategically employs rhetoric, linguistics, and performance to resonate with as large an audience as possible—inevitably a central goal for megachurch pastors in general.[12] Citing Aristotle, Abrams (1999) defines rhetoric as "the art of 'discovering all the available means of persuasion in any given case'" and as intrinsically connected to "the means and devices that an orator uses in order to achieve the intellectual and emotional effects on an audience that will persuade them to accede to the orator's point of view" (268). In Osteen's case, this includes repetition and humor as well as, linguistically, simple sentence structures and the frequent use of imperative clauses. Consider the following excerpt from the beginning of the sermon:

> Soon it's going to be over. Soon you're going to see the breakthrough. Soon your health is going to turn around. Soon you're going to meet the person of your dreams. Soon you're going to break that addiction. You may not see how this can happen, everything in your reasoning says, "It's not possible." You're looking at it in the natural—we serve a supernatural God.

The word "soon" occurs five times in as many sentences, and the sermon as a whole is peppered with it. The sentences are short and simple so that the audience can follow easily. The larger, thematic repetitions throughout the sermon are constructed similarly: After introducing the topic, revealing the "forever mindset" as a dead-end street, and emphasizing the power of positive thinking and declarations, Osteen threads the story of Job into his own narrative as a biblical example, as discussed in the previous section. He continues in this vein, alternating between paragraphs on the "forever mindset," Job's trials, the "soon mentality," Job's rewards, the task of not getting stuck in the "forever mindset," the promises of the "soon mentality," how this message is revealed in the Book of Job, his own challenge of not getting stuck in the "forever mentality" when the lawsuit against Lakewood was pending and when he was experiencing turbulence on the plane to India, how liberating and rewarding the "soon mentality" is, and so on. This type of repetition—both within sentences and paragraphs and in the sermon's larger structure—is typical of all Osteen's sermons.

In her analysis of Osteen's rhetoric of hope, Sødal (2010) points out that repetition as a well-known rhetorical tool "may lead to recognition and the feeling of being an insider" (44). While she connects this first and foremost to the numerous examples from the Osteen family that Joel Osteen frequently cites in his speeches and writings, I would argue that the feeling of being an insider goes beyond a perceived familiarity with the Osteen family to include broader notions of being a member of the Lakewood family, and is thus a central identity marker for congregation members. Osteen's rhetorical strategy of using repetition on different levels—within sentences and paragraphs but also within the larger structure of his sermons, as well as in the structure of his worship services, including the customary kick-off joke and the communally cited Bible pledge—arguably creates a feeling of familiarity on the part of his audience regarding both the content of what he is saying and the style in which he communicates. Recognition, in other words, serves to reinforce the in-group/out-group boundaries Osteen discursively constructs with the claims to collective validity and the rhetorical strategies he employs to do so.

Another rhetorical device Osteen frequently uses to buttress his claim is to interweave rhetorical questions posed by imaginary others to himself, which he answers with ease and humor, showing his experience as a public speaker. Consider the following rhetorical back-and-forth with himself in the sermon "Trouble Is Temporary":

> When is your health going to turn around?
>
> "I don't know, Joel, the medical report doesn't look good."
>
> That's one report, I'm giving you another report: Soon things are going to change in your favor.
>
> When are you coming out of debt?
>
> "Looks like it's going to take me 112 years to pay everything off."
>
> You're going to be in heaven by then, how about: Soon I'm coming out of debt. Soon I'm going to lend and not borrow.
>
> How can that happen? God owns it all!

On a metalevel, this dialogue with an imaginary other points to Osteen's use of narrative experientiality as "the quasi-mimetic evocation of real-life experience" (Fludernik 1996: 12). Osteen activates a range of parameters in his listeners that Fludernik (2003) defines as constituting narrative experientiality, particularly understanding intentional action, perceiving temporality and emotionally evaluating experiences. He develops a narrative in which he incentivizes intentional action on the part of his listeners—that is, to develop a positive mentality and can-do mindset—and into which he weaves a specific perspective on temporality—that is, developing this mindset and mentality now will lead to God changing your life for the better soon—all the while tapping into affect instead of cognition to be as persuasive as possible. Interestingly, he switches back and forth frequently between the narrating I and the experiencing I (Stanzel 1986) throughout the sermon, framing his message by relating both stories that happened to others as well as experiences that he himself has had.

Regardless of the specific rhetorical device he might be employing, Osteen's messages are always comprised of short, simple sentences and straightforward instructions, often using the grammatical imperative, to render his claims intelligible to his broad range of listeners: "Don't stay in the ashes. Don't stay defeated." "Switch over to a soon mentality." "Keep the right perspective: the trouble is temporary, it's not going to last as long as it looks. Live with this soon mentality." Sødal (2010) notes that Osteen "does not use advanced imagery, allusions or symbols" in his speech or writings to avoid being "socially excluding" (45). Again, this is indicative of the church growth framework in which megachurches must be understood: In order to attract as broad a range of people as possible, it is important to tap into the lowest common denominator in terms of what is intelligible and appealing to the audience (von der Ruhr 2020).

Interwoven with rhetoric and linguistics, but analytically distinguishable from both, is performativity. Michaels and Sax (2016) note that "performative approaches to social and cultural phenomena tend to emphasize embodiment over cognition, situated communication over linguistic structure, and contextual meaning over propositional content" (304). The focus is on the doing, they argue: Performative acts are embodied, scripted, staged, mediatized, and, thus, public. For the final part of this chapter, not only the sermon transcript but the video of the entire service has been included in the analysis. Because the service was an event broadcast live (instead of one recorded, edited, and then released), I watched it as a non-participant observer, taking notes throughout and after the service and then categorizing them deductively with content analysis (Julien 2008). Following Michaels and Sax (2016), the categories include performativity as embodied, scripted/staged, and mediatized/public. Because Osteen's worship services are typically very similar in structure, the remarks below sometimes generalize beyond the performance analyzed for this chapter.

Osteen's high popularity arguably stems not only from his claim that optimism and hope will turn one's life around and from his rhetorical and linguistic style, but is also a result of the way he performs and embodies what he preaches.

Consider his appearance: He is fifty-eight years old but looks at least fifteen years younger, and is the embodiment of good health and positivity. Slim and erect, he wears a dark suit, a white shirt, a tie in muted colors, and shiny leather shoes when preaching. His hair is carefully styled, and he sports a friendly smile. His body language is relaxed, with one hand occasionally in his pocket. Taken together, he is immaculately groomed in an understated way, arguably coming across less as rich and famous than as an everyday guy in his Sunday best. Sødal (2010) compares his appearance to his simple but persuasive linguistic style. As such, Osteen may be considered a role model by many segments of his large audience, who can both admire him as the ideal father, husband, or friend, and strive to become more like him.

Osteen seems to preach freely, without even a teleprompter, only occasionally returning to the lectern at the center of the stage for a glance at his notes. He moves around the stage with ease, one hand in his pocket, suggesting that he is very comfortable speaking in front of large audiences. He modulates his voice, lowering it when telling a joke or a story from his experience, raising it when talking about positive declarations. He smiles often, looking directly at the camera, and is not shy of tearing up when talking about God's power. To what degree this emotionality is a performative act and to what degree it is genuine cannot be determined here, but it is very apparent that Osteen's performance is as professionally scripted and staged as it may seem genuine and spontaneous. While the secular joke and the Lakewood Bible pledge which mark the beginning of each worship service are obviously scripted, his performance during the sermon is much less obviously so. Whether he memorizes his sermons in advance or uses other strategies, such as noting key terms to jog his memory in specific places, his words flow smoothly, sentences slotting together easily to build his argument. Throughout his sermons, he interweaves accounts of his personal experiences and stories from the lives of people he knows with biblical examples to support his validity claims. Introductory expressions such as "One time I was …," "A friend of mine once …," and "The Bible says …" mark whether the story to follow is based on personal experience or Scripture. This suggests that his sermons, like most instances of public speech, are scripted at least to a certain extent.

At the close of the sermon "Trouble Is Temporary," Osteen emphasizes the importance of developing a personal relationship with Jesus and renewing the Christian bond with God. After inviting everyone to "accept the free gift of Christ's salvation this morning," he encourages his television and online viewers to take up the challenge and join Lakewood Church for one year, suggesting they "plug in" to the church's online beginners' course and promising that "your life will never be the same for the better." Here, the mediatized nature of his performance is particularly evident, as those viewers that are not yet members of Lakewood or that are not present physically at the church are directly addressed. Furthermore, the various camera perspectives as well as the Lakewood logo and additional information (such as Joel Osteen's name and URLs for further resources) that are inserted on the bottom of the screen at the beginning and end of the worship service are also markers of mediatization.[13]

Osteen's performativity suggests that he is highly conscious of his positive effect on viewers. His style of dress, his comportment, and the way he structures and delivers his sermon reveal that he draws on his wide popularity to reinforce his message that believing in the power of God and declaring this belief will make his listeners as prosperous as he himself appears. In so doing, Osteen maintains a fine balance between appearing humble but not modest and actively claiming what God has in store at the same time. He is the embodiment of his claim that expressing optimism and hope in thought and speech and adhering to the Bible as the Word of God will lead to divine intervention for the better in people's lives.

Conclusion

Lakewood's Sunday worship is an anchor point in the church's week. Osteen's sermons attract thousands of in-person attendees and millions of television and online viewers into what can be considered an imagined community (Anderson 1983) of the faithful, hopeful, optimistic, blessed, and victorious. In this chapter, I have shown how Osteen frames and presents his claims of collective validity and discursively constructs in-group/out-group boundaries, how he reinforces this framing with rhetorical, linguistic, and performative strategies, and how this fits into his adaptation of the Prosperity Gospel.

His central validity claims are that positive thinking and positive declarations, paired with faithful adherence to the Bible as the Word of God and trust in the Holy Spirit as a powerful force in the world will result in God changing believers' lives for the better. In communicating the importance of optimism and hope, Osteen taps into affect rather than cognition and draws clear discursive boundaries between "successful" believers—those who have managed, as it were, to move God to act on their behalf (the faithful in-group)—and "unsuccessful" believers, who have, according to the implicit message, not yet fully accepted the scope of God's promise for them (the out-group, regarded as not being faithful enough). He substantiates his claims by using both stories from the Bible and examples from everyday life to illustrate their relevance for his audience.

The rhetorical strategies of humor and repetition that he uses throughout his sermons lead to recognition on the part of his audience, arguably reinforcing their identity as members of Lakewood Church and thus serving to increase cohesion in the in-group. The linguistic strategies of using simple sentence structures and frequent imperative clauses also function as inclusionary, meeting people where they are in terms of their educational background and their vocabulary. Taken together, Osteen's rhetoric and linguistics serve to evoke real-life experience in what has been called narrative experientiality in literary studies (Fludernik 1996). Osteen develops an emotional narrative that incentivizes intentional action, encouraging his listeners to maintain a positive mindset and verbally articulate this mentality, and casting a specific perspective on temporality, namely that cultivating this mindset and mentality now will lead to God changing one's life for the better soon. Presenting a carefully crafted and highly professionalized image of himself as successful, accomplished, and happy, Osteen combines popularity with normativity by presenting himself as the best evidence of the truthfulness of his validity claims. From a performative perspective, he embodies his claims physically, mentally, emotionally, and in terms of his wealth. The fact that his worship services are professionally staged and highly scripted, a fact his audience is arguably fully aware of, casts no doubt on his appearance of sincerity and candor. On the contrary, their orchestrated and mediatized nature only reinforces their appeal in the eyes of the church's members.

Osteen's version of the Prosperity Gospel brings together the fourfold idea of positive thinking, positive declarations, providence of positive outcomes, and the physical, mental, and emotional body as a site of improvement with the neo-Pentecostal belief in the all-encompassing power of the Holy Spirit and the Bible as the inerrant Word of God. As a charismatic leader in the Weberian sense, Osteen has perfected his use of a variety of media to communicate his message and successfully market Lakewood Church as "a model for harmony and diversity" (Lakewood undated), as a "heaven on earth" (Carney 2012: 66) that is available to everyone who is faithful and willing to accept Jesus as Lord and Savior, live by the Bible, and cultivate a mindset of optimism, hope, and positivity. In this way, Osteen has managed to construct personal health and individual wealth as religiously mandated commodities that are framed as the ultimate goals of human existence.

Notes

1 The sermon transcript can be found here: https://sermons.love/joel-osteen/7587-joel-osteen-trouble-is-temporary.html (accessed July 23, 2021).

2 On different kinds of authority at play in neo-Pentecostal megachurches, see Freudenberg (2022). For an overview of the concept of authority in the sociology of religion, see Freudenberg, Radermacher, and Schüler (2022).

3 Norwegian scholar Helje Kringlebotn Sødal published an article in the *Journal of Contemporary Religion* in 2010 entitled "'Victor, not Victim': Joel Osteen's Rhetoric of Hope." I was not aware of this publication until finalizing this chapter, and while there are smaller overlaps, I pursue a different research question and line of argumentation. Nevertheless, Sødal's paper has been helpful in refining some of my arguments after the empirical analysis was concluded.

4 To my knowledge, there is no current information on how Lakewood's membership has been affected by the pandemic. It is likely that it has increased, due to the church's easy online accessibility and range of digital resources.

5 The other types are "'old' or programmed-based megachurches," "'seeker' churches" and "New Wave/Re-envisioned churches" (quoted in Hunt 2020b: 5).

6 See Freudenberg and Weitzel (2019) for an overview of the concept of charisma and its reception and use in the sociology of religion.

7 Sødal (2010) notes the likelihood of a majority of congregational members being less well-off economically as indicated by their racial diversity and the fact that Osteen's message of wealth and health resonates so strongly with them. A thorough study of Lakewood's membership body would be necessary to substantiate this seemingly sensible assumption, however, as it has been established that neo-Pentecostals suffer less from absolute than from relative deprivation (see Hunt [2002] for an instructive overview).

8 For an analysis of the moral economy at work at Lakewood as a result of Joel Osteen's teachings on prosperity, see Freudenberg, Lutz, and Radermacher (2020).

9 According to Lee and Sinitiere (2009), this popular description goes back to an article by Lois Romano in the *Washington Post* (Romano 2005). The nickname is also noted in the entry on Joel Osteen in the *Encyclopedia Britannia* (Hollar 2021).

10 Early on as Lakewood's lead pastor, Osteen changed the more Christian-sounding expression "positive confession" into "positive declarations" to address a wider range of potential followers (Bowler 2013).

11 All quotes in this section are from the sermon transcript (https://sermons.love/joel-osteen/7587-joel-osteen-trouble-is-temporary.html) (accessed July 23, 2021) unless indicated otherwise.

12 See Hunt's *Handbook of Megachurches* (2020a) for an instructive overview.

13 For a useful survey of mediatization theory, which cannot be addressed here for reasons of scope, see Lövheim and Hjarvard (2019).

References

Abrams, Meyer Howard (1999), *A Glossary of Literary Terms*, 7th ed., Boston: Heinle & Heinle.

Anderson, Benedict (1983), *Imagined Communities: Reflections on the Origins and Spread of Nationalism*, London: Verso.

Bowler, Kate (2013), *Blessed: A History of the American Prosperity Gospel*, Oxford: Oxford University Press.

Carney, Charity R. (2012), "Lakewood Church and the Roots of the Megachurch Movement in the South," *Southern Quarterly*, 50: 61–78.

Coleman, Simon (2016), "The Prosperity Gospel: Debating Charisma, Controversy and Capitalism," in Stephen J. Hunt (ed.), *The Handbook of Global Contemporary Christianity: Movements, Institutions, and Allegiance*, 276–96, Leiden: Brill.

Einstein, Mara (2008), *Brands of Faith: Marketing Religion in a Commercial Age*, London: Routledge.

Fludernik, Monika (2003), "Natural Narratology and Cognitive Parameters," in Davis Herman (ed.), *Narrative Theory and the Cognitive Sciences*, 243–67, Stanford: CSLI Publications.

Fludernik, Monika (1996), *Towards a "Natural" Narratology*, London: Routledge.

Freudenberg, Maren (2022), "Explaining Glossolalia Instead of Speaking in Tongues: Emotional Energy and Authority Relations at a Midwestern Pentecostal Megachurch," *Research in the Social Scientific Study of Religion* (32): 534–58.

Freudenberg, Maren, Martin Lutz, and Martin Radermacher (2020), "Gospels of Prosperity and Simplicity: Assessing Variation in the Protestant Moral Economy," *Interdisciplinary Journal of Research on Religion*, 16. Available online: https://www.religjournal.com/articles/article_view.php?id=156 (accessed July 28, 2021).

Freudenberg, Maren, Martin Radermacher, and Sebastian Schüler (2022), "Introduction to Special Section 3: Religious Authority in Practice in Contemporary Evangelical, Charismatic, and Pentecostal Christianity," *Research in the Social Scientific Study of Religion* (32): 471–81.

Freudenberg, Maren, and Thomas Weitzel (2019), "Introduction to the Special Issue on 'Charisma,'" *Journal of Religion in Europe* 12: 99–114.

Gauthier, François, and Thomas Martikainen (eds.) (2013), *Religion in Consumer Society: Brands, Consumers and Markets*, Farnham: Ashgate.

Hunt, Stephen J. (2002), "Deprivation and Western Pentecostalism Revisited: Neo-Pentecostalism," *PentecoStudies*, 1: 1–29.

Hunt, Stephen J. (ed.) (2020a), *Handbook of Megachurches*, Leiden: Brill.

Hunt, Stephen J. (2020b), "Introduction: The Megachurch Phenomenon," in Stephen J. Hunt (ed.), *Handbook of Megachurches*, 1–20, Leiden: Brill.

Julien, Heidi (2008), "Content Analysis," in Lisa M. Given (ed.), *The SAGE Handbook of Qualitative Research Methods*, 120–1, Los Angeles: SAGE.

Lee, Shayne, and Philipp L. Sinitiere (2009), *Holy Mavericks: Evangelicals Innovators and the Spiritual Marketplace*, New York: New York University Press.

Lövheim, Mia, and Stig Hjarvard (2019), "The Mediatized Conditions of Contemporary Religion: Critical Status and Future Directions," *Journal of Religion, Media and Digital Culture*, 8: 206–25.

Marshall, Ruth (2016), "Destroying Arguments and Captivating Thoughts: Spiritual Warfare Prayer as Global Praxis," *Journal of Religious and Political Practice*, 2: 92–113.

Michaels, Axel, and William S. Sax (2016), "Performance," in Michael Stausberg and Steven Engler (eds.), *The Oxford Handbook of the Study of Religion*, Oxford: Oxford University Press.

Osteen, Joel (2014), *Your Best Life Now: 7 Steps to Living at Your Full Potential*, New York: Faith Words.

Porterfield, Amanda, John Corrigan, and Daren E. Grem (2017), *The Business Turn in American History*, Oxford: Oxford University Press.

Pruisken, Insa, Josefa Loebell, Nina Monowski, and Thomas Kern (2022), "From Denominationalism to Market Standards: How Does the Religious Market Affect Authority Relations in Protestant Congregations?," *Research in the Social Scientific Study of Religion*, (32): 508–33. Available online: https://doi.org/10.1163/9789004505315_026 (accessed July 26, 2023).

Sinitiere, Phillip L. (2011), "From the Oasis of Love to Your Best Life Now: A Brief History of Lakewood Church," *Houston History*, 8: 1–9.

Sinitiere, Phillip L. (2015), *Salvation with a Smile: Joel Osteen, Lakewood Church, and American Christianity*, New York: New York University Press.

Sødal, Helje K. (2010), " 'Victor, not Victim': Joel Osteen's Rhetoric of Hope," *Journal of Contemporary Religion*, 25: 37–50.

Stanzel, Franz K. (1986), *A Theory of Narrative*, Cambridge: Cambridge University Press.

Thornberg, Robert, and Kathy Charmaz (2014), "Grounded Theory and Theoretical Coding," in Uwe Flick (ed.), *The SAGE Handbook of Qualitative Data Analysis*, 153–69, Thousand Oaks: SAGE.

Von der Ruhr, Marc (2020). "Megachurches in the Religious Marketplace," in Stephen J. Hunt (ed.), *Handbook of Megachurches*, 131–51, Leiden: Brill.

Weber, Max (1978 [1922]), *Economy and Society: An Outline of Interpretive Sociology*, Berkeley: University of California Press.

Wellman Jr., James K., Katie E. Corcoran, and Kate J. Stockly (2020), "Megachurches as Total Environments," in Stephen J. Hunt (ed.), *Handbook of Megachurches*, 152–71, Leiden: Brill.

Internet References

Hollar, Sherman (2021), "Joel Osteen: American Televangelist, Theologian, and Author," *Encyclopedia Britannia*, June 8. Available online: https://www.britannica.com/biography/Joel-Osteen (accessed July 28, 2021).

Kumar, Anugrah (2018), "Joel Osteen's Lakewood Church Has Annual Budget of $90 Million: Here's How That Money Is Spent," *Christian Post*, June 3. Available online: https://www.christianpost.com/news/joel-osteen-lakewood-church-annual-budget-90-million-money-spent.html (accessed July 23, 2021).

Lakewood Church (undated), "Our History," *Lakewood Church*. Available online: https://www.lakewoodchurch.com/about/history (accessed July 29, 2021).

Osteen, Joel (2021), "Trouble Is Temporary," *Sermons.love*. Available online: https://sermons.love/joel-osteen/7587-joel-osteen-trouble-is-temporary.html (accessed July 23, 2021).

Romano, Lois (2005), "'Smiling Preacher' Builds a Huge Church," *Washington Post*, January 30. Available online: https://www.washingtonpost.com/archive/politics/2005/01/30/smiling-preacher-builds-a-huge-church/6b046a0a-10d0-4c01-812b-b00decbac893/ (accessed July 30, 2021).

6

A Case on Behalf of the Routine Listener

Julian Millie

Ethnographic studies of preaching have revealed a variety of in situ responses from listeners, including utterances, bodily movements and gestures, acts of questioning or challenging, and weeping. This chapter is about these responses, and specifically about the associations to be made between listeners' responses and the concepts of agency and routineness. The ethnographic study of preaching has made progress in exploring the signs of agentive listening, but at the same time, the figure of the "routine listener" is hardly known. In what follows, I wish to introduce the routine listener by proposing some embodied aspects of her participation in preaching events.

I contrast agentive listening with routine listening. In using this terminology, I draw on the agentive/routine dyad.[1] Following the contours of this dyad, we can identify particular embodied responses as signs of listening practices that appear to act efficaciously upon the listener's self or collective. Routine listeners, I suggest here, do not show those signs, and might even show contrasting responses that point to repetitive submission with no intentionality beyond participation. If social scientists are to understand how religious listening sustains socially embedded routines of participation, we ought not exclude this figure from analysis. For one thing, overt focus on listener agency overlooks engagement in preaching events that—despite its non-agentive nature—nevertheless constitutes an individual's project of pious cultivation and might even represent the projects of a significant listening segment. Apart from that, a focus on the signs of routine listening enables us to relativize the agentive listener and avoid the risk of creating a hierarchy in which the agentive listener is somehow privileged above their routine co-listener.

Why does the routine listener have such a low profile in scholarship about pious listening? It is partly because this figure is inimical to the projects of many religious activists as well as social scientists. As I argue below, religious activists usually take the position that participation in preaching projects ought to provide listeners with the means to achieve personal and group transformations, and as such, the listener who is satisfied with mere attendance is a failure. For social scientists, the recent challenge has been to rescue practical observance from a tradition of analysis that understood it to be an experience of mindless indoctrination (Asad 1993). On that basis, observers have been keen to equate pious listening with processes such as challenging, questioning, reflection, and the struggle for self-empowerment.

These innovations in scholarship rescue the listener from being misunderstood as an automaton, but at the same time, the reification of the agentive listener seems to be at least in part a product of typically modernist ideologies of language and subjectivity (Bauman and Briggs 2003; Keane 2007) that attempt to purify listening of the constraints of the social order within which the listener dwells. By training the spotlight on the routine listener, I observe how listening practices are constrained by the social order in which listeners live and worship, and on that basis, I argue on behalf of styles of pious listening that indicate ambivalence about transformation and manifest themselves in embodiments pointing to the wrong end of the agentive/routine dyad. In other words, I am open to the recent suggestion by Stephen Cummins and Max Stille (2021: 20) that "boredom may be a very important part of the experience of sermon-going."

I intend this chapter to be a contribution to a broad conversation about the methodology of studying preaching and listening, and for this reason, my goal is to create relevance beyond one tradition or setting for listening. In what follows, I refer to a wide range of ethnographies of preaching originating in diverse religious currents. Nevertheless, my experiences as researcher have much to do with the development of the ideas expressed here. I studied Islamic oratory in West Java, a densely populated province of Indonesia, between 2007 and 2014 (Millie 2017). Around 98 percent of this province's population of around 43 million people are Muslim, and the level of support for frequent preaching and pedagogical events in public and private locations is very high. I studied preaching and pedagogical events held for audiences that were plural in terms of age, social status, gender, and political affiliation. Most of these events were held as commemorations of events of the Islamic calendar and life cycle, and were held in locations such as villages, places of employment, civic spaces, and educational institutions. The successful maintenance of these routines is entrusted to popular preachers who are highly skilled in nonreligious performance genres and do not hesitate to make use of these in their preaching.

Without such attractive preaching styles, it is doubtful whether such high participation could be achieved.

I mention this background because it provides the foundation for the ideas presented here. I observed in West Java that listeners' individual desire for pious transformation does not by itself enable such high participation in preaching routines. Instead, it is enabled by collaboration between a number of social actors committed to provide listening experiences suitable to listeners' social realities (preachers, event organizers, government, event-holders, and sponsors). As a result, I not only ask, "How does the listener participate in the discursivity of this interaction with the spoken word?" and "How does this listening provide a path to the shaping of a pious self?" I also ask questions such as "How do listening bodies arrive at preaching events in routines that might be out of their control, and what embodiments are specific to this unintentional listening?"

In what follows, I first reflect on an encounter with a listener that prompted me to think about routine listening. In this encounter, the listener talked about his preaching experience not as attendance at a discursive event, but as embodied participation in the routine commemoration within which the preaching event was embedded. I then focus on signs of routine listening in two modes, discursive and emotional. In both these sections, I refer to ethnographies that have described the signs of agentive listening, and then compare those with the signs of the routine listener.

Routine Listening

In 2016 I met a friend named Agus, a lawyer, at a social function in Bandung, West Java. Our conversation turned to preaching and listening. I asked him some casual questions about his own listening habits. The following exchange took place, in which Agus refers to the *'id ul-fitri* celebration held at the conclusion of the fasting month. This is a national holiday in Indonesia. Typically, Indonesians residing in cities return to their villages to celebrate the feast day and holiday with their extended families. Islamic ritual regulations require that a sermon be delivered at the celebration (see Wensick 2016):

Julian: Hey Gus, do you often listen to preachers?
Agus: Yes, of course!
Julian: What was the last time you listened to a preacher?

Agus: I guess it was when I went back to our village with my family for the *'id ul-fitri* celebration last month. It is a three-hour trip from here. We do this every year.
Julian: What was the sermon like?
Agus: I don't remember … just the usual stuff.

He did not recall anything more about the sermon beyond this.

What is noticeable in this exchange is that Agus did not recall the discursive experience of listening. He mentioned a collective ritual, routine in nature, within which the discursive experience was one part. It cannot be doubted that Agus must have participated in the preaching as a discursive experience on that day, for after all, the listening part of the ritual involved a speaker making reference to shared knowledge of Islamic norms. Nevertheless, Agus's recollection foregrounded the routinized commemoration in which the preaching event was just one part. He equated the discursive part with bodily fulfilment of what is collectively regarded as an important ritual obligation involving himself and others. His answer points to routinized listening. It does not negate agentive listening but draws our attention to preaching events as actions that include parts other than the discursive one.

West Javanese Muslims often end up listening to preaching as an inherent component of participating in other activities, in which the discursive part is embedded. Incidental listening occurring within wedding celebrations is a good illustration of this. Participants enjoy the moments of discursive engagement with religion alongside moments of eating, listening to music and other ritual performances, and socializing. Incidental listening also occurs in workplaces, educational institutions, government agencies, civic spaces where government and companies sponsor events, and so on. It is not impossible that incidental attendance at preaching events embedded within larger structures of routinized action might provide opportunities for agentive listening. Nevertheless, by reflecting on how one listens to speech that one did not intend to listen to, we can relativize the ideal of the pious listener seeking transformation of self and group through agentive listening. Routine listeners draw our attention to the other social circumstances prevailing in such activities. Perhaps the paradigmatic question might be, What processes bring bodies together for pious listening?

Three points arise from Agus's representations and my broader experience in West Java. The first is that participation of the kind described briefly by Agus does not deviate from the general models about observance and pious cultivation that have emerged in recent ethnographic studies of preaching (Hirschkind

2006; Mahmood 2005; Stille 2020). The holding of preaching events in diverse settings is supported and valued widely in West Javanese society because people regard them as opportunities to cultivate a pious self and collective. Like many Muslims of West Java, Agus is a lifelong student of Islam. Some of that learning will be acquired in formal learning processes, and much of it will be acquired in unfocussed and incidental processes. Nevertheless, attendance at preaching events is highly valued as an opportunity to cultivate the virtues and internal states revealed in the Qur'an, and to encourage younger generations to do the same. This conviction unites listeners with the organizers of events.

Furthermore, listening takes a number of different embodied forms, many of which I was able to observe during my attendance at so many preaching events in West Java. Some listeners will stroke an unlit cigarette in anticipation of leaving the preaching space at its conclusion; some will check messages and postings on their digital devices; some are overcome by sleep while listening; others laugh and chat. If we compare these listening embodiments with the images of agentive listeners encountered in the ethnographic literature (some of which I cite below), these modes of engagement clearly cannot be called agentive. Nevertheless, they are modes of cultivation of the pious self that analysts ought not to derogate below agentive modes. Of course, the preacher or teacher will criticize them, and other listeners might also castigate the listener who sleeps or checks their social media. Analysts, however, ought to observe these embodiments as strategies implemented by individuals wanting to fulfil their deeply felt conviction that attendance at preaching events is an essential resource for pious self-cultivation.

The third point is that experienced preachers are well aware of routines and incidental listening (Millie 2017).[2] Preachers are skilled at analyzing and anticipating the reception of their messages by listeners, and know which preaching styles are appropriate for the incidental listener. They mediate Islam in ways that are calibrated to maintain attention and support from listeners. Invariably, this means that preachers work not only with their listeners' religious knowledges, but also with their shared cultural experience. Preachers will establish a rapport and maintain listeners' attention through shared knowledge of the circumstances of everyday life in West Java, and of the symbolic forms mediated through television, radio, and cinema. So, apart from being engaged affectively and cognitively as *religious subjects*, routine listeners are engaged by the skillful speaking of mediators possessing intimate knowledge of their cultural subjectivity. This accommodation of non-agentive listeners sits uneasily beside the hopes of activists, state planners, and educators for agentive engagement (Millie 2017). Nevertheless, these ensure high participation in routines.

Some might object that in relativizing the agentive listener, I am being enticed by Agus to return to a previous chapter of social science reasoning, to the image of society and subject proposed by Émile Durkheim (1887–1917). In that image, the moral order is synonymous with collective action, and the space for individuals to be efficacious is narrow, if it exists at all. This image has been surpassed as a general explanatory model, partly because of the way it radically subsumes capabilities of the individual subject into the organized whole (an exemplary critique is Laidlaw 2002). My reading of Agus's experience might seem Durkheimian because I am representing Agus as someone engaged in something discursive, but only in his capacity as a "mere listener." Yet the problem for the analyst is this: If we banish the non-agentive listener from analysis, derogating their listening embodiments beneath agentive ones, are we not conniving with the teacher and activist by affirming their purified visions of successful preaching outcomes? Agentive engagement in the discursive part of preaching should not push routine listening out of our attempts to understand preaching as a feature of social life.

Agentive Listening

In this section I discuss the listening practices that ethnographers have interpreted as signs of the agentive listener. As noted, scholarly identification of this subject is a relatively recent development. Traditional scholarship had considered participation in ritual observances as work being done for the collective. Yet ritual observances are not one-way processes in which passive participants are fitted with normative attributes. More recently, scholars have begun to approach observances as discursive practices (Asad 1986). Yet once a preaching or pedagogical event is framed as discursive practice, this has implications when it comes to constructing the subjectivity of participants. In the case of pious listening, analysis tends to privilege certain attributes of listening—those that point to agentive listening—over those displayed by a listener such as Agus. As the agentive listener emerged, the stage was set for the routine listener to become a second-rate listening subject, more by analytical neglect than by explicit naming as such.

A groundbreaking analysis of agentive listening is Saba Mahmood's (2005: chapter 3) ethnographic study of preaching and pedagogy attended by women from Cairo's Islamist communities. In these communities, women strive to implement religious norms that place constraints on their mobility and freedom in comparison with those enjoyed by men. One of the goals of Mahmood's study is to refute negative stereotypes about such women. Their rejection of the norms of secular liberalism does not mean, Mahmood shows, that they are passive participants in their own subjugation. Agency has other modalities than those that point to secular liberalism.

Agentive listening is a central part of this argument. Mahmood (2005: 100–5) describes a pedagogical event at which female teachers discuss the norm of avoiding eye contact with males outside a women's immediate kin. A youthful listener challenges the stringent level of avoidance advocated by the teachers, quoting alternative religious texts that support a less stringent interpretation. Mahmood points out that these objections are expressed not in the conceptual repertoire of secular liberalism, but in the argumentative modes of the Islamic textual tradition. On this basis, we observe a religious discursive tradition that encourages listeners to challenge, object, argue, and engage in processes of exchange and dialogue. This is what agentive listeners do. The stereotype of passive indoctrination is refuted by observation of these listening practices. In short, "The pedagogical space of *da'wa* [Islamic predication] is often constituted by debate and disagreement" (Mahmood 2005: 105).

It is striking how Mahmood's specification of the signs of agentive listening overlaps with the concerns of an influential strand of Islamic activism in Indonesia (Millie 2017). Since before independence in 1945, Muslim reformists have advocated for an Islamic subject that displays the critical autonomy described by Mahmood.[3] Reformists have long criticized the conventional routines of pious listening enjoyed by Indonesian listeners because they appear to involve listeners who lack the capacity for agentive listening. For intellectuals and activists within this group, preaching is a media form to be compared with other media and communications forms that constitute the contemporary public sphere. In comparison with these they invariably find the traditional styles of preaching to be lacking. The reformists idealize literate, newspaper-reading subjects who reflect on the common good with the critical perspective of an enlightened and educated citizen. Islamic education processes are to produce the same subject, and against that background, the Muslim who "merely listens" is one who is failing to develop.[4]

Furthermore, reformists typically hold that Islam is a resource upon which a prosperous and modern Indonesia could develop, and fulfilment of this aspiration seems out of reach while Muslims are being thrilled and amused by clever preachers. Listeners who laugh—or are easily emotionally aroused in response to invocations of group symbols—are Muslims who do not show the detachment seen as a necessary attribute of contemporary citizenship. Indonesia's Muslim feminists are particularly concerned at the effects of routine listening upon women's political subjectivity. Feminist NGOs conduct empowerment programs to enable women to agentively engage in traditional frames for listening that they see as cultivating passive subjectivity in women participants (Millie 2021). For the Muslim feminist project, female listeners who can object, challenge, and argue are empowered to make progress in women's issues generally.

It is striking that in Mahmood's analysis of the Cairo women's study groups, and also in the critiques of listening made by Indonesian reformists, we find no references to the conditions that propel bodies to events in which preaching is embedded. No one asks, "How did the body of this listener come to attend this event?" It is as if the discursive engagement with religion needs to be separated from the patterns and cycles that lead to the construction of temporary stages and the assembling of audiences. The discursive aspect is abstracted from the schedules that move bodies to become listeners.[5] This leads to another question: Is it possible that when engagement in preaching is framed as discursive practice, the embodied routines and conventions become problematic for the analysis? What are the implications for a listener's agency if it is known that the listener has arrived at the event incidentally upon participating in a routinized ritual practice in which the listening is embedded? If agency implies an element of forethought or intentionality, then surely incidental listening is a compromised agency? If agency is the socially mediated capacity to act (Ahearn 2001), then this capacity might be limited when the mode of arrival at the discursive event lacks attributes of agency.

Routine Emotions

In some religious contexts, listening is construed through language ideologies that understand the listening body to be permeated, entered, or taken over by the Divine presence, Holy Spirit, Divine word, and so on. These ideologies provide striking foundations for embodied responses by listeners, for the affective transformation of the listener's interiority materializes as embodied listening acts recognized as such within the context. Such engagement is frequently observed in the practices of Pentecostal and Charismatic Christians. Pentecostal practice is short on canonical liturgical practices and is relatively unconstrained by a need to reenact specific ritual models and concepts. For many Pentecostals and Charismatics, the most authoritative index of the Holy Spirit's presence is the personal sensation of the individual, brought on as emotional responses to worship practices and notably by sermons (Coleman 2000; Meyer 2010). Listeners make bodily gestures and actions that index this presence. One such action is glossolalia (speaking in tongues), an embodied response to listening that is cultivated within Pentecostal circles. Coleman (2000) observed a number of other distinctive bodily gestures that signal the listener's reception of the spirit, including the altar call. Upon being inspired to do so by the preacher's mediation of the Holy Spirit, listeners physically approach the preacher to renew their spiritual commitment. Another is the listener's assumption of distinctive bodily stances that indicate reception: raised arm, closed eyes, and head tilted back.

Hirschkind's (2006) analysis of a pious Islamic listening subculture in Cairo is striking because the gestural responses that signal the desired emotional states are practices to be studied and learned by listeners. A vocabulary of gestures signals emotions that are associated with the pious and ethical dispositions objectified in the Qur'an. Emotional states such as pious fear, regret, humility, and repentance remind and oblige listeners to perform ethical bodily practices and acts and to develop moral skills (Hirschkind 2006: 107–17). A successful preacher will bring on these states, which may be signaled by weeping, an approved bodily response that forms "a kind of emotional response appropriate for both men and women when, with humility, fear, and love, they turn to God" (Hirschkind 2001: 630).

What is striking is that the listening ideology cultivated in the community studied by Hirschkind specifically requires more than "mere listening." Muslims ought to listen with care and intention, and these attributes characterize "listening with attention" as pious practice beyond and above mere hearing (*al-sam'*). A shared vocabulary of gestural responses are signs of the listener's openness to the transformation that is the goal of ethical piety. According to this ideology of listening, "one is capable of hearing the sermon in its full ethical sense only to the extent one has already cultivated the particular modes of sensory responsiveness presupposed in the discourse's gestural vocabulary" (Hirschkind 2006: 101).

The above analyses reveal two points about the bodily signs of an emotionally affected listener. First, the signs all point to effects located in the interior self of the listener. They confirm the modern notion that the true locus of religion is the inner self (Keane 2007). Second, the embodied signs are structuring devices for the creation of a hierarchy of listeners. It might not be enough to "merely listen." In Hirschkind's observation (2006: 101), gestural responses reveal the listener who is "hearing the sermon in its full ethical sense." This ideology of listening distinguishes between routine listening and the listening of true transformation.

What about the emotional transformation of the routine listener? There are many embodiments of affect that point to the routine listener, but perhaps the most frequently encountered is her laughter. In my ethnographic work on preaching in West Java, I was constantly attending sermons delivered by preachers skilled in "affective communication that creates surprise, laughter, sympathy, and feelings of comfort and belonging" (Millie 2017: 135). The embodied sign of this species of affect is also physical movement; the audience ripples as laughing listeners lean sideways, forwards or backwards, seeking support with their hands from their sibling or neighbor sitting beside them, sometimes striking them gently to relieve their urge to laugh. In discourse about preaching in West Java, it is rarely admitted that a preacher's success might be due to their skill in making listeners laugh. This would have a negative effect on the dignity of the preacher's mission (Millie 2017a). But in fact, there are many popular preachers who succeed with preaching styles in which humor is the dominant content.

This species of affect does not point to transformations indicating progress in individual ethical projects. Rather, it points to a context where the commitment of the collective to the frequent holding of preaching events is high. The organizing committees I met in West Java desired strongly that their events attract large audiences consisting of people of all ages. Preachers who specialize in speaking for women's groups, for example, are aware that levity offsets the normative pressure of Islamic textual study. Organizers of workplace sermons did not want unwilling or recalcitrant listeners to suffer unduly during the sermon. After all, employees were attending under duress. Skillful mediation of humorous affect encourages audiences with flagging commitment to attend. This collaborative project of making preaching suitable for the incidental listener keys into collective rather than individual religious commitments, for preachers are not only working upon listeners' awareness of their religious obligation. Rather, the preacher is working with cultural knowledge shared by members of the audience (knowledge of everyday lifeways, cultural stereotypes, media figures, etc.). The normative obligations of religious conviction are not absent from such preaching, but they are softened through inversions and contextualizations that lighten the burden of piety.

Preachers vary in their dispositions toward strategies of softening (Millie 2021). Some base their careers upon performative skill without being troubled by such reflections. I met many who were ambivalent about them, accepting that creating a sense of belonging through affective preaching is a necessary thing that ought to be constrained. For some activists and progressives, however, preaching styles that appear to cater for non-agentive listeners are a problem. The country's Muslim feminists, for example, hope that preaching events and study groups might become means for women's empowerment. In their view, a listener's laughter is a sign of their failure to transform into the empowered subject idealized by the women's movement. Reformist activists lament the missed opportunities, imagining that listeners could become agents of social and political progress if their listening practices became serious (Millie 2017: 116–19).[6] That aspiration, however, affirms a narrow conception of pious listening that necessitates that listening routines be purified of non-agentive listening styles. In contrast, everyday preaching practices in Indonesia reveal that preachers accommodate rather than reject listeners who are bored, recalcitrant, eager to leave, tired, and disinterested. In this way, they achieve something critical on behalf of the collective: They ensure that the cycles and routines of commemoration and ritual attract high participation.

Concluding Words

It might seem misdirected to argue that it is legitimate religious practice to laugh one's way through a sermon, or to use the phrase "pious listener" to refer to someone who checks her social media during a sermon that she never intended to attend. Yet these are realities of pious practice in many communities, and by what right does the analyst claim that laughter and message-checking vitiate projects of ethical cultivation? By introducing the routine listener, I hope to draw attention to a listening subject that might disappoint the hopes of those who identify listening as a means to group and individual transformation, but is nevertheless engaged in a project of religious cultivation, drawing on the resources available to her. I also hope to draw attention to cultures of preaching that foster the routine listener.

I have also highlighted the contrasting analytical approaches that recognize and distinguish the routine and the agentive listener. We see the agentive listener most clearly when she is abstracted from the conditions that might threaten her intentionality and the scope of the project that she could achieve through listening. When discussing agentive listening, we shy away from mentioning, for example, the collective routines that brought her to the point of listening. In contrast, we observe the routine listener clearly when we observe the dependencies and constraints in her environment, and when we inquire about how her body came to be present in a listening audience. We see her in routines that accommodate and enable pious practice for believers with little intent beyond participation and "mere listening."

Notes

1 This definition—or a variant of it—can be found in Ahearn (2001), Ortner (2006), and Mahmood (2005).
2 An equivalent meta-preaching awareness is described in Stille's discussion of Bangladeshi preaching cultures (Stille 2020).
3 Key sources about Indonesia's Muslim reformist movement include Bowen (1993) and Nakamura (2012).
4 Some reformists have deep concerns about the negative effects of preaching routines on the development of Muslim political attitudes. Some have even promoted programs to encourage Muslims to develop skills in *writing* about Islamic tradition and doctrine. This is directly connected to perceptions about the kind of Islamic subject that is shaped through listening as opposed to written modes of discourse (Millie 2017: 104–11).
5 A growing body of literature has observed that ideologies of language associated with modern rationality insist on abstracting linguistic practices from their dependence upon specific social and material conditions (e.g., Bauman and Briggs 2003; Keane 2007).
6 A similar critique within Bangladeshi Islamic society is described by Stille (2020: 168–74).

References

Ahearn, Laura (2001), "Language and Agency," *Annual Review of Anthropology*, 30: 109–37.
Asad, Talal (1986), *The Idea of an Anthropology of Islam*, Georgetown: Occasional papers series, Georgetown University.
Asad, Talal (1993), *Genealogies of Religion: Discipline and Reasons of Power in Christianity and Islam*, Baltimore, MD: Johns Hopkins University Press.
Bauman, Richard, and Charles L. Briggs (2003), *Voices of Modernity: Language Ideologies and the Politics of Inequality*, Cambridge: Cambridge University Press.
Bowen, John (1993), *Muslims through Discourse: Religion and Ritual in Gayo Society*, Princeton, NJ: Princeton University Press.
Coleman, Simon (2000), *The Globalisation of Charismatic Christianity: Spreading the Gospel of Prosperity*, Cambridge: Cambridge University Press.

Cummins, Stephen, and Max Stille (2021), "Religious Emotions and Emotions in Religion: The Case of Sermons," *Journal of Religious History*, 45 (1): 3–24.

Hirschkind, Charles (2001), "The Ethics of Listening: Cassette-Sermon Audition in Contemporary Egypt," *American Ethnologist*, 28 (3): 623–49.

Hirschkind, Charles (2006), *The Ethical Soundscape: Cassette Sermons and Islamic Counterpublics*, New York: Columbia University Press.

Keane, Webb (2007), *Christian Moderns: Freedom and Fetish in the Mission Encounter*, Berkeley: University of California Press.

Laidlaw, James (2002), "For an Anthropology of Ethics and Freedom," *Journal of the Royal Anthropological Institute*, 8 (2): 311–32.

Mahmood, Saba (2005), *Politics of Piety: The Islamic Revival and the Feminist Subject*, Princeton, NJ: Princeton University Press.

Meyer, Birgit (2010), "Aesthetics of Persuasion: Global Christianity and Pentecostalism's Sensational Forms," *South Atlantic Quarterly*, 109 (4): 741–63.

Millie, Julian (2017a), *Hearing Allah's Call: Preaching and Performance in Indonesian Islam*, Ithaca, NY: Cornell University Press.

Millie, Julian (2017b), "The Public Metaculture of Islamic Preaching," in Matt Tomlinson and Julian Millie (eds.), *The Monologic Imagination*, 231–50, New York: Oxford University Press.

Millie, Julian (2021), "Men's Politics, Women's Piety: The Gendered Asymmetry of Indonesia's New Public Islams," *Australian Journal of Anthropology*, 32 (2): 135–49.

Nakamura, Mitsuo (2012), *The Crescent Arises over the Banyan Tree: A Study of the Muhammadiyah Movement in a Central Javanese Town c.1910–2010*, 2nd ed., Singapore: ISEAS.

Ortner, Sherry (2006), *Anthropology and Social Theory: Culture, Power, and the Acting Subject*, Durham, NC: Duke University Press.

Stille, Max (2020), *Islamic Sermons and Public Piety in Bangladesh: The Poetics of Popular Preaching*, London: I.B. Tauris.

Internet References

Wensinck, Arent (2016), "K̲huṭba," in Peri Bearman, Thierry Bianquis, Clifford Edmund Bosworth, Emeri van Donzel, and Wolfhart Peter Heinrichs (eds.), *Encyclopaedia of Islam, Second Edition*, Leiden: Brill Online. http://dx.doi.org/10.1163/1573-3912_islam_SIM_4352 (accessed June 28, 2023).

Part 3

Ritual and Religious Speech

7

"Words against Death": Religious Speech—Perspectives from Ritual Ambivalences and Trends

Paul Post

Introduction

In July 1996, a military transport plane was returning members of the Royal Netherlands Air Force brass band to the Eindhoven air base after a performance in Modena, Italy. During the landing, the plane crashed and burst into flames. Four crew members and twenty-eight members of the band died in the crash. Two days later, a national memorial service was held at the Eindhoven air base. The service included a three-part religious ceremony with contributions from humanist, Roman Catholic, and Protestant chaplains.

As part of a large-scale research project on disaster rituals, I analyzed this memorial service extensively, focusing on the three speeches by the religious representatives (Post, Nugteren, and Zondag 2002: 101–14; Post et al. 2003: 100–15). I noticed remarkable differences between their speeches. Without calling into question the speakers' sincerity, it is notable how often in such ceremonies a speaker starts by saying that it is impossible to find words, and yet goes on to devote many, many words to the catastrophe. Accordingly, the Roman Catholic chaplain delivered a long and rather bombastic speech, while the Protestant Baptist pastor presented a short, reformed liturgy in the limited time available to him.

The contribution of the humanist chaplain was entirely different. His speech impressed the attending families and friends, especially the deceased soldiers' comrades. He entered the pulpit and delivered a short poem without any introduction or conclusion. The anonymous poem, "The Stone Is Strong"

(Dutch: “De steen is sterk”), is as follows (Post, Nugteren, and Zondag 2002: 104 [Dutch]; Post et al. 2003: 104):[1]

Stone is strong, but iron breaks it.
Iron is strong, but fire melts it.
Fire is strong, but water extinguishes it.
Water is strong, but sun evaporates it.
The sun is strong, but cloud hides it.
The cloud is strong, but wind drives it onward.
The wind is strong, but man can withstand it.
Man is strong, but death strikes him down.
Death is strong, but love is stronger than death.
Love never passes away.

The central message was clear: “Death is strong, but love is stronger than death. Love never passes away.” This speech, in fact this poem, was subsequently copied and hung in many rooms around the military base’s barracks.

Why was this poem so well received? Why was its impact so great? In general, it can be explained by the use of what is known as “second language,” or visual, symbolical, evocative language—the language of ritual and poetry. Here, the poem and the ritual performance coincided, where the poem was the ritual and the ritual the poem. There was no introduction and no explanation afterward: just the poem, nothing more, nothing less. We are then left with an interesting question: Was it a religious statement? It contributed to the liturgical part of the ceremony, but was it religious? Furthermore, how does this relate to the fact that it was the humanist chaplain, called in Dutch the *humanistisch raadsman*, who gave the most powerful and impressive speech according to the experience of the ceremony’s participants?

For me, this memorial service twenty-five years ago is a good place from which to explore religious speech from the perspective of ritual and ritual studies. The ceremony was a “game changer” in the field of national memorial rituals in the Netherlands. There was a broad feeling that these public rituals must be done differently. And in the new millennium, we see another ritual language in national ceremonies, with a dominant place for poetry and music, for stories told by next of kin, with basic symbols and acts. Often the national memorial for the MH17 Ukraine air crash in 2014 is considered exemplary of this development in the Netherlands (Post 2014).

The Stone poem at the 1996 Eindhoven ceremony was a prelude to those changes. In this chapter, I will therefore consider this poem as an example of changing ritual language.

Scope and Outline of This Chapter

In this chapter, I plan to explore the ritual dimension of religious speech using two lenses. First, I view it from the perspective of ritual's ambivalence and ambiguity, and second, I consider current trends that influence our rituals and give rise to the dynamics of ritual. With this choice of ambivalences and trends, I bring in two important perspectives of ritual acting and ritual study. On the one hand, through ambivalence we have a more internally oriented perspective, an approach linked to the specific nature of ritual. On the other hand, through the discussion of trends, a more externally oriented contextual perspective emerges. However, the two approaches are not separate trajectories to approach ritual, which can never be studied independently of context (Post 2019b, 2021a, 2021b, 2022).

In my exploration, I include ritual criticism, a critical and normative view of ritual (Post 2013a; Post and Van der Beek 2016). Ritual study is never only descriptive or analytical, but also has a critical function and task—that criticism can be informed and oriented in different ways. It can focus on the ritual performance, the acting competence or lack thereof at the level of the presentation, the "craft" of performing the ritual, or on norms and values, ideology of politics, and religion. Recently, the importance of authenticity in ritual acting is emerging. Or insights informed by research as presented in Ritual Studies.

In line with my opening, death rituals are my main focus here.

Some Preliminary Notes on Concepts

Before exploring the ritual dimension of religious speech, I will briefly describe how I use some central concepts: ritual, ritual language, religious language, and the sacred. In a very general sense, I use all these terms and concepts openly and dynamically.

Ritual

In the *Handbook of Disaster Ritual* (Post 2021a: 2–6), I offer the following open description of ritual:

> Ritual is a more or less repeatable sequence of action units which take on a symbolic dimension through formalization, stylization, and their situation in

> place and time. On the one hand, individuals and groups express their ideas and ideals, their mentalities and identities through these rituals; on the other hand, the ritual actions shape, foster, and transform these ideas, mentalities, and identities. (Post 2021a: 3)

To keep the working definition of ritual open and dynamic, we also need to recognize all kinds of ritualizations. By ritualization or ritualizing, I do not refer to the use of the term by Ronald Grimes, who sees ritualizing as a particular mode of ritual, that is, actions that are on the way to becoming ritual but have not yet been culturally accepted as such (Grimes 2014: 192–3). Instead, I observe that there are many practices with a ritual dimension that never become "full" rituals. Here, I am in line with the theoretical legacy of the late American ritual studies scholar Catherine Bell (1953–2008), who mainly connects ritualizing with what she labels "ritual-like activities." By this, she refers to common activities that are ritualized to a greater or lesser degree (Bell 1997: 138–69). More specifically, Bell argues that "examples of ritual-like activity suggest that what's going on in ritual is not unique to religious institutions or traditions" (Bell 1997: 164). There are thus many ways of acting ritually and many degrees of ritualizing. For ritual and religious language, I take a similarly open and dynamic approach.

Ritual Language

Let us begin with ritual language. As we will see with religious language, there are several perspectives or parameters that can compose its identity. For instance:

a. In addition to space/place, time, acting, and objects, language can be the designation of an element of ritual (or of ritualizations as practice with a ritual dimension, as seen above; Grimes 2014: 274–9).
b. Context can be an important designator for language as ritual language. For example, a text read or spoken in a ritual context in a ceremony or in a crematorium, church, or mosque becomes ritual language.
c. Additionally, performance can make a text or words ritual. In my definition, I mentioned the importance of stylization and formalization. This also concerns the performance of words, language, the spoken word, and speech. You can read a text as you quote a newspaper or telephone directory, or you can recite and declaim it.
d. The religious identity of language and words is directly related to designation and appropriation and can therefore be highly variable. For

example, there may be a distinction between the scope of language by the authorities and the appropriation by the hearers.

e. Finally, the denominator "ritual" is related to what we could call language genres. Grimes lists several kinds of ritual language (Grimes 2014: 274–9), and some concern genres with a direct and inherent ritual dimension, such as a sermon, prayer, spell, or incantation.

Religious Language

I offer a parallel series of perspectives for religious language. To start, I propose here, too, an open and dynamic concept of religion, encompassing a spectrum with institutional religion on the one hand and religiosity and spirituality on the other. Thus, religious language also knows defining perspectives as an element of religion, context, performance, designation and appropriation, and genre.

The Sacred

Ritual and religiosity, and in this context also ritual and religious language and speech, are linked to the sacred. My concept of the sacred is also open and dynamic, extending from what is special and set apart by people. There can be different parameters for the sacred: It can be supernatural or natural, personal or collective, and so on (Evans 2003).

In this chapter, I use ritual, religious, and sacred language side by side.

Ritual Ambivalences

Rituals are often ambiguous and leave us ambivalent (Post 2019b, 2021a, 2022; Post and Hoondert 2019).[2] Because of their paradoxical nature, rituals are difficult to pin down; they are elusive and frequently uncontrolled and unplanned. Religious authorities in particular frequently have difficulty with how rites are not subject to normal control mechanisms. Attempts at control are commonly made through written scenarios, directives, and instructions, but ultimately, the ritual is the action itself, the performance, the play. There is thus an interesting tension here between spoken and written words.

I will mention briefly some of the important ambivalences with which ritual presents us and focus on the role of words, speech, and language.

The Traditional and the New

First, there is a tension between ritual as a known and "old" tradition and a newly created act. This ambivalence between the old and the new directly impacts religious speech. Few have escaped the endless debate as to whether liturgical language should be traditional or modern (e.g., Latin or the vernacular). Does religious communication require traditional sacred language? Must religious speech be traditional in the sense of being repeatable? In the context of ritual, is religious language not primarily *found* in tradition rather than being *created* by men?

Referring to the case with which I opened this chapter I think religious speech can be both traditional and, at the same time, fresh and modern. The "Stone" poem (circulating on the internet on Dutch poetry websites in the 1990s; for instance, it was found in 1999–2000 on the Dutch poetry website poetryalive.nl under the pseudonym Oase Eerbeek) is based on a moralistic poem from 1889, *Het Sterkste* (The Strongest) by J. A. Goeverneur (1809–1889) that was recast in fresh and modern language (Post 2022, chapter 9). Like ritual itself, ritual language and religious speech need to be involved in an ongoing process of inculturation and recasting or, to use terminology better tailored to language, they need to be part of a translation process (Post 2019a).

The Individual and the Community

A second ambivalence lies in the relationship between the individual and the community. We struggle constantly with this tension in our rituals. To take again a funeral as a case in point, a (post-)modern funeral liturgy focuses on *this* dead person and *this* group of relatives. However, we find it difficult to locate harmony between the emerging dominance of the "culture of self," with its strong personalization, and the desire for solidarity within a group.

This ambivalence is often reflected in ritual speech. How do we create a community language? How general can ritual language be? Rituals can be created as spaces open to different appropriations. In the humanist chaplain's speech the poem was just such an open space, going beyond the dichotomy of the individual versus the community.

Inclusive and Exclusive

The communal dimension touches directly on the ambivalence of ritual as both inclusive and exclusive. It is inviting, accessible, and hospitable, but it is also closed, strange, secret, and exclusive. These two polar extremes play an important role in the ritual and its sacred character, which includes both acting and speech. Recently, in the context of various movements criticizing language which they regard as discriminatory or offensive, the issue of the inclusivity or exclusivity of our words has become topical. I could mention here the gender perspective, or "gender trouble," as in the title of Judith Butler's work (Butler 1990).

Again referring to our "Stone" poem, it is open, with well-known symbols and short sentences, yet enigmatic and puzzling as to where it goes and where it ends. It has all the characteristics of a spell or an incantation.

Useless and Useful

Fundamental to the ritual is its ambiguity as a useless action and, simultaneously, as a powerful, productive, and efficient instrument. Any reflection on ritual must struggle with this paradox. Johan Huizinga strongly emphasizes in his famous study *Homo Ludens* that the useless dimension of cult and ritual is directly related to play, and the playing of man is closely related to that of a child or an animal (Huizinga 1949: esp. ch. 1). It is just for fun. However, other scholars of ritual argue that its most basic dimension is that of incantation. Rituals are powerful tools that allow us as humans to cope with setbacks and contingencies; they can keep us going in a world full of dangers and evil. In facing this dichotomy, we must go beyond the "useless/useful trap" (Wepener et al. 2019: 27–46) because these polar opposites are two sides of the same coin. Are rituals not powerful coping mechanisms precisely because they are of a different order? And the other way around? (Post 2019a: 73–6)

This paradox is evident in religious language and everyday speech. Religious language forms part of a ritual, which, although often unproductive to understanding, at the same time carries the nature of a spell or incantation. Douglas Davies, an expert in studies on death and dying, calls funeral rites "words against death" (Davies 2017). Looking back at the speech by the humanist chaplain, the poem he delivered was a powerful word of hope. It was indeed a "word against death."

Some Current Tendencies and Trends in Rituals

Due to external stimuli, rituals change; they come under pressure to inculturate and transform (Hoondert and Post 2021). General trends in a culture are reflected in trends in its rituals. Sometimes these relate directly to the ambivalences described above. I will illustrate that process through a few trends that I have identified in the Western European context. I will also provide a brief critical evaluation in the tradition of ritual criticism (Post 2013a, 2019a; Post and Van der Beek 2016).

Casualization

The first trend that has had a direct impact on our rituals is what I describe as casualization (Schippers 2015). This describes the emergence of a casual approach to ritual that manifests itself primarily in external design, but I think goes deeper and expresses something about our attitudes toward the sacred. For example, at funerals, I often see that people no longer dress for the event, but are dressed casually in jeans and an old sweater.

This is not the place to elaborate on a tendency toward the "domestication" of ritual. I note only that language and speech are important vehicles of this process of casualization. With reference to Martin Stringer, I see a relationship between the warm, emotional side of ritual and "an increasing sense of comfortableness and intimacy" in enacting rituals in the global setting of discourses on consumerism and individual well-being. Stringer notices in contemporary Christian worship "carpets on the floor, a crèche for the children, power-point technology providing reassuring images, language that does not offend, and music aimed to speak to our emotions and calm us down" (Stringer 2005: 239).

The poem "The Stone" and everlasting love transcend this tendency toward reassuring and casual language and symbolism through the strict poetic format and the context in which rather casual phenomena, like a stone, fire, water, and wind, become sacred and cosmic symbols.

Explaining

Another emerging trend is that of explanation and commentary. Many things in our modern culture are accompanied by words of explanation. We are increasingly didactic and like to explain. However, explaining can invade the ritual. If a pastor is constantly explaining and commenting on a ritual—what he or she is doing, what it means, and where it comes from—a new genre of ritual speech is introduced, that of explanation and comment. But for the ritual itself, that is disastrous: It can be destroyed by the explanation. Your lighting of a candle and the light it gives need no explanation, for the act is sufficient. My colleague Wouter van Beek put this aptly: "In a functional ritual catechesis is superfluous, for an incomprehensible ritual, it comes too late" (Van Beek 2007: 49). Regarding religious speech in a ritual context, we need to make a distinction between ritual speech and speech about the ritual. Catechesis, or speaking about the ritual, explaining it, and commenting on it, must not be confused with the ritual speech itself. Ideally, catechesis has its place *outside* of the ritual act and after the acting, as was the case in early Christian mystagogical catechesis performed after the Easter ceremonies.

The Emergence of the Basic Sacred

Finally, I mention the increase of what I call basic symbolism, or basic sacrality, in ritual (Schippers 2015). Due to many changing circumstances, such as the superdiversity of our globalized and networked culture, rites and symbols arise that are both open and very basic. Ritual can thereby provide an open hermeneutic space. Here, the enormous success of the Camino, the old medieval pilgrims' way to Santiago de Compostela, provides a clear example. That path is literally a space within which you walk, it is a vessel that the pilgrim fills her- or himself while journeying (Post 1998; Post and Van der Beek 2016).

The emergence of basic sacrality is reflected through ritual speech and language. Open language, with basic sacred symbols, can play a role in religious rituals that have an institutional Christian identity or in a more open setting of religious seeking and spirituality (Post 2013b). Indirect references, such as those to the Bible, can play an important role as accents or details: Indeed, God can be in the details, as Mies van der Rohe famously said. Once again, I refer to the "Stone" poem: It is a striking example of such an open space and basic symbols with which we all can identify: iron, fire, water, sun, cloud, wind, man, death, and love.

Conclusion

I opened this chapter with a Dutch poem that became a popular funeral poem. I conclude by referring to two poems by the Welsh poet Dylan Thomas (1914–1953) that have similarly played and still play a prominent role in the international repertoire of funeral rituals.[3] In 1951, when his father was dying and two years before his own death, Thomas wrote what is perhaps his most famous poem: "Do Not Go Gentle into That Good Night." Almost twenty years earlier, in April 1933, he wrote another famous poem: "And Death Shall Have No Dominion."[4] He was nineteen at the time. The poem was published in May that year and again in his second volume of poetry in 1936.

In this poem, we can identify much of what I have suggested about the ritual dimension of religious speech. This becomes all the more powerful when the text is recited as a performance. Thomas often did so himself, and there are several recordings of him reading his poetry. He was known primarily for his spoken word performances, and others, including pop stars such as Iggy Pop, have presented his poems in this way. Thomas's performance is strikingly convergent with the religious speech of his period, when one considers the performance of sermons and prayers of prominent preachers from the interbellum. The connections between poetry and ritual speech are also exemplified by Amanda Gorman, who read her poem "The Hill We Climb" at Joe Biden's inauguration, and who performed her poetry first in the liturgies of the Roman Catholic St. Brigid's parish church in Los Angeles.

At first glance, the contrast with "The Stone" is great. Thomas's poetry is complex and layered. His poems are full of references and intertextuality, with the Bible and mythology playing an important role in understanding the metaphors. The recurring first line of "And death shall have no dominion" (which is also the poem's title, because Thomas never gave his poems titles) comes from Rom. 6:9, while other parts are drawn from the Sermon on the Mount and 1 Cor. 15:40-44. "The Stone," meanwhile, is notable for its simple language and images.

Yet there is a direct relationship between both forms of poetry, especially when we see them in a ritual context, in this case a funerary setting. They are lyrics brought to life in that ritual context through performance. As language, as ritual expression, both texts become open spaces in which mourners can express their feelings, their anger, protest, and hope. In both cases, the dimension of "words against death" (Davies 2017) dominates, and the incantation dimension that calls on death is exorcised.

That dimension of a powerful word against death is best expressed when the poems, both "The Stone" and "And death shall have no dominion," are performed.

I invite the reader of this chapter to finish reading my chapter by listening to a historical recording of the poem read by Thomas himself that underlines this ritual incantation dimension.[5]

Notes

1 Translation by D. H. Mader; this version of the poem is an adaptation of an older poem, also referred to in this chapter; it was circulating on the Dutch poetry website poetryalive.nl under the pseudonym Oase Eerbeek.

2 I reuse here parts of my work—Post (2021a: 68–73 and 2022).

3 Cf. Poems for Funerals. Available online: https://poets.org/poems-funerals (accessed June 26, 2023); Poems for Funerals: Poetry Foundation. Available online: https://www.poetryfoundation.org/articles/69937/poems-for-funerals (accessed June 26, 2023) and Dying Matters. Available online: https://www.dyingmatters.org/page/poetry-about-dying (accessed June 26, 2023).

4 Texts: Dylan Thomas, "And Death Shall Have No Dominion" (1943) and "Do Not Go Gentle Good Night" (1937). Recitation: Dylan Thomas, "And Death Shall Have No Dominion" (2014) and "Dylan Thomas reads `Do Not Go Gentle into That Good Night'" (2011).

5 Recitation: Dylan Thomas, "And Death Shall Have No Dominion" (2014).

References

Ackerman, John (1991), *A Dylan Thomas Companion*, London: Palgrave Macmillan.

Bell, Catherine (1997), *Ritual, Perspectives and Dimensions*, New York: Oxford University Press.

Butler, Judith (1990), *Gender Trouble. Feminism and the Subversion of Identity*, New York: Taylor & Francis.

Davies, Douglas (2017), *Death, Ritual and Belief. The Rhetoric of Funerary Rites*, New York: Bloomsbury.

Evans, Matthew (2003), "The Sacred: Differentiating, Classifying and Extending Concepts," *Review of Religious Research*, 45 (1): 32–47.

Ferris, Paul (2006), *Dylan Thomas: The Biography*, 3rd rev. ed. New York: Dial Press.

Grimes, Ronald (2014), *The Craft of Ritual Studies*, New York: Oxford University Press.

Hoondert, Martin, and Paul Post (2021), "Editorial. Introduction to Special Issue: Exploring Ritual Fields Today," *Religions*, 12 (3). Available online: https://doi.org/10.3390/rel12030210 (accessed July 27, 2023).

Huizinga, Johan (1949), *Homo Ludens. A Study of the Play-Element in Culture*, London: Routledge & Kegan Paul, reprint 1980; orig. Dutch ed.: "Homo ludens. Proeve eener bepaling van het spel-element der cultuur (1938)," in L. Brummel et al. (eds.) (1950), *J. Huizinga: Verzamelde werken V: Cultuurgeschiedenis III*, 26–246, Haarlem: Tjeenk Willink & Zn.

Post, Paul (2013a): "Ritual Criticism. Een actuele verkenning van kritische reflectie ten aanzien van ritueel, met bijzondere aandacht voor e-ritueel en cyberpilgrimage," *Yearbook for Liturgical and Ritual Studies*, 29: 173–99.

Post, Paul (2013b), "From Identity to Accent. The Ritual Studies Perspective of Fields of the Sacred," *Pastoraltheologische Informationen*, 33 (1): 149–58.

Post, Paul (2014), "Nederland is ritueel competent (Vliegramp Malaysia Airlines)," *Brabants Dagblad*, July 29: 32–3.

Post, Paul (2015), "Ritual Studies," in *Oxford Research Encyclopedia of Religion*, New York: Oxford University Press. Available online: http://religion.oxfordre.com/view/10.1093/acrefore/9780199340378.001.0001/acrefore-9780199340378-e-21 (accessed June 27, 2023).

Post, Paul (2019a), "Rituele herbestemming als recasting. Rituele dynamiek voorbij inculturatie en syncretisme" (valedictory lecture Tilburg University), Tilburg: Tilburg University.

Post, Paul (2019b), "Ein Panorama der Ritualdynamik. Bereiche und Trends," in Ulrike Wagner-Rau and Emilia Handke (eds.), *Provozierte Kasualpraxis. Rituale in Bewegung*, 21–43, Stuttgart: Kohlhammer.

Post, Paul (2021a), "Introduction. Some Conceptual and Historiographical Explorations on Ritual, Disaster, and Disaster Ritual," in Martin Hoondert, Paul Post, Mirella Klomp, and Marcel Barnard (eds.), *Handbook of Disaster Ritual. Multidisciplinary Perspectives, Cases, and Themes*, 1–48, Leuven: Peeters.

Post, Paul (2021b), *Rituelen: Theorie en praktijk in kort bestek*, Almere: Parthenon.

Post, Paul (2022), "Ritual Studies," in Birgit Weyel, Wilhelm Gräb, Emmanuel Lartey, and Cas Wepener (eds.), *International Handbook of Practical Theology. A Transcultural and Transreligious Approach*, 743–60, Berlin: De Gruyter.

Post, Paul, Ronald Grimes, Albertina Nugteren, P. Pettersson, and Hessel Zondag (2003), *Disaster Ritual: Explorations of an Emerging Ritual Repertoire*, Leuven: Peeters.

Post, Paul, and Martin Hoondert (eds.) (2019), *Absent Ritual. Exploring the Ambivalence and Dynamics of Ritual*, Durham, NC: Carolina Academic Press.

Post, Paul, Albertina Nugteren, and Hessel Zondag (2002), *Rituelen na rampen. Verkenning van een opkomend repertoire*, Kampen: Gooi en Sticht.

Post, Paul, Jos Pieper, and Marinus van Uden (1998), *The Modern Pilgrim: Multidisciplinary Explorations of Christian Pilgrimage*, Leuven: Peeters.

Post, Paul, and Suzanne van der Beek (2016), *Doing Ritual Criticism in a Network Society. Online and Offline Explorations into Pilgrimage and Sacred Place*, Leuven: Peeters.

Schippers, Inez (2015), *Sacred Places in the Suburb: Casual Sacrality in the Dutch VINEX-District Leidsche Rijn*, Amsterdam: Institute for Ritual and Liturgical Studies.

Stringer, Martin (2005), *A Sociological History of Christian Worship*, Cambridge: Cambridge University Press.

Van Beek, Wouter (2007), "De rite is rond. Betekenis en boodschap van het ongewone" (inaugural lecture Tilburg University), Tilburg: Tilburg University.

Wepener, Cas, Ignatius Swart, Gerrie ter Haar, and Marcel Barnard (2019), *Bonding in Worship. A Ritual Lens on Social Capital in African Independent Churches in South Africa*, Leuven: Peeters.

Internet References

Dying Matters. Available online: https://www.dyingmatters.org/page/poetry-about-dying (accessed June 26, 2023).

"Poems for Funerals," *Academy of American Poets.* Available online: https://poets.org/poems-funerals (accessed June 26, 2023).

"Poems for Funerals (2013)," *Poetry Foundation.* Available online: https://www.poetryfoundation.org/articles/69937/poems-for-funerals (accessed June 26, 2023).

Thomas, Dylan (1937), "Do Not Go Gentle Good Night," *Academy of American Poets.* Available online: https://poets.org/poem/do-not-go-gentle-good-night (accessed June 26, 2023).

Thomas, Dylan (1943), "And Death Shall have No Dominion," *Academy of American Poets.* Available online: https://poets.org/poem/and-death-shall-have-no-dominion (accessed June 26, 2023).

Thomas, Dylan (2014), "And Death Shall Have No Dominion," *YouTube.* Available online: https://www.youtube.com/watch?v=G-30VGYyLVo (accessed May 14, 2023).

8

Arabic Oration in Early Islam: Religion, Ritual, and Rhetoric

Tahera Qutbuddin

Across the mosques, homes, battlefields, and open town spaces of the Middle East in the seventh and eighth centuries AD, religion, politics, and aesthetics coalesced in the richly artistic public performance of spontaneous Arabic oration (*khuṭba*). Exquisite in rhetorical craftsmanship, these interactive speeches and sermons by the Prophet Muhammad (d. 632), Imam Ali (d. 661), and other political and military leaders were also the major vehicle of policymaking and persuasion, and the primary conduit for dissemination of ethical, religious, and legal teachings. The Friday sermon that is an intrinsic part of Muslim ritual across the globe in our present time has a long history rooted in the first Friday sermon delivered by Muhammad in Medina, and more broadly in these multifunctional orations of the early Islamic world. In this chapter, I consider Arabic-Islamic oration across different social domains in its foundational age and situate religious speech within them. Drawing on a decade of research for my book published in 2019, *Arabic Oration: Art and Function*, I discuss the major features of classical Arabic oration, with a focus on religion, ritual, and the rhetoric of orality; further details for each of the points discussed below may be found in my book. I begin with a section on rhetoric, discussing the oral milieu of early Islamic oration and its aesthetic memory-based techniques. In a second section focusing on religion, I then discuss the pious themes of the early oration, and their diffusion across political and military speechmaking, which shows how boundaries between religion and other spheres of life were fluid in the early Islamic period. In the third section, on ritual, I say a few words about ceremonial aspects of the oration that served, among other things, as a mode of authority assertion. Altogether, I present the religious face of Arabic oration in early Islam, and some of its interconnections with art and society.

"Oration" is the English term I have used to translate the Arabic word *khuṭba*, which refers in the early period to speeches, sermons, and other forms of public address at a variety of religious, political, military, and other important functions, and which follows a standard structure and certain formal conventions. In modern times, *khuṭba* refers almost entirely to the Friday sermon, but that was not the case in its original iteration. At that time, the Friday sermon was just one of many types of oration declaimed across the Middle East. The first generations of Muslims and their forebears in the Arabian Peninsula lived in a largely oral realm, and they cultivated the art of the rhythmic spoken word. On the one hand, oration in this period was a fundamental art form. Rather than focusing on painting or sculpture or music, the early Arabians focused their aesthetic talents on eloquent verbal creations. Oratory, together with the Qur'an and poetry, was foundational in the earliest Arabic literary tradition and reigned supreme for more than a century as the preeminent genre of prose. Oration's artistic formulation was also the loom on which the community's movers and shakers wove their religious and political discourse. It was the chief form of public address, with central administrative, social, and devotional functions. It was the primary means of government, the major tool for negotiating authority, and the main vehicle for doctrinal instruction. It roused warriors to battle, codified legislation on civil and criminal matters, and raised awareness of the imminence of death and the importance of leading a virtuous life. It called listeners to the new religion and formed part of its ritual worship. In addition to being a vital piece of the Arabic literary landscape, it was an essential component of political, military, and spiritual leadership.

Rhetoric

To persuade, to convince, to achieve its exhortative goals, oration needed to pack a powerful aesthetic punch, and oration texts found in the medieval sources include some of the most beautiful and powerful expressions of the Arabic literary canon. But wherein lay its beauty and power? Did orators randomly pick and choose aesthetic features, or were there characteristics that they privileged? More importantly, what drove their choices? I argue that the classical Arabic oration's stylistic choices stem from its oral culture.

From the vantage point of the twenty-first century, we access early Arabic oration through historical and literary sources, and from many genres of books from the medieval library. In other words, we engage with it as written text. Because of this, and because of our experience with how our own modern-day speeches and sermons are produced, we fall into the trap of unconsciously assuming for early Arabic oration a similar mode of being. We look at it with the anachronistic eyes of people from a fully reading and writing society. For us, the presence of written texts all around is given fact. Even when we encounter orality today, it is a secondary orality that is dependent on writing and print. We measure orality against literacy, never on its own terms. But although early Arabic orations have come to us on paper, it is important to acknowledge that they were not created as written texts. When we read orations in the medieval sources, we are in fact reading texts that were produced, and initially transmitted, orally. We must keep in mind the oral milieu of Arabic oration. Unless we recognize its orality, we cannot fully appreciate its character.

It is also important to keep in mind the limitations of this orality, because the pre-Islamic and early Islamic milieu was no stranger to writing. However, although Arabic oration lay between orality and writing, it was closer to the oral end of the spectrum. Let us imagine a sliding scale between pristine orality, in which there is absolutely no writing, and a fully literate society, in which writing is an integral part of the culture—for example, certain tribes living in isolation in the Congo and Amazon rainforests today versus the contemporary United States and Europe. Although writing was known in Middle Eastern lands in the period of our study, it was a skill limited to a tiny proportion of the populace. They laboriously employed crude instruments of writing such as rock, bone, and skin, and later, parchment and papyrus, and they reserved their writing for momentous occasions. Pre-Islamic and early Islamic society was predominantly oral.

A major aspect of the artistic verbal production of an oral milieu is mnemonic design, meaning that its aesthetic format helps the brain to remember it. In his pioneering study, *Orality and Literacy*, Walter Ong (1982) demonstrated that artistic expression in an oral culture is essentially mnemonic. He explains these mnemonics thus (Ong 1982: 34–5):

> In a primary oral culture, to solve the problem of retaining and retrieving carefully articulated thought, you have to do your thinking in mnemonic patterns, shaped for ready, oral recurrence. Your thought must come into being in heavily rhythmic, balanced patterns, in repetitions or antitheses, in alliterations and assonances, [and so on] … Serious thought is intertwined with memory systems.

Ong goes on to say that an orality-rooted speaker will ground his ideas in the material world around him. He will represent his ideas graphically and visually, rather than in abstract forms. He will speak about a ball, for example, rather than a sphere, or about a plate, rather than a circle. He will repeat his core message, sometimes using the same language, sometimes using different words.

These ideas map on to early Arabic oration, in which two essential mnemonic features are vivid imagery and pulsating rhythm.

Here are some examples of imagery. Much of it relates to desert flora, fauna, and natural phenomena, and much of it is based on animals:

- Ali ibn Abi Talib was the cousin, ward, and son-in-law of the Prophet Muhammad, the Prophet's successor according to the Shia, and the fourth Rightly Guided caliph according to the Sunnis. He was a master orator renowned as the sage of Islam. In various sermons, he compared the world to "the sneeze or fart of a goat," to "a leaf being chomped in the mouth of a locust," and to the "bones of a pig in the hand of a leper" (Qutbuddin 2019: 122–3; Qutbuddin and Raḍī forthcoming: 1.3.4, 1.183.4, 3.221). Instead of stating that the world has little worth, Ali illustrated its low worth through graphic images that conveyed this abstract idea in concrete physical terms.
- Abu Sufyan (d. 653), in pre-Islamic times, compared two brothers from the Amir tribe, as being of equal stature: "You are like two knees of a fleshy camel" (Qutbuddin 2019: 121; Safwat 1933: 1:43).
- The Umayyad governor of Iraq, Hajjaj (d. 714), spoke of his subjects' rising stages of wickedness, saying: "Truly, Satan penetrated you, permeating flesh, blood, and nerves, ears and fingers, limbs and hearts. Then he rose into brain-marrow and inner ear. Then he climbed further and made a nest. Then he laid eggs and hatched chicks" (Qutbuddin 2019: 117; Safwat 1933: 2:293). Hajjaj's extended metaphor here may be described as a form of dramatization, as can the next example.
- The rationalist theologian Wasil ibn Ata (d. 748) began an *ubi sunt* sermon by asking, "Where are the kings who built Ctesiphon?" and answered, "Death grabbed them along with their howdahs, it crushed them with its breast, it chomped on them with its canines!" (Qutbuddin 2019: 112; Safwat 1933: 2:502).

These graphic images familiar to the audience helped the orator bring abstractions into the realm of the immediate audiovisual, and fix the texts in the audience's memory.

Another key feature of the oration's style was rhythm. Modern neuroscientists explain memory formation through the brain's propensity to organize information in patterns; they call the process neuronal entrainment. Children learn the ABC, for example, through a melody. Imagine how much more difficult it would be to memorize a random list of letters. Rhythm is present in many forms even in a society that communicates regularly through writing, but in the artistic expressions of an oral society, it is a primary characteristic. Among the features that create rhythm, classical Arabic oration is especially shaped by the consistent, almost relentless use of parallelism, where two sentences possess identical grammar; their structural units are "parallel" to each other, and thus rhythmic. Here is an example:

- The Umayyad governor Ziyad (d. 673) warned the rebellious people of Basra about severe punishments for criminal activity. He said: "Whoever drowns people, I shall drown him. Whoever burns people, I shall burn him. Whoever breaches a house, I shall breach his heart. Whoever digs up and robs a grave, I shall bury him in it alive" (Qutbuddin 2019: 347; Safwat 1933: 2:272–3).
- The pre-Islamic Christian bishop of Najran, Quss ibn Sa'ida (d. *c.* 600), is said to have orated from the back of his red camel at the Ukaz Market outside Mecca, "Whoever lives dies. Whoever dies is lost. Everything that could happen will happen" (Qutbuddin 2019: 238; Safwat 1933: 1:38).

Religion

All types of orations in our period, including battle and political speeches, contain religious themes. Among the various types, the three that are most focused on religious speech are the Friday sermon, the similar Eid sermon, and the ad hoc sermon of pious counsel. Additionally, the marriage oration, the legislative oration, the theologically oriented oration, and the oration that supplicated for rain, also have well-defined religious functions.

Pious Themes

The sermon of pious counsel contains three core themes. The first is piety, more specifically, consciousness of God, and obedience to him; the second is the imminence of death; and the third is a comparison of this world and the hereafter. A handful of pieces are attributed to the pre-Islamic period, while hundreds are recorded for the first two centuries of Islam.

Pre-Islamic pieces focus on the transience of human life. We have seen an example in my presentation of rhythm earlier, namely the sermon by the Christian Bishop Quss, which warns of the imminent end of life. Here is the full sermon (Qutbuddin 2019: 238–9; Safwat 1933: 1:38–9):

> People! Gather around, listen and retain!
>
> Whoever lives dies. Whoever dies is lost. Everything that could happen will happen.
>
> Truly, there are messages in the earth. There are lessons in the sky. Firm signs. Rain and plants. Fathers and mothers. One who goes and one who comes. Light and darkness. Piety and sin. A garment and a mount. Food and drink. Stars that rise and set. Seas that do not dry out. A firmament elevated. An earth laid out. A dark night. A sky with zodiacal signs.
>
> Where do people go, and why do they never return? Have they been given satisfaction and chosen to reside? Or have they been confined and compelled to sleep?

The opening rhythmic lines after the address drive home the inevitability of death. "Whoever lives dies." The body paragraph directs the audience to observe the natural world and take lessons from it. "Truly, there are messages in the earth. There are lessons in the sky." And so on. The final lines pose rhetorical questions that leave the audience to ponder for themselves: "Where do people go, and why do they never return?"

The Islamic sermons of pious counsel, while continuing the theme of mortality, build on it to exhort the audience to perform good deeds and prepare for the eternal life to come. An example is a sermon by Imam Ali in which he urges preparation for the hereafter, translated rather literally here to highlight its parallel structure (Qutbuddin 2019: 153; 2023: 1.28):

> Truly! The world has indeed turned back and proclaimed its departure.
> And truly! The hereafter has come forward and announced its arrival.
> Hark, truly! Today is the day of training, and tomorrow is the race:
> The goal is paradise, and the end is hellfire!
> Is there no one who would repent from his sin before his death?
> Is there no one who would perform good deeds for his soul before his day of hardship?
> Hark! These are your days of hope, right behind them is death.

> Whoever performs deeds during his days of hope, before the arrival of his death—his deeds will benefit him, and his death will not harm him.
> Whoever falls short during his days of hope, before the arrival of his death—his deeds he will lose, and his death will harm him.
> Hark! Perform good deeds from fondness as you perform them from fear.
> Hark, truly! I have not seen the like of paradise, one who desires it sleeping, nor the like of hellfire, one who flees it sleeping.
> Hark, truly! Whomsoever right does not benefit, wrong will harm.
> Whomever guidance does not put on the straight [path], error will drag to destruction.
> Hark! You are commanded to depart and directed toward provisions.
> And truly! The most fearful thing I fear for you is following of desires and length of yearning.
> Take provisions in the world, from the world, with which you can nourish your souls tomorrow.

The first two pairs of parallel lines compare this world with the hereafter. The parallelism persists through the sermon, all but the final line being parallel in structure. I have analyzed the rhetorical features of this sermon in some detail in an article titled "A Sermon on Piety by Imam Ali: How the Rhythm of the Classical Arabic Oration Tacitly Persuaded" (2018a), using Richard Lanham's (1983) term, "tacit persuasion." There, I argued that the oration's artistry played a vital role in achieving the orator's goal of persuasion, and that together with rational argumentation, the orator achieved much of his stirring of hearts and prodding of minds through literary techniques. The parallelism underscores the stark dichotomy between two opposing entities. It sets up this world against the hereafter, and it highlights the choice of good versus evil, hope versus fear, and paradise versus hellfire. In the final line, the sermon breaks from the parallelism and crescendos in a longer, non-parallel finale, encapsulating the gist of the sermon's overall message, "Take provisions in the world, from the world, with which you can nourish your souls tomorrow."

Connected with reminders of death and the imminence of the hereafter, the most important theme, an umbrella theme in Islamic sermons of pious counsel, is consciousness of God. The Arabic word is *taqwā*. Expressing a fundamental concept in Islam, *taqwā* is among the most frequent lexemes in the Qur'an and in Muhammad's traditions. The term is ubiquitous in Muslim sermons, whose lines are permeated by the formula "I counsel you to piety" and which frequently quote the Qur'anic verse 2:197 "Gather your provisions! The best of provisions is piety." *Taqwā* is often translated imprecisely as "fear of God."

Muslims understand it to mean something more than simple fear. As with many signifiers that are culture-specific, no English word or phrase exactly conveys its full range of implications, but its scope comes close to the English (Christian) usage of "godfearing," or the Biblical Mosaic command in Lev. 19:2 to "be holy" (Hebrew: *kedoshim*), "You shall be holy, for I, the Lord your God, am holy." In Islam, *taqwā* means to desist from evil deeds, to fear God's retribution for any wrongs you may do, to be aware that God sees and knows everything, and indeed, most importantly and paradoxically, to be in awe of him while always taking comfort from his presence. This attitude entails believing in God, being ever conscious of him, and thus always thinking and acting righteously.

Among leaders in early Islam, some are singled out as prolific and effective orators of pious counsel. Muhammad is for Muslims the foremost guide, and, in addition to the Qur'an, which he is believed to have brought from God, his own words—called "hadith"—are revered as the product of divine inspiration. All his sermons are framed by the injunction to *taqwā*, and one of his Friday sermons will be presented shortly.

In addition to Muhammad's sermons, the sermons of Ali are held up as the gold standard for brilliant eloquence and sage advice. We have seen one already. Here is another famous sermon by Ali on piety (Qutbuddin and Raḍī forthcoming: 1.191):

> The pious in this world are people of virtue. Their speech is rational, their garments simple, and their walk the embodiment of humility. They lower their eyes avoiding things God has forbidden them to see, and dedicate their ears to hearing words of wisdom that bring them benefit. Their hearts are at peace in times of tribulation and in times of prosperity. If not for the lifespans decreed for them by God, their souls would not tarry in their bodies the blink of an eye, but would instantly depart, yearning for God's reward and fearing his punishment. The creator's majesty in their hearts makes all else small in their eyes. Paradise is before their eyes—they see it as clearly as though they themselves were enjoying its blessings. Hellfire too is before their gaze—they see it as clearly as though they themselves were being tortured in it. Their hearts are sorrowful, their malice never feared, their bodies emaciated, their needs few, and their persons chaste. They patiently endure these few days here, awaiting the long comfort of the hereafter. Theirs is a profitable trade bestowed in ease and security by their lord. The world approached them but they turned away. It shackled them but they ransomed their souls and set them free.
>
> In the night they stand in worship reciting sections of the Qur'an, chanting it in sweet melody, moving their own hearts to tears and finding in it the cure for their illness. If they come across a verse that rouses yearning, they latch on

to it hungrily and their hearts stretch out toward it in longing. They see—its promised blessings are visible right in front of their eyes. If they come across a verse that stokes fear, they incline their hearts toward its warning—the hiss and crackle of the inferno fills the innermost recesses of their ears. They bow their backs, laying their forehead, palms, knees, and toes on the earth, beseeching God to free their necks from the fire.

In the day they are kind, wise, good, and pious. Fear has emaciated them like arrow shafts. The observer thinks them ailing, but they are not ill. He says, "They are crazy!," but they are crazed only by something immensely grave. They are not satisfied with a few good deeds, and they do not think their numerous endeavors too many. They constantly chide themselves and fear the consequence of their actions. If one of them is praised he is apprehensive, and replies: I know myself better than you know me, and my lord knows me even better. Lord, do not hold me to what they say about me, make me more virtuous than they think I am, and forgive those of my actions they do not know.

Their hallmark is strength in faith, resolve with gentleness, belief with conviction, voracity for knowledge, knowledge with maturity, temperance in affluence, humility in worship, forbearance in indigence, patience in hardship, seeking the licit, enthusiasm in following guidance, and aversion to greed. They perform good deeds while always being on guard. They spend the night thanking God and the morning praising him. They sleep vigilant and awake in joy, vigilant because they have been warned against neglect and joyful because they have gained blessings and mercy. If their ego bucks against doing something it dislikes, they do not allow it full rein in letting it do what it desires. Their joy is centered on things which bring lasting reward, while they care little for commodities which will not remain. They combine maturity with learning and words with action.

You will see this—their needs are few, their slips are rare, their hearts are humble, their souls are content, their fare is meager, their manner is easygoing, their faith is protected, their appetite is dead, and their rage is held in check. Their goodness is always anticipated, and their evil never dreaded. If they sit with the heedless they are still numbered among the heedful, and if they sit with the heedful they are not numbered among the heedless. They forgive those who oppress them, give to those who refuse them, and foster those who cut them off. Lewdness is far removed from them, gentleness imbues their words, and wrongdoing is absent from their actions. Their decency is ever present, their goodness always forthcoming, and their evil always distant and removed.

In calamities they remain calm and dignified, in catastrophes they remain patient, and in happy times they remain thankful. They never wrong an enemy or transgress to help loved ones. They acknowledge the dues they owe to another

> before testimony is given against them. They never squander something they have been given in trust. They never forget a thing of which they have been reminded. They never call others vile names. They never harm a neighbor. They never gloat at another's misfortune. They never enter into wrongdoing and never leave the truth.
>
> If they are silent their silence is not burdensome. If they laugh they are not raucous. If attacked in treachery they are patient—God himself avenges them. They weary themselves by constant chiding while never causing others unease. They push themselves to prepare for the hereafter and never cause others harm. Chaste and upright, they stay away from those who distance themselves. Kind and merciful, they draw near to those who seek to come close. Their detachment is not from arrogance or grandiosity, and their drawing near is not from cunning or trickery.

In this long sermon, Ali describes the pious, the people of *taqwā*, and lays out in minute detail the virtuous characteristics, the hereafter-focused aspirations, and the entirely godly way of life of those who truly deserve the epithet. He presents virtue and piety as two indivisible sides of the same coin. Just as virtue is incomplete without piety, piety is incomplete without virtue. The sermon begins with a general statement: "The pious in this world are people of virtue." It goes on to give a list of ethical and religious traits: They "speak sensibly," "dress simply," and "walk humbly." They are "deeply conscious of God's greatness and bounties," and "do not care for the world." It is as though they "see paradise and hell in front of their eyes." Their "bodies are emaciated, their needs few, their souls chaste." They pray all night, standing before God, and reciting the Qur'an. They possess amazing virtues, including "strength in religion, maturity with gentleness, belief with conviction, passion for knowledge, and moderation in wealth." They are kind to their fellow humans, for they "forgive those who oppress them, give to those who refuse them, and show compassion to those who shun them." They are "dignified in times of calamity, patient in times of misfortune, and grateful to God in times of ease." In sum, according to Ali, *taqwā* governs the totality of a believer's life, grounding her relationship with God, and encompassing her relationship with all of God's creation.

In an earlier article, "Piety and Virtue in Early Islam: Two Sermons by Imam Ali" (2018b), I cataloged a hundred virtues of the pious noted in this sermon. In it, I separated them into the two categories of religious and humanitarian virtues, to highlight the strong presence of both in Ali's description of piety. Indeed, for Ali, they are all religious and they are all humanitarian. There is no substantive difference between the two. Virtues in Ali's sermon that we now deem religious speak of God, of spiritual practices, and the hereafter, twenty-three in all. Virtues in Ali's sermon that are now usually deemed humanitarian relate particularly to humans' behavior toward each other, fifty-seven in all. Taking the middle ground between secular humanism and insular faith, Ali propagates a holistic model, combining individual devotion with dynamic social engagement. All this comes together in the notion of *taqwā*.

In line with Ali's advocacy of balance in all things, here is another dimension of his philosophy of *taqwā*, that of living with joy in this world, yet preparing all the while for the hereafter. He says (Qutbuddin and Raḍī forthcoming: 2.27.2):

> The pious (the people of *taqwā*) partake of the joys of this world and those of the next. They share the world with the worldly, but the worldly do not share the hereafter with them. In this world, they reside in the most splendid of residences and consume the finest of delicacies. They possess the sumptuous comforts of the wealthy and partake of the lavish luxuries of the mighty. Yet, when they depart, they leave with full provisions and a large profit.

I have analyzed both these last sermons in some detail in various articles (2016, 2018b). Here, I cite them to show the broad scope of *taqwā*.

The theme of *taqwā*, as you would expect, is an essential component of the Muslim Friday sermon, the weekly communal prayer service of Islam. The following is said to be the Prophet Muhammad's first Friday sermon, delivered in a hamlet on the outskirts of Medina, when he emigrated there from Mecca (Qutbuddin 2019: 287–9; Safwat 1933: 1:148–9):

> [A] God be praised! I praise him, and beseech his aid, forgiveness, and guidance. I believe in him, I do not disbelieve in him, and I abhor those who disbelieve in him. I bear witness that there is no god but God, one without peer; and that Muhammad is his servant and messenger, whom he sent with guidance, radiance, and counsel, after a period had gone by without messengers, when knowledge had become scarce and people had gone astray, when the age had neared its conclusion, the hour had drawn close, and the end had approached. Whoever obeys God and his messenger has been guided. Whoever disobeys them has sinned and gone far astray.
>
> [B] I counsel you to be conscious of God—that is the best counsel a Muslim can give a Muslim: urging him to seek the hereafter and commanding him to be conscious of God. Beware God's retribution, of which God himself has warned you. There is no better advice, nor better recommendation. Consciousness of God—if you act upon it, heeding and fearing your lord—is the best aid for obtaining what you desire of the hereafter.

[C] If someone is righteous in doing the things God has commanded him to do, the things that are between himself and God, in public and in private, intending by them only God's pleasure—they will become a memorial for him in this world, and a treasure for him after death, at the time when a man is truly in need of the deeds he has set by. As for the things which he has done otherwise, he will wish that a great distance divided him from them. God warns you of himself, yet he is kind to his servants. I swear by the one who speaks truth and fulfills his pledge, that there is no dispute in this—he, the high and mighty, has said: "My word never changes, and I never oppress my servants."

[D] Remain conscious of God, now and later, in private and in public. If someone is conscious of God, God erases his bad deeds and magnifies his reward. If someone is conscious of God, he has attained a great victory. Consciousness of God protects you from his aversion. It protects you from his punishment. It protects you from his wrath. Consciousness of God makes faces gleam, pleases the lord, and raises rank.

[E] Seize your share, but do not be remiss in tendering God's due. He has taught you his book and laid out for you his path, in order to differentiate between those who speak truth and those who are liars. Do good, for God has been good to you. Bear enmity to his enemies and strive truly for him. He has singled you out and named you Muslims. "Anyone who perishes does so having seen clear proof, and anyone who lives does so having seen clear proof."

[F] There is no power save God's. Always remember God and act for what will come after today. Indeed, if someone is righteous in doing the things that are between himself and God, God suffices him the things that are between him and others. This is so because God ordains things for people, they do not ordain things for him. He rules over them, they do not rule over him. God is greatest. There is no power save God's.

Notice that immediately after the opening benediction, in the section marked [B], Muhammad says, "I counsel you to be conscious of God—that is the best counsel a Muslim can give a Muslim: urging him to seek the hereafter, and commanding him to be conscious of God." Seen in this sermon and elsewhere, the invitation to piety, *taqwā*, frames the entire oration. Muhammad's first Friday sermon is a blueprint for the main doctrines of Islam, and it also forms the exemplar for one of the Muslim community's defining rites of worship. It sets the standard for the ritual Friday sermon of Islam in terms of its exhortative tone, its standard structure, and its pious content and religiopolitical themes. In all these areas, perhaps most significantly in its pious themes—including directions to be conscious of God and remember him, to obey God and his Prophet, to perform good deeds and prepare for the hereafter—we see echoes in the vast majority of Friday sermons to come.

Friday sermons most often had a political and military side to them. In the texts from our period, we see religious advice assimilating with the evolving political aims of the nascent Islamic state. Political themes of the Friday sermon include administrative and fiscal policies and their justifications, executive commands, statements asserting the legitimacy of various power groups, and instructions to the subject populace, primarily regarding obedience to the leadership. In a classic combination of administrative and spiritual themes, the second Sunni caliph Umar ibn al-Khattab (d. 644) said in a Friday sermon, "By God, I do not send governors to flay your skin or to seize your wealth. I send them to you so they may teach you your religion" (Qutbuddin 2019: 282–3; Safwat 1933: 1:219). Note also the political implications in the Prophet's Friday sermon, at the end of section [A], for example, which enjoins obedience to God and His Messenger.

Military themes are also observable in Friday and Eid sermons, in the form of exhortations to fight in the path of God and to defend the community. A famous oration full of military themes that Ali delivered when his enemies raided a town in Iraq is flagged by one source as a Friday sermon (Qutbuddin and Raḍī forthcoming: 1.29). Note also the military implications of the Prophet's Friday sermon in the middle of section [E], where Muslims are directed to take God's and Muhammad's enemies as their own enemies.

Diffusion of Religious Themes across Oration Types

As we have seen, Friday sermons combine pious themes with secular themes. Conversely, as I mentioned earlier, a religious component can be observed in all major types of oration in early Islam, including the battle oration and the political speech. Friday sermons are an obvious repository of devotional material, but battle speeches and political orations are also frequently framed in terms of piety. Injunctions to piety, invocation of prayers, and testamentary Qur'an citations shored up the orator's authority (Qutbuddin 2017), and they helped him persuade the audience to accept and deploy his policies. A preponderance of leaders, including the Prophet, caliphs, governors, and commanders, delivered orations in various political, military, and liturgical contexts, and these real-world contexts coexisted and intermingled. Ali is said to have seldom ascended the pulpit, for any purpose, without saying at the beginning of his oration these words of counsel, "People, always remain conscious of God. Humans are not created in vain—do not waste your lives in frolic" (Qutbuddin and Raḍī forthcoming: 3.351). Further examples include the first Sunni caliph Abu Bakr's (d. 634) speeches in Medina early in his caliphate, which disparaged material wealth and pomp (Safwat 1933: 1:173–5). His successor Umar intoned in one of his first caliphal speeches a series of prayers for himself to be a good caliph and a good Muslim (Safwat 1933: 1:213–4). The accession speech of Umar's successor Uthman included censure of the world, along with a large number of Qur'an quotations (Qutbuddin 2019: 339; Safwat 1933: 1:271).

Qur'an citation was an important mode of pious counsel in political speech. It provided religious sanction to political claim and secured public support. In *The Use of the Qur'an in Political Argument* (1988), Ibrahim Jomaih writes that Muslims used Qur'anic allusion to imply comparisons between themselves and their opponents.

Quran citation was also frequent in the Battle Oration, where orators used verses from the Holy Book to endorse their point of view. Two Qur'anic verses that were commonly cited in military contexts advocate endurance:

- "God is with those who endure" (Qur'an 2:153).
- "With God's permission, many a small contingent may overpower a larger one; God is with those who endure" (Qur'an 2:249). This verse adds the element of hope in the face of challenging odds.

Two other verses that were also cited in battle orations often refer to the inevitability of death, and the ultimate victory of the pious:

- "We belong to God, and to him we shall return" (Qur'an 2:156).
- "The earth belongs to God. He bequeaths it to whomsoever he chooses among his servants. The good outcome is reserved for the pious" (Qur'an 7:128).

The theme of death's imminence is especially suited to warfare, and as we might expect, it is often connected with martyrdom. The Umayyad commander Attab ibn Warqa' (d. 696) is reported to have urged his army to be conscious of God and patiently endure, and then to have spoken of the rewards enjoyed by martyrs, in the following battlefield homily (Qutbuddin 2019: 321; Safwat 1933: 2:464):

> Martyrs have the fullest share of paradise. God is pleased to reward none other in the manner in which he is pleased to reward those who endure. Do you not see that he says "Endure, for God is with those who endure" (Qur'an 8:46)? If God is pleased with your action, what a high station you will have! God hates

> no one as much as he hates the treacherous. Do you not see that your enemy is putting Muslims to the sword, believing all the while that it will garner them closeness to God? They are the most evil of all the people of the earth.

Ritual and Authority

Early Arabic oration was delivered from a position of power. Its practitioners were leaders—caliphs, commanders, governors, or people with religious weight. Through speeches and sermons, these leaders articulated policy, solicited support for military and religiopolitical initiatives, and recruited people to a particular set of ethics and values. Hannah Arendt (1968) has argued for the importance of language as an integral medium in constructing political identity, and this was certainly true for the orator-leaders of the early Islamic world, where language, and particularly the language of oratory, was vital in the construction of religiopolitical identity. In addition to a Muslim leader's other qualifications, such as nobility of lineage, wisdom, courage, early conversion to Islam, and service in its cause, effective leadership entailed nuanced interpersonal communication; the communal aspect of high-level power brokerage was enacted largely through public oration. Orations were the vehicle of state policy and religious legislation, for important decisions were conveyed to the public almost solely through this medium. They were also the platform of religiopolitical decision-making, for policy was communally negotiated through them. In many ways, Arabic oration shaped the religious and political landscape of the pre-Islamic and early Islamic period, and was a prime locus of authority.

So, what were the ways in which the ritual of the oration reinforced the authority of the orator? The preaching of the Friday sermon was itself a symbol of authority, and attending it was tantamount to accepting that authority. In an exception that demonstrates the rule, the people of Iraq wrote to the Prophet's grandson Husayn (d. 680) in Medina and urged him to take up arms against the Umayyads, and the way these people indicated their disavowal of Umayyad authority was by saying to Husayn, "We have dedicated ourselves to you, and we do not attend the Friday service anymore with the Umayyad governor" (Qutbuddin 2019: 285; Safwat 1933: 2:35). Moreover, the Friday sermon, and many kinds of religiopolitical orations, were delivered from a pulpit. The battle orator often spoke from the back of a horse. The orator's higher positioning, in addition to its practical benefits of enabling better seeing and hearing, was also emblematic of his authority over the audience. Additionally, the preacher carried a ceremonial staff, or sword, or bow in his right hand as an emblem of authority. This was rooted in pre-Islamic practice, and for Muslims it connects also with the staff wielded by the Prophet Moses to perform miracles (Qur'an 7:107); Muhammad perpetuated this practice, and it became part of his exemplary *Sunnah*. Yet further, the language register of the early oration was usually classical Arabic, which conveyed an official and authoritative ambiance. Also, the use of religious formulae to open and end lent the oration an air of holiness. Since early times, many preachers opened with a verbatim recitation of the Prophet Muhammad's standard praise invocation. Furthermore, citation of Qur'an verses infused the oration with the grace and authority of God's revelation. And finally, the standard structure of the oration—blessings, the phrase "now to the point" (*ammā baʿd*), the vocative address (e.g., "O Muslims"), main body, and ending formulae of prayer—also gave the oration an air of sacred convention.

These physical accoutrements and ritual practices in early Muslim oration all exuded formality and authority. Going forward, the Friday sermon's physical context symbolically invoked the authority of the Prophet's mantle and the divine word. The present volume contains Abdulkader Tayob's chapter (Ch. 3) on performance aspects of present-day Friday sermons in Cape Town, Linda Jones's chapter (Ch. 9) on ritual dimensions of rain-supplication orations in tenth-century Cordoba, and Julian Millie's chapter (Ch. 6) on embodied ritual in today's Islamic preaching. These rituals, and the rituals of all Muslim sermons across the ages, are rooted in the Arabic oration of early Islam. As we have seen, the interaction between religious and secular spheres of oration shows that boundaries between religion and other spheres of life were fluid in the early period of Islam. Early Arabic oration was located at a rich nexus of religion, ritual, and rhetoric.

References

Arendt, Hannah (1968), *Between Past and Future: Eight Exercises in Political Thought*, New York: Penguin.

Al-Jomaih, Ibrahim (1988), "The Use of the Qurʾan in Political Argument: A Study of Early Islamic Parties (35-86 A.H./656-705 A.D.)," PhD dissertation, University of California, Los Angeles.

Lanham, Richard (1983), *Analyzing Prose*, New York: Charles Scribner.

Ong, Walter (1982), *Orality and Literacy: The Technologizing of the Word*, London: Routledge.

Qutbuddin, Tahera (2016), "ʿAlī's Contemplations on This World and the Hereafter in the Context of His Life and Times," in Alizera Korangy, Wheeler Thackston, Roy Mottahedeh, and William Granara (eds.), *Essays in Islamic Philology, History, and Philosophy*, 333–53. Berlin: De Gruyter.

Qutbuddin, Tahera (2017), "Qurʾan Citation in Early Arabic Oration (khuṭba): Mnemonic, Liturgical and Testimonial Functions," in Nuha Alshaar (ed.), *The Qurʾan and Adab: The Shaping of Literary Traditions in Classical Islam*, 315–40, Oxford: Oxford University Press.

Qutbuddin, Tahera (2018a), "A Sermon on Piety by Imam ʿAlī ibn Abī Ṭālib: How the Rhythm of the Classical Arabic Oration Tacitly Persuaded," in Sabine Dorpmüller, Jan Scholz, Max Stille, and Ines Weinrich (eds.), *Religion and Aesthetic Experience: Drama–Sermons–Literature*, 109–23, Heidelberg: Heidelberg University Publications.

Qutbuddin, Tahera (2018b), "Piety and Virtue in Early Islam: Two Sermons by Imam Ali," in Jennifer Frey and Candace Vogler (eds.), *Self-Transcendence and Virtue: Perspectives from Philosophy, Psychology, and Theology*, 125–53, London: Routledge.

Qutbuddin, Tahera (2019), *Arabic Oration: Art and Function*, Leiden: Brill Academic Publishers.

Qutbuddin, Tahera, and Sharīf Raḍī (forthcoming), *Nahj al-balāghah, The Wisdom and Eloquence of ʿAlī*, Leiden: Brill Academic Publishers.

Safwat, Ahmad Zaki (1933), *Jamharat khuṭab al-ʿArab fī l-ʿuṣūr al-ʿArabiyyah al-zāhirah*, 3 vols., Cairo: al-Maktabah al-ʿIlmiyyah.

9

The Rain Rogation *Khuṭba*: A Case Study of the Reciprocal Relationship between Islamic Ritual and Religious Speech

Linda Gale Jones

Introduction

The Umayyads were the dynasty that ruled Muslim Iberia (al-Andalus) from its foundation in the eighth century until the civil war that overthrew the regime in 1031, splintering the country into numerous petty kingdoms. Al-Andalus reached its political and cultural zenith as the "ornament of the world" during the reign of al-Nāṣir ʿAbd al-Raḥmān III (r. 912–61), who made history by declaring al-Andalus to be an independent caliphate in 929, thereby severing its allegiance to the Abbasids, the temporal rulers of the Sunni Islamic world (Kennedy 1996; Safran 2000). Medieval Muslim chroniclers wrote with admiration about the accomplishments of the Umayyads and the kingdom of al-Andalus, located in the far western region of the Islamic world. At a time when the Mediterranean empires shared a common "scenography of power" (Cardoso 2017), the diplomatic relations the Umayyads maintained with Byzantium and the Holy Roman Empire, as well as the Iberian Christian kingdoms, assured that the country's fame spread throughout Christendom as well.

One of the many memorable anecdotes about the Umayyad rulers of al-Andalus relates that when a severe drought afflicted the people of Cordoba during the reign of the first caliph, al-Nāṣir ʿAbd al-Raḥmān III, the caliph summoned his chief liturgical preacher and the Supreme Judge of al-Andalus, Mundhir b. Saʿīd al-Ballūṭī (d. 966), to lead the people in the rain rogation ritual (*salāt al-istisqā'*), which includes a communal prayer and a sermon. Accounts of this ritual survive in four Arabic premodern texts of diverse literary genres dating from the fourteenth to the seventeenth centuries. Hence all the available sources were compiled centuries after the preaching event and none includes a complete transcription of Mundhir b. Saʿīd's sermon. The accounts largely coincide in depicting the drought as a divine punishment for the caliph's hubris in constructing his new palatial capital city, Madīnat al-Zahrāʾ, while neglecting his religious duties. They also agree in portraying the preacher leading the rituals of humiliation and his evocative sermons as the catalyst for the caliph's repentance and the subsequent end of the drought.

The rain rogation ritual belongs to the subcategory of rites or rituals of affliction, which seek to "rectify a state of affairs that has been disturbed or disordered; they heal, exorcise, protect, and purify" (Bell 1997: 115). Codified in Islamic law, the rogation ritual was prescribed for occasions of severe drought and featured various ritualized acts of repentance and humiliation before God in order to elicit divine mercy in the form of rainfall. This ritual offers a particularly apt case study for exploring the interplay between ritual and religious speech because it highlights the interdependency and synergy between religious utterances (prayers and sermons) and ritual embodiment and affect. Moreover, literary accounts of the outcome of these practices, whether in the form of rainfall or continued drought, allow us to gauge the efficacy of the ritual.

This chapter will analyze the reciprocal relationship between religious speech and ritual through a comparison of four literary accounts of the rain rogation ritual led by the Cordovan judge and preacher Mundhir b. Saʿīd al-Ballūṭī (El Hour 2006: 177–82). The rain rogation ritual will be treated as a ritual complex or ritual drama in which each of the ritual agents (the preacher, the caliph, and the community) has a distinct role to play. The four versions depict the ritual agents carrying out a confluence of discreet symbolic acts and gestures and religious speech performances that must be examined individually to understand how each is positioned in relation to the other and to account for the ritual's efficacy or failure. In keeping with this volume's theme, I am especially interested in elucidating the role that the rogation sermon (*khuṭba*) plays in the larger ritual complex. Specifically, I will demonstrate that the rogation *khuṭba* plays a generative role in the processes of embodied and affective ritual humiliation that are intended to provoke the repentance and ritual humiliation of the ruler and to produce an emotional community of purified penitential Muslims.

Methodological Challenges and Research Questions

Studying the relation between ritual and religious speech using premodern sources presents several methodological challenges. The first of these is what could be called the danger of interpreting rituals described in medieval texts. Clearly, the proposed analysis of the rain rogation ritual led by a tenth-century Andalusi preacher based on sources composed in the thirteenth and fourteenth centuries cannot claim to be an anthropological interpretation of the ritual ceremony. Rather, in line with Philippe Buc, it will be an analysis of the "medieval practices that the historian has reconstructed using texts, with full and constant sensitivity to their status as texts" (Buc 2001: 259; Watts 2007: 1).

Many of the concerns Buc raised about "data-poor" medieval sources are mitigated by the fact that the rain rogation ritual is a prescribed act that is codified in the Prophet's *Sunna* (custom, example) and Islamic legal texts. Since Malikism was the official *madhhab* (legal school) in Umayyad al-Andalus, I have consulted descriptions of this ritual in Maliki legal compendia, such as *al-Muwaṭṭa'* (The Well-trodden Path), by Mālik ibn Anas (d. 795) the founder of the Maliki school of law, and in other canonical hadith collections that circulated widely in al-Andalus. These texts preserve some of the earliest descriptions of how the Prophet Muhammad performed this ritual, and reports of and about Muhammad's speech. Moreover, the ritual stability of the rogation ceremony is confirmed by the extensive accounts of how the Moriscos conducted the *ṣalāt al-istisqā'* in sixteenth-century Spain, which were translated by the Spanish Arabist Pedro Longás (1915: 123–65).

All of this data can be usefully contrasted with the information contained in the four literary descriptions of the *ṣalāt al-istisqā'* ritual led by Mundhir b. Sa'īd al-Ballūṭī. Despite the obvious methodological limitations of relying upon non-contemporaneous medieval literary accounts of the rogation sermon and ritual, there is sufficient data to address several key questions that are relevant to the present volume, beginning with whether or how the rogation sermon and the ritual reaffirm one another. If so, what role does the religious speech play within the larger rain rogation ritual context? What is the ritual significance of the sermon vis-à-vis the other parts of the rogation ritual? How is the sermon ritualized? Finally, do the authors refer to any specific verbal, linguistic, gestural, affective, or corporeal markers that signal the ritualization or ritual significance of the sermon?

I argue that the rogation sermon and the larger *ṣalāt al-istisqā'* ritual do indeed mutually reaffirm one another. This reciprocal relationship is actualized through specific ritualizing strategies affecting the bodies, emotions, and affective disposition of the preacher, the caliph, and the audience. I will demonstrate how the intense ritualization of the bodies of the ritual participants operates in tandem with the *khuṭba* to provoke and produce the emotions and affective dispositions of abject humility, humiliation, and contrition that are deemed necessary for the ritual's successful outcome. To develop this argument, I draw upon the insights of various ritual theorists specializing in rites of affliction and rites of passage, ritual and social dynamics, rituals and the emotions, and ritual speech (Bell 1997, 2009; Durkheim 1995; Katz 1995; Tavárez 2014; Turner 1969). None of the premodern authors (al-Dhahabī, al-Ḥimyārī, or al-Maqqarī) provide anything resembling a detailed anthropological "thick description" of the rain rogation ritual. Nevertheless, as literary sources they are useful because the authors attribute the severe drought explicitly or implicitly to the caliph's hubris and religious negligence and because their narrative editorializing of the results of the rogation ritual provides us with an indirect means of assessing the impact of Mundhir's preaching. Their narratives illustrate how the rogation ceremony's rites of affliction and Mundhir's sermons triggered the collective emotions that produced the social transformation—the community's and especially the caliph's public repentance, which was the preacher's immediate goal and the indispensable social change needed to elicit divine relief.

The second methodological challenge concerns the perennial problem of medieval sermon studies: navigating the relationship between the written text that preserves the sermon and the sermon as a public oral discourse addressed to a live audience. The advice that Louis-Jacques Bataillon (1980) gave regarding medieval Christian sermons may be fruitfully applied here as well: One must first assess the genre of the text in which the sermon was preserved. For example, was the sermon preserved as an independent manuscript of sermons or did it belong to a larger collection of texts of other genres? The four sources to be analyzed are literary or chronicle renderings of a preaching event that took place within a larger ritual complex, yet none of the texts preserve a verbatim account of al-Ballūṭī's *khuṭbas* and, as noted, they were all composed centuries after the event. They merely summarize the gist of what he said in varying degrees of detail; however, importantly, they also comment on the impact of his preaching upon the general audience and the caliph in particular. Hence it is especially important to interrogate the roles played by the description of the rogation ritual and the sermon in particular in the various literary accounts. This, in turn, requires the use of literary critical methods to account for the literary genre, historical context, authorship, and authorial intent of each source.

Sources and Authorial Intent

I have consulted four texts of diverse literary genres and provenances that record the preacher Mundhir b. Saʿīd's rain rogation rituals. The first text, entitled *Siyar aʿlām al-nubalā'* (The Lives of Noble Figures), is a biographical compendium of Muslim elites compiled by the Damascene scholar and historian Muḥammad al-Dhahabī (d. *c.* 1348) (al-Dhahabī 2006). Al-Dhahabī's comprehensive biographical obituary of Mundhir b. Saʿīd attests to Mundhir's profound piety, his prodigious talent as a preacher, and his illustrious career as a religious judge (al-Dhahabī 2006, vol. 12: 238–40; Bencheneb and de Somogyi 1999).

The second source is the *Kitāb al-Rawḍ al-miʿṭār fī khabar al-aqṭār* (The Book of the Fragrant Garden of Geographical Regions), a geographical dictionary compiled by Ibn ʿAbd al-Munʿim al-Ḥimyārī (d. 1321) (al-Ḥimyārī 1963, 1980). Virtually nothing is known about al-Ḥimyārī, except that he was a North African jurisprudent and notary who may have had Andalusi ancestors. Al-Ḥimyārī accompanied each geographical entry with historical and biographical details of the key events and personalities associated with the location. He placed his notice about Mundhir b. Saʿīd al-Ballūṭī under the geographical reference for Mundhir's place of birth, Faḥs al-Ballūṭ, a small administrative district (*kūra*) north of Cordoba city, which today is known as Los Pedroches.

The two remaining sources were written by the same author, Algerian scholar and belletrist Aḥmad al-Maqqarī (d. 1632) (Lévi-Provençal and Pellat 1999, vol. 6: 187–8). Both works are literary anthologies-cum-chronicles about the Maghreb and al-Andalus, respectively, which showcase the oeuvre of a famous polyglot from each region. *Azhār al-riyāḍ fī akhbār ʿIyāḍ* (The Fragrant Flowers of the Garden of Reports about ʿIyāḍ) is dedicated to ʿIyāḍ ibn Mūsā (d. 1149), a celebrated Maliki judge and preacher from Ceuta who served under the Almoravids (*c.* 1062–1150) (al-Maqqarī 1978). Al-Maqqarī's second publication, *Nafḥ al-tīb min ghusn al-Andalus (*The Breath of Perfume from the Branch of Flourishing al-Andalus and Memories of its Vizier Lisān ad-Dīn ibn al-Khaṭīb) (al-Maqqarī 1995), consists of a history of al-Andalus since its origins in the early eighth century and a bio-bibliography of the Nasrid vizier and polyglot Ibn al-Khaṭīb (1313–1374), arguably the most celebrated literary and political figure in Andalusi history (Bosch-Vila 1999; Molina López 2001). Based on the comments in the prologue of his works, al-Maqqarī's accounts of the encounters between Mundhir b. Saʿīd and the Umayyad caliph al-Nāṣir ʿAbd al-Raḥmān III should be read in light of the author's nostalgia for al-Andalus as a paradise lost (Elger 2002; Elinson 2009) that had once been the home of one of the most powerful Islamic dynasties and the most illustrious paragons of Islamic culture.

As for the relationship among the four texts, al-Dhahabī alone provides the name of the source of the anecdote about the rain rogation rituals led by Mundhir b. Saʿīd, a certain al-Ḥasan b. Muḥammad, whom, unfortunately, I have not been able to identify. The similarities between the accounts strongly suggest that the authors relied upon this common source. Moreover, al-Maqqarī self-plagiarizes, copying virtually verbatim the earlier account in *Aẓhār al-riyāḍ* in his later work, *Nafḥ al-tīb*. In sum, the four versions do not constitute multiple attestations of the rogation ritual and sermon but rather editorial reworkings of the same source.

The Textual Analysis: Mundhir b. Saʿīd's Rain Rogation *Khuṭbas*

With the exception of Nadia Abu-Zahra (1988), the few existing studies on the *istisqāʾ* ritual (Başgöz 2007; Doutté 1908; Goldziher 1962; Fahd 1999) have paid scarce attention to how speech is ritualized and the specific role the *khuṭba* plays in this ceremony. I will address these issues in the following analysis of the depictions of Mundhir b. Saʿīd's celebration of the *istisqāʾ* ritual preserved in the four aforementioned Arabic primary sources. When relevant, I will indicate the similarities and the salient differences between the various versions.

The Syrian historian al-Dhahabī and the Algerian chronicler al-Maqqarī both begin the anecdote by stating: "The people were deprived of rain (*qaḥiṭa al-nāss*) in the latter years of Caliph al-Nāṣir's reign. So the caliph ordered the qadi Mundhir b. Saʿid to come out [in procession] and lead the people in the rain rogation ceremony. So Mundhir fasted several days and prepared himself" (al-Dhahabī 2006, vol. 12: 239; al-Himyarī 1963: 234; al-Maqqarī 1978, vol. 2: 279; al-Maqqarī 1995, vol. 1: 572). Al-Maqqarī specifies that Mundhir fasted for three days "as a voluntary supererogatory devotion, which he frequently did in veneration of God" (al-Maqqarī 1978, vol. 2: 279; al-Maqqarī 1995, vol. 1: 572). The mention of this preparatory fasting affirms that Mundhir performed the "preliminal" rites of separation prior to leading the rogation ritual. The expression al-Dhahabī and al-Maqqarī use, "*qaḥiṭa al-nāss*," implies that God withheld the rain from the people, which resonates with Qur'anic motifs associating rain with divine mercy or blessings for repenting of one's sins (cf., Qur'an 11: 51 and 71: 10–11), and, by inference, casting drought as a divine castigation. Thus al-Dhahabī and al-Maqqarī were signaling to their readers that God had deprived the people of Cordoba of rain as a punishment for sins committed by the caliph in the final years of his caliphate without stating so explicitly.

This period coincided with the final phase of construction of the magnificent palatial city-fortress, Madīnat al-Ẓahrā', which the caliph built as a second capital and where he hosted opulent gatherings (Fierro 2005; Ruggles 2000; Vallejo Triano 1992). Al-Himyarī and al-Maqqarī's texts evoke this causality by placing the rain rogation narrative immediately after extensive anecdotes attesting that Caliph al-Nāṣir had become so engrossed in the construction and ornamentation of Madīnat al-Ẓahrā' in order to display "the power of his caliphate, the might of his sovereignty" and "spread his fame" worldwide, that Mundhir b. Sa'id felt compelled to intervene to "humble and publicly shame him" for his hubris and religious neglect by preaching "homiletic exhortations … and reminders of the need to repent and return to God" (al-Himyarī 1963: 282; al-Maqqarī 1978, vol. 2: 277; al-Maqqarī 1995, vol. 1: 570). In these previous Friday *khuṭbas*, Mundhir rebuked the caliph for his arrogance and defiance of God by accusing him of emulating the "infidels" and "tyrants" who built monuments to their vanity and treated these ephemeral structures as if they were "signs (*ayāt*) of God" (al-Maqqarī 1978, vol. 2: 277; al-Maqqarī 1995, vol. 1: 570).

The four versions of Mundhir b. Sa'id's rogation *khuṭba* coincide in stating that after Caliph al-Nāṣir ordered Mundhir to organize the *istisqā'* ritual, the people gathered at the al-Rabaḍ outdoor oratory (*muṣallā*) "coming out in procession in a great multitude (*bārizīna ilā Allāh ta'ālā fī jam'in 'aẓīm*)," according to al-Maqqarī and al-Ḥimyārī (al-Ḥimyārī 1963; 234; al-Maqqarī 1978, vol. 2: 279; al-Maqqarī 1995, vol. 1: 572). Al-Maqqarī and al-Dhahabī mention that Caliph al-Nāṣir climbed to the highest point of his castle so that he could observe the crowd, and al-Maqqarī adds that this was in order that the caliph could "participate with them in going out to meet God Almighty and humbly implore Him (*al-ḍarā'atu la-hu*)" (al-Dhahabī 2006, vol. 12: 239; al-Maqqarī 1978, vol. 2: 279; al-Maqqarī 1995, vol. 1: 572). (One cannot help but wonder whether there was an intentional irony in al-Maqqarī pointing out that the caliph climbed up to the highest point of his castle to humble himself before God.) Al-Maqqarī seemingly addresses this not in the narrative of this rogation *khuṭba* but rather in a subsequent notice in which we read that the caliph sent an emissary to Mundhir to order him to lead the people in another *istisqā'* ritual. Al-Maqqarī thereby informed his readers indirectly that the underlying causes of the drought afflicting the community—the caliph's neglect of his religious duties and his vanity and hubris before God—had yet to be fully expiated. Significantly, when the people gathered at the *muṣallā* the second time, Mundhir asked someone about the caliph's conduct, who responded, saying:

> I have never seen anyone more humbled than him (*akhsha' min-hu*) in our time. He has isolated himself in spiritual retreat, wearing the shoddiest clothing and … covering his head and beard with ashes. He has wept and confessed his sins, saying, "My life is in Your hands. Do You see fit to torment my subjects because of me? You are the most Wise of the wise. Nothing I have done has escaped You." (al-Dhahabī 2006, vol. 12: 239; al-Maqqarī 1995, vol. 1: 573)

Upon hearing that Caliph al-Nāṣir had admitted his culpability in provoking the drought, performed the rites of separation to purify himself, and wept in repentance of his sins, Mundhir "beamed with joy" and predicted that "God would allow the rain to fall because the mighty one of the earth has humbled and humiliated himself (*khasha'a jabbār al-arḍ*) and in response "the Mighty One of the Heavens has had mercy (*fa-qad raḥima jabbār al-samā'*)." Thus al-Maqqarī makes explicit the underlying political context and causes of the drought and the political dimension of the *khuṭba*.

To return to the narrative of the first rogation ceremony, al-Dhahabī and al-Maqqarī indicated that Mundhir waited "until the people had gathered together crowded in the courtyard of the *muṣallā* and then came out [dressed and] walking in a lowly manner: (*kharaja rājilan mutakhashshi'an*)." Al-Maqqarī intensifies the sense of pathos by inserting two additional nearly synonymous adverbs. His text reads: *mutaḍarru'an, mukhbitan, mutakhashshi'an*, meaning that Mundhir came out "submissively imploring [God], humbling himself, debasing himself before Him" (al-Maqqarī 1978, vol. 2: 279; al-Maqqarī 1995, vol. 1: 572). All the texts report that Mundhir stood up to preach "weeping, humbling himself before God (*qāma Mundhir b. Sa'īd bākiyan khāshi'an li-Llāh*)," according to al-Ḥimyārī (1963: 234 and 1980: 95). In al-Dhahabī's version Mundhir stood up to preach "but when he saw the situation he wept and sobbed" (2006, vol. 12: 239). Al-Maqqarī describes the situation that provoked Mundhir's tears: "But when he saw the complete abasement and submission of the people toward God, their fear of God, their humility toward Him, and their humble imploring of Him, his heart softened, his eyes clouded over, and he shed tears and sobbed for a while" (al-Maqqari 1978, vol. 2: 279; al-Maqqarī 1995, vol. 1: 572).

To sum up thus far, the foregoing passages highlight the importance of authorial editorializing in establishing the narrative framework that allows us to interpret the events as a "rite of affliction" (Turner 1967: 282; Katz 1995: 58). All four narratives attribute the underlying cause of the extended drought to the social conflict occasioned by Caliph al-Nāṣir's hubris and obsession with his own power and prestige, exemplified in his fixation with the construction of his lavish palatial city and the concomitant neglect of his religious obligations. Whether explicitly or implicitly, the accounts coincide in portraying the drought as a divine punishment visited upon the entire community due to the caliph's sins. This social affliction could only be redressed through rituals of repentance and humiliation undertaken by the preacher, the audience, and particularly the caliph as the instigator of the calamity. In line with Catherine Bell's premise that "ritualization is first and foremost a strategy for the construction of certain types of power relationships effective within particular social organizations" (Bell 2009: 197), I suggest that al-Dhahabī and al-Maqqarī are particularly effective in depicting Mundhir b. Saʿīd's *istisqāʾ* ritual as a strategy to restore the correct power relationship between God and the caliph through the performance of collective rituals of purification, humiliation, and repentance.

This is precisely the intention of the preliminal rites of separation described earlier: Mundhir's fasting three days and staying awake at night in prayer prior to the ritual. The reports that Mundhir went out walking toward the *muṣallā* "submissively imploring [God], humbling himself, debasing himself before Him (*kharaja mashiyan mutaḍarruʿan, mukhbitan, mutakhashshiʿan*)" (al-Dhahabī 2006, vol. 12: 239; al-Maqqarī 1978, vol. 2: 279; al-Maqqarī 1995, vol. 1: 572) deliberately recall the paradigmatic hadiths affirming that when the Prophet went out to perform the rain rogation ritual he "went out (dressed) in a state of humility, beseeching and humble (*kharaja…mutabadhdhilan, mutawāḍiʿan, mutaḍarriʿan*)" (al-Nasāʾī: Book 17, hadith nos. 3 and 5). The goal of these preliminal rites of separation is to attain the emotional states of humility, submission, repentance, and debasement before God and render them visible (through one's humble dress and gait), as well as audible, which is connoted by the adverb *mutaḍarriʿan*, meaning imploring, beseeching, and begging God. The term *mutaḍarriʿan* suggests a performative alteration of voice intonations that distinguishes this form of speech from the normative supplications that are denoted by the verb *yadʿū* or the noun *duʿāʾ*).

Not only do the accounts of Mundhir's prefatory rites of separation establish deliberate parallels between Mundhir and the Prophet Muhammad, but they also simultaneously magnify the contrast between the humble, pious, ascetic Cordovan judge and the haughty vainglorious caliph who initially stood aloft observing the preparations for the rogation ritual from the rooftop of his palace. That Mundhir's ritualization also provides a model for channeling the emotions of the community is seen in al-Maqqarī's description of the ritual dialectic of God-consciousness, humility, and abject helplessness before God that is forged between Mundhir and his audience: As Mundhir observed the people watching him, he witnessed their sincere God-consciousness, their debasement of themselves toward Him, and their supplications of God, which emotionally overwhelmed Mundhir and reduced him to tears. It was in this heightened emotional state that Mundhir rose to deliver the *khuṭba*. Even though al-Ḥimyārī and al-Dhahabī do not include these details of pathos, they both note that Mundhir rose to preach "crying and sobbing" (1963: 234; 2006, vol. 12: 239, respectively).

Mundhir began his *khuṭba* by saying, "Peace be with you." According to al-Dhahabī and al-Maqqarī, "then he became silent as if he were exhausted or overwhelmed (*sakita shibha al-ḥasīr*), and this was not his custom" (al-Dhahabī 2006, vol. 12: 239; al-Maqqarī 1978, vol. 2: 279; al-Maqqarī 1995, vol. 1: 572). The four versions coincide in stating that Mundhir began with the following words: "Your Lord has decreed upon Himself mercy: that any of you who does wrong out of ignorance and then repents after that and corrects himself—indeed, He is Forgiving and Merciful" (al-Dhahabī 2006, vol. 12: 239; al-Ḥimyārī 1963: 234; al-Maqqarī 1978, vol. 2: 279; al-Maqqarī 1995, vol. 1: 572). This is a quotation of Qur'anic verse 54 from Sūrat al-Anʿām (the Cattle), which Mundhir immediately followed with the recitation of verse 51 of Sūrat Hūd: "seek your Lord's forgiveness and turn in repentance to Him" and/or verse 10 of Sūrat Nūḥ: "seek your Lord's forgiveness, for He is the most forgiving."[1] The Muslim readers of these texts would know that both verses end in exactly the same way, promising that repenting and seeking God's forgiveness will result in rainfall: "He will send you celestial rain in torrents" (Qur'an 11:51 and Qur'an 71: 10–11).

All four narratives portray Mundhir as a ritual agent and mediator between God and the community, which he enacted rhetorically by following the recitation of these authoritative Qur'anic exhortations with his own incitements "to curry His favor by performing good deeds (*wa-tazallafū bi-iʿmāl al-ṣāliḥāt laday-hi*)" or, according to al-Dhahabī, "to draw nearer to God (*taqarrabū*) by performing good deeds" (2006, vol. 2: 239). Although no further details are recorded about the content of the sermon, all the sources report that Mundhir's words made an immediate and profound emotional impact upon his audience: "The people broke out in loud tears (*wa-ḍajja al-nāss bi-al-bakā'*)" and "supplicated [God] fervently with sighs (*ja'arū bi-al-du'ā'*)." Without providing more specific details, all the narrators state that Mundhir went on to finish his "eloquent *khuṭba*" and affirm that before the end of the day God sent the rain (al-Dhahabī 2006, vol. 2: 239; al-Maqqarī 1978, vol. 2: 280; al-Maqqarī 1995, vol. 1: 572).

Having analyzed the main aspects of Mundhir b. Sa'id's rain rogation *khuṭba*, I shall now address the relationship between ritual and religious speech. The four narratives demonstrate the reciprocity and mutual reinforcement between the *khuṭba* and the larger rogation ritual complex, the latter of which also included the prefatory rites of separation (supererogatory fasting and prayers, wearing old, worn-out clothing, and processional walking toward the *muṣallā* in an attitude of abject humility). This reciprocity was focused toward the evocation of profound collective sentiments of sorrow, contrition, and humility toward God, which climaxed in a Durkheimian "collective effervescence" of the entire congregation's eruption into loud sobbing, fervent sighs and supplications for God's mercy and merciful rainfall.

I concur with Edmond Doutté's view that the ritualized body plays a role in the rain rogation ritual, through the practice of dressing in humble old clothing, in generating the heightened emotions and affective dispositions of humility and submission to God (Doutté 1908: 592). The four narratives corroborate that this practice ritually exteriorized the community's and, belatedly, the caliph's complicity with Mundhir in these collective emotional experiences, which made visible their sense of belonging to an emotional community of ritually purified, God-conscious, humble, penitential Muslims. Yet the four narratives also illustrate the essential role played by religiously motivated speech in channeling these emotions, beginning with Mundhir's audible beseeching and imploring God "submissively" and "humbly" as he walked toward the *muṣallā*, which was mirrored in the congregation's ritually embodied debasement toward God and their vocal "humble imploring of Him," causing Mundhir's heart to soften and his eyes to cloud over, until he "shed tears and sobbed for a while" even before he began preaching the *khuṭba*.

This scene powerfully illustrates that the "'dialectic of emotion' between the preacher and the audience, whereby displays of piety and humility in the one mimetically reproduce these sentiments in the other" (Jones 2012: 234), had already begun prior to the delivery of the *khuṭba* and would be intensified during the course of Mundhir's preaching. Yet while the dialectic of emotion was established immediately between Mundhir and the community, the caliph's response was delayed due to his hubris and vanity. Hence the contrasting emotional dialectic al-Maqqarī depicted between Caliph al-Nāṣir's weeping in repentance for his sins and Mundhir's "beaming with joy" over the caliph's contrition.

Historians of the emotions refer to the "contagiousness of emotions," the capacity of ritual agents to provoke complementary emotional responses in others within a community that "adheres to the same norms of emotional expression and values" and shares a common understanding of how specific emotions motivate specific social behaviors (Keltner and Haidt 2001: 200; Rosenwein 2006: 25). In the particular case of the rain rogation ritual as a rite of affliction, the triggering of the emotions of sorrow, contrition, and humility before God through the ritualization of the body and ritualized speech seeks its culmination in the shedding of tears. For this reason, it is especially relevant to note that all four narratives confirm that when Mundhir stood up to preach he was already "weeping and sobbing," and that his preaching and exhortations caused the people to burst into loud weeping and sighs of supplication toward God.

As I have discussed elsewhere, premodern Islamic sermons and related literature recognize religiously motivated weeping as spiritually meritorious, ritually efficacious, and emblematic of sanctity, divine favor, or privileged spiritual gnosis (Jones 2011: 111–12). Gaudefroy Demombynes characterized weeping during the *istisqā'* ritual as a form of sympathetic magic intended to stir God's compassion to send down rain from heaven (Jones 2011: 225). While Abu-Zahra' takes issue with such interpretations, she records that in contemporary Tunisia babies were separated from their mothers shortly before the initiation of the *istisqā'* ritual, based on the Prophet's belief that God would respond favorably "to the weeping of such helpless creatures" (Abu-Zahra 1988: 516). An exhortation in an anonymous sixteenth-century Morisco rogation sermon also associated ritual penitential weeping with the divinity's positive response to one's supplications: "Multiply your prostrations and humiliation toward Him, and weep until you shed tears, for a supplication is never closer to being answered than when a man turns toward God in abject humiliation with a contrite heart in repentance" (Longás 1915: 152). Similarly, I suggest that the weeping of Mundhir, the congregation, and the caliph immediately prior to and during the *khuṭba*, and especially the collective sobbing and sighs provoked by his exhortations, fulfilled the same ritual function of manifesting the utter helplessness before God necessary to elicit His mercy in the form of rainfall.

Regarding the content of Mundhir's sermon, the sources agree that he began the rain rogation *khuṭba* with Qur'anic recitations. Mundhir b. Sa'īd selected Qur'anic verses expressed in the form of exhortations to repent and beseech God's forgiveness in order to obtain the desired celestial rainfall. The significance of this religious speech is obvious but bears underscoring: Qur'anic recitation is the most sacred form of ritual speech because it is considered to be the literal word of God and is distinguished from normal human speech by its special rules of cantillation. Numerous hadiths and devotional texts on "the spiritual merits of the Qur'an" (*faḍā'il al-Qur'ān*) avow that reciting and listening to the recitation of the sacred text bestows God's mercy, blessings, and tranquility and brings one closer to paradise. As ritual speech, Qur'anic recitation is inherently authoritative and uniquely empowered to engender emotional experiences due to its singular sacred authority and inimitable aesthetic beauty. In particular, Qur'anic verses articulated in the form of direct second-person commands and exhortations lend themselves to a mimetic mode of reception that actively encourages the listener to model and transform their conduct accordingly (Jones 2012; Stille 2021).

It is also important to emphasize the power of the social institution in which these verses were recited. The fact that these verses, and indeed, the entire sermon, were spoken within the institutional setting of the canonical rain rogation ritual by Mundhir b. Sa'īd, the person authorized to preach by the caliph and whose authority as a pious ascetic "whose prayers were answered" was recognized by the entire community, enhanced the "conditions of felicity" (Bourdieu 1999: 9) needed for the ritual's efficacy. In the emotionally charged ritual setting of the *istisqā'* ceremony, Mundhir's initial recitation of these exhortatory Qur'anic verses, which explicitly command listeners to repent and seek God's forgiveness so that "He will send you celestial rain in torrents," illustrates the capacity of ritual action and language to collapse the time between the mythic past and the present (Connerton 1989: 41–71). Mundhir's Qur'anic recitation conjures up the divine presence and reestablishes the correct dialogical relationship between God, who issues these sacred exhortations, and the audience, which immediately and obediently acts upon them. Through their loud tears of repentance and supplications of forgiveness, the people hope to inspire, in a sympathetic magical way, God's forgiveness and mercy expressed as "celestial torrents of rain." As the preacher, reciter, and transmitter of these sacred commands, Mundhir fulfills the role of ritual conduit-intercessor between the community and God.

Mundhir's famed rhetorical eloquence and booming voice, especially when he preached the *khuṭbat al-istisqā'*, further enhanced the emotional impact of his preaching. Al-Maqqarī stated that Mundhir "had the most amazing beginnings in his rain rogation *khuṭba* (*kāna li-Mundhir fī khuṭbat al-istisqā' iftitāḥ 'ajīb*)," which caused "tears to stream forth from the people's eyes" (al-Maqqarī 1978, vol. 2: 280; al-Maqqarī 1995, vol. 1 573). What did this "amazing beginning" consist of? It seems to have entailed a pronounced vocal shift, since Mundhir would speak in a loud voice, "bellowing like a town crier." It entailed specific gestures, because he would address the people by repeating the customary vocative "O people!" while pointing with his hand in their direction. And it entailed beginning the sermon proper with Qur'anic recitation. Al-Maqqarī cited one verse to illustrate: "O people! It is you who are the poor, in need of God; while God is the Rich, the Praiseworthy. If He wills, He can do away with you, and produce a new creation. And that would not be difficult for God" (Qur'an 35: 15–17) (al-Maqqarī 1978, vol. 2: 280; al-Maqqarī 1995, vol. 1: 573).

The references to Mundhir's booming voice as he recited this particular Qur'anic verse further illustrate this preacher's ritual mastery in reenacting the mythic script established by the Prophet Muhammad. According to a hadith preserved in *Saḥīḥ Muslim*, "when [Muḥammad] preached (*idhā khaṭaba*), it was as if he were the exhorter of an army" (Ibn al-'Aṭṭār 1996: 115). It is also worth recalling the hadith transmitted by Muhammad's wife 'Ā'isha affirming that when Muhammad invoked God during the *istisqā'* ritual, he would say, "O Allah, you are God, there is no deity but You, the Rich/Self-Sufficient, while we are the poor/the needy" (Abū Dāwūd: Hadith: Book 13, hadith 13). Hence the Qur'anic verse that Mundhir recited at the beginning of his rogation *khuṭba* (Qur'an 35: 15–17) also echoed words Muhammad pronounced in his rain rogation *khuṭba*. In sum, the sources suggest that Mundhir's *khuṭbas* contained many of the characteristics of ritual speech: enaction and personification of sacred authority and sacred paradigms, repetitive utterances from divine sources, symbolic gestures, and voice modulation calibrated to provoke specific collective emotional responses (Tavárez 2014). Since al-Maqqarī implied that these words and gestures were characteristic of Mundhir's performance of rain rogation *khuṭbas*, he likely conducted himself similarly in the episode discussed above.

To complete the analysis of Mundhir's rogation sermon, all four versions simply note that Mundhir concluded his "eloquent *khuṭba*." Al-Maqqarī alone adds that the remainder of the *khuṭba* consisted of exhortations and warnings that profoundly impacted the audience: In *Nafḥ al-ṭīb* he writes, "The people were stricken with terror because of his exhortations (*fa-fazza'a al-nufūs bi-wa'ẓi-hi*) and his warnings triggered in them sincere devotion to God (*inba'atha al-ikhlāṣ bi-tadhkīri-hi*)" (al-Maqqarī 1995, vol. 1: 570). In *Azhār al-riyāḍ* we find a minor change: "*fa-qaraʿa al-nufūs bi-waʿẓi-hi*," meaning they rebuked or reproached themselves due to his exhortation (al-Maqqarī 1978, vol. 2: 279–80). Finally, the four narratives confirm the ritual efficacy of Mundhir's *istisqāʾ* oration: "The day had not finished before God sent water from the sky pouring forth, quenching the soil, chasing away the drought, and calming [the people's] distress" (al-Dhahabī 2006: 239; al-Ḥimyārī 1963: 234; al-Maqqarī 1978, vol. 2: 280; al-Maqqarī 1995, vol. 1: 570). The statement evokes the collective memory of the ritual efficacy of the Prophet Muhammad's rain rogation invocations. Numerous hadiths testify that God answered Muhammad's supplications for rain. According to one incident, when the people came to him and urged him to "ask Allah to bless us with rain … he invoked Allah for it, and it rained so much that we could hardly reach our homes and it continued raining till the next Friday" (al-Bukhārī: Book 15, hadith 10).

Conclusion

The foregoing analysis of four accounts of a premodern Islamic rain rogation *khuṭba* has served as a case study to explore the role that religious speech plays within a larger ritual complex. The various sources considered confirm the relationship of reciprocity and mutual reaffirmation between the rogation *khuṭbas* and the rain rogation rites. This reciprocity operates at various levels. The first and most obvious link is juridical: The rogation *khuṭba* is an established mandated part of the ceremony. The Maliki school of law considers its performance to be one of the conditions of the validity and ritual efficacy of the *ṣālat al-istisqā*. Maliki law stipulates at what point in the rogation ritual the *khuṭba* should be delivered, the form it should take (the double *khuṭba*), the performative and ritual embodiment aspects (wearing old clothing, processional walking in abject humility) (Ibn Anas 2014: 157–8), while the hadiths and other sources allude to Muhammad's gestures, the words he spoke as he invoked God, and the Qur'anic verses he recited while performing the rites. All these practices derived from the Prophet's *Sunna* and the legal conventions of a given *madhhab* mark the *khuṭba* as ritualized or religious speech.

As a rite of affliction, the efficacy of the *istisqāʾ* ritual depends on the ritual agent's capacity to generate the collective sentiments and affective dispositions of contrition, humiliation, and submission to God to atone for the underlying social sins (the caliph's hubris and religious neglect), which caused the divine affliction. The four versions of the rogation ritual led by Mundhir b. Saʿīd reveal how the reciprocity between the larger *istisqāʾ* ritual (including the prefatory rites of supererogatory fasting, prayer, and donning old clothing) and the religious speech of Mundhir's sermons and invocations formed part of a "dialectic of emotions" or an emotion "contagiousness" focused on penitential weeping. As we saw, the congregation burst into tears of sorrow and repentance upon hearing Mundhir's sermons, exhortations, and invocations, but this was precipitated by Mundhir's own penitential weeping as he rose to deliver his sermon, which, in turn resulted from his contemplation of "the complete abasement and submission of the people toward God, their fear of God, their humility toward Him, and their humble imploring of Him" (al-Maqqari 1978, vol. 2: 279; al-Maqqarī 1995, vol. 1: 572), which softened his heart and reduced him to sobs. Although the full text of Mundhir's sermons is not preserved, the literary sources attest to the ritual impact of Mundhir's preaching on the audience, generating collective sentiments of "terror" of the divine castigations in this life (the continuance of the drought) and the afterworld, sincere devotion and renewed humility and submission to God, externalized in their weeping, wailing, and pleading for God's mercy.

Significantly, the four literary sources explicitly associate the climactic eruption of the congregation into tears with Mundhir's preaching and exhortations, and each attests to the ritual efficacy of the rogation ritual, since it subsequently rained. In other words, the sources corroborate the sympathetic magical association between penitential tears—Mundhir's tears, the congregation's tears, and the caliph's tears—as pleas for divine mercy, and rainfall as the actualization of that mercy, and they highlight the *khuṭba*'s role in this larger ritual process. Finally, since the sources frame the severe drought as a divine castigation for the caliph's sins, the narratives of the rain rogation ritual could be read as a social drama pitting the ever humble, pious, ascetic Mundhir b. Saʿīd against the vainglorious Caliph al-Nāṣir. Thus, what Mundhir achieved through his ritual speech and actions was a rectification of the power relations and hierarchical positioning between God, the caliph, Mundhir, and the people.

Note

1 Al-Maqqarī only cites Q 11: 51 in *Azhār al-riyāḍ*, vol. 2:280; however, according to *Nafḥ al-ṭīb* (vol. 1:572) Mundhir first recited Q 71:10 followed by Q 11:51. Al-Dhahabī only records Q 11:51, while al-Ḥimyārī only cites 71:10.

References

Abū Dāwūd, Sulaiman b. A. S. (undated), "Sunan Abī Dāwūd," *Sunnah.com*. Available online: https://sunnah.com/abudawud (accessed September 26, 2022).

Abu-Zahra, Nadia (1988), "The Rain Rituals as Rites of Spiritual Passage," *International Journal of Middle Eastern Studies*, 20 (4): 507–29.

Başgöz, Ilhan (2007), "Rain Making Ceremonies in Iran," *Iranian Studies*, 40 (3): 385–403.

Bataillon, Louis-Jacques (1980), "Approaches to the Study of Medieval Sermons," *Leeds Studies in English*, 11: 19–35.

Bell, Catherine (1992), *Ritual Theory, Ritual Practice*, Oxford: Oxford University Press.

Bell, Catherine (2009), *Ritual Theory, Ritual Practice*, Oxford: Oxford University Press.

Bencheneb, Mohamed, and Joseph de Somogyi (1999), "Al-Dhahabī, Shams al-Dīn Abū 'Abd Allāh Muḥammad b. 'Uthmān b. Ḳaymāẓ…al-Shāfi'ī," in Martinus Theodorus Houtsma (ed.), *Encyclopaedia of Islam*, 2, 2nd ed., 214–16, Leiden: Brill.

Bosch-Vila, Jacinto (1999), "Ibn al-Khaṭīb, Abū 'Abd Allāh Muḥammad. b. 'Abd Allāh b. Sa'īd…al-Salmānī," in Martinus Theodorus Houtsma (ed.), *Encyclopaedia of Islam*, 3, 2nd ed., 185–7, Leiden: Brill.

Bouchiba, F. (undated) "Legal Aspects of the Khuṭba."

Bourdieu, Pierre (1999), *Language and Symbolic Power*, trans. Gino Raymond and Matthew Adamson, Cambridge, MA: Harvard University Press.

Buc, Phillipe (2001), *The Dangers of Ritual: Between Early Medieval Texts and Social Science Theory*, Princeton, NJ: Princeton University Press.

Al-Bukhārī, Muhammad b. I. (undated), "Ṣaḥīḥ al-Bukhārī. Arabic text and English translation by M. M. Khan," *Sunnah.com*. Available online: https://sunnah.com/bukhari (accessed 26 September 2022).

Cardoso, Elsa (2017), "The Scenography of Power in al-Andalus and the 'Abbasid and Byzantine Ceremonials: Christian Ambassadorial Receptions in the Court of Cordoba in a Comparative Perspective," *Medieval Encounters*, 24: 390–434.

Connerton, Paul (1989), *How Societies Remember*, Cambridge: Cambridge University Press.

Al-Dhahabī, Tahqiq (2006), *Siyar a'lām al-nubalā*, Cairo: Dār al-Hadīth.

Doutté, Edmond (1908), *Magie et religion dans l'Afrique du Nord*, Algiers: Typographie Adolphe Jourdan.

Durkheim, Émile (1995), *The Elementary Forms of Religious Life*, trans. by Karen E. Fields, New York: Free Press.

Elger, Ralf (2002), "Adab and Historical Memory: The Andalusian Poet/Politician Ibn al-Khatīb as Presented in Aḥmad al-Maqqarī (986/1577–1041/1632), Nafḥ al-ṭīb," *Die Welt des Islams*, 42 (3): 289–306.

Elinson, Alexander E. (2009), *Looking Back at al-Andalus: The Poetics of Loss and Nostalgia in Medieval Arabic and Hebrew Literature*, Leiden: Brill.

Fahd, Taufiq (1999), "Istisḳā," in Martinus Theodorus Houtsma (ed.), *Encyclopaedia of Islam*, 4, 2nd ed., 269–70, Leiden: Brill.

Fierro, Maribel (2005), *'Abd al-Rahman III, Makers of the Islamic World*, London: Oneworld Publications.

Goldziher, Ignaz (1962), *Muslim Studies*, Samuel Miklos Stern (ed.), Chicago: Taylor & Francis.

Al-Ḥimyārī, A. 'A. A. ibn 'Abd al-Mun'im (1963), *Kitāb ar-Rawḍ al-mi'tār*, trans. Maria P. Maestro González, Valencia: Gráficas Bautista.

Al-Ḥimyārī, A. 'A. A. ibn 'Abd al-Mun'im (1980), *Kitāb al-Rawḍ al-mi'tār fī khabar al-aqṭār*, 'Abbās, Beirut: Maktabat Lubnān.

El Hour, Rachid (2006), "Ibn Sa'id al-Balluti, Mundhir," in Jorge Lirola (ed.), *Biblioteca de al-Andalus*, 5, 177–82, Almería: Fundación Ibn Tufayl.

Ibn Anas, Malik (2014), *Al-Muwatta' of Imām Mālik*, trans. Aisha A. Bewley, 3rd ed., Norwich: Diwan Press.

Ibn al-'Aṭṭār, Ibrāhīm ibn Dāwūd (1996), *Kitāb Adāb al-Ḫaṭīb*, intro. Mohammed Ibn Hocine Esslimani, Beirut: Dār al Gharb al-Islāmī.

Ibn al-Ḥajjāj, Muslim (undated), *Ṣaḥīḥ Muslim*. Arabic text and English translation by Abdul H. Siddiqi. Available online: https://sunnah.com/muslim (accessed September 26, 2022).

Jones, Linda G. (2011), "'He Cried and Made Others Cry': Crying as a Sign of Pietistic Authenticity or Deception in Medieval Islamic Preaching," in Elina Gertsmann (ed.), *Crying in the Middle Ages: Tears of History*, 102–35, London: Routledge.

Jones, Linda G. (2012), *The Power of Oratory in the Medieval Muslim World*, New York: Cambridge University Press.

Katz, Paul R. (1995), "The Pacification of Plagues: A Chinese Rite of Affliction," *Journal of Ritual Studies*, 9 (1): 55–100.

Keltner, Dacher, and Johnathan Haidt (2001), "Social Functions of Emotions," in Tracy Mayne and George Bonanno (eds.), *Emotions: Current Issues and Future Directions*, 192–213, New York: Guilford Press.

Kennedy, Hugh (1996), *Muslim Spain and Portugal*, London: Longman.

Lévi-Provençal, Évariste, and Charles Pellat (1999), "Al-Maḳḳarī, Shihāb al-Dīn Abū l-'Abbās Aḥmad b. Muḥammad b. Aḥmad b. Yaḥyā al-Tlimsānī al-Fāsī al-Mālikī," *Encyclopaedia of Islam*, 6, 2nd ed., 187–8, Leiden: Brill.

Lewicki, Tadeusz (1999), "Ibn 'Abd al-Mu'nim al-Ḥimyārī," in Martinus Theodorus Houtsma (ed.), *Encyclopaedia of Islam*, 3, 2nd ed., 675–6, Leiden: Brill.

Longás, Pedro (1915), *Vida religiosa de los moriscos*, Madrid: Imprenta Ibérica.

Al-Maqqarī, Ahmed M. (1978), *Azhār al-riyāḍ fī akhbār 'Iyāḍ*, 2, Rabat: Ṣundūq Aḥyā'a al-Turāth al-Islāmī.

Al-Maqqarī, Ahmed M. (1995), *Nafḥ al-tīb min ghusn al-Andalus al-raṭīb wa-dhikr waziriha Lisān al-Dīn ibn al-Khaṭīb*, 1, Beirut: Dār al Kutub al-'Ilmīyya.

Molina López, Emilio (2001), *Ibn al-Jatib*, Granada: Comares.

Al-Nasāʾī, Ahmad (undated), "Sunan an-Nasāʾī," *Sunnah.com*. Available online: https://sunnah.com/nasai (accessed September 26, 2022).

Qutbuddin, Tahera (2019), *Arabic Oration: Art and Function*, Leiden: Brill.

Rosenwein, Barbara H. (2006), *Emotional Communities in the Early Middle Ages*, Ithaca, NY: Cornell University Press.

Ruggles, Fairchild D. (2000), *Gardens, Landscape, and Vision in the Palaces of Islamic Spain*, Philadelphia: Pennsylvania State University Press.

Safran, Janina (2000), *The Second Umayyad Caliphate: The Articulation of Caliphal Legitimacy in al-Andalus*, Cambridge, MA: Harvard University Press.

Stille, Max (2021), "Public Piety and Islamic Preaching in Bangladesh," *South Asian History and Culture*, 12 (1–2): 295–309. https://doi.org/10.1080/19472498.2021.1878790.

Tavárez, David (2014), "Ritual Language," in Nick J. Enfield, Paul Kockelman, and Jack Sidnel (eds.), *The Cambridge Handbook of Linguistic Anthropology*, 496–516, Cambridge: Cambridge University Press.

Al-Tirmidhi, Muhammad (undated), "Jāmiʿ al-Tirmidhī," *Sunnah.com*. Available online: https://sunnah.com/tirmidhi (accessed September 26, 2022).

Turner, Victor W. (1967), *The Forest of Symbols. Aspects of Ndembu Ritual*, Ithaca: Cornell University Press.

Turner, Victor W. (1969), *The Ritual Process*, London: Penguin.

Vallejo Triano, Antonio (1992), "Madīnat az-Zahrāʾ: The Triumph of the Islamic State," in Jerrylin D. Dodds (ed.), *Al-Andalus: The Art of Islamic Spain*, 27–39, New York: Metropolitan Museum of Art.

Watts, James W. (2007), *Ritual and Rhetoric in Leviticus: From Sacrifice to Scripture*, New York: Cambridge University Press.

Wensinck, Arent J. (1999), "*Khuṭba*," in Martinus Theodorus Houtsma (ed.), *Encyclopaedia of Islam*, 5, 2nd ed., 74–5, Leiden: Brill.

Appendix 1

Bishop Dr. Wolfgang Huber (Berlin-Brandenburg)

Sermon on Mk 10:42-45

[St. Nicholas Church, Potsdam, October 3, 2005]

Grace and peace to you from God our Father and the Lord Jesus Christ. Amen. Dear participants of our celebration!

Under the dome of the St. Nicholas Church, we pause before God to give thanks to him and ask him to show us the way. We are delighted and honored that so many guests have chosen to join us. We are united in the word of Jesus: *whoever wishes to become great among you must be your servant, and whoever wishes to be first among you must be slave of all* (Mk 10:43-44).

Germany has already been unified again for fifteen years, half a generation, but for many of us the time feels much shorter. Because two different things are encompassed by this timespan: Often our hopes have been fulfilled beyond our explicit pleas. After all, some of us no longer expected unity in freedom, at least not then. At the same time, some wishes remain, and some paths were rockier than expected.

We take stock and weigh up the tasks ahead of us. They have been described again and again. Our state carries so much debt that this will be an intolerable burden for our children. Permanent unemployment means that millions of people's potential is going unused, leading to bitterness. Fewer and fewer working people have to provide for the old age of more and more senior citizens. The joy brought by children is being replaced by fear of the future. Any answers we can find have to prove their worth in the face of worldwide competition over who will win out in the future. The weight of responsibility shouldered by politicians is enormous.

In my mind's eye, I see Atlas with the globe on his shoulders. He can be found on one of the three domes which shape the image of Potsdam. Standing on the top of the town hall, he continues even today to carry the heavy responsibility of the whole world. When Atlas looks from the town hall at the other two domes of Potsdam, he can choose between Fortuna and the cross. These two insignia surround him. Fortuna, the moody diva, pours luck out of her horn of plenty over the places she chooses. Today some may see in her the goddess of globalization, the amulet of capital which yields its own interest. They might think that the burden of the globe can only be carried by someone who bows to the currents of capital which encircle the earth, controlled by an invisible hand.

However, Atlas could also direct his gaze at the cross which crowns the St. Nicholas Church. This sign expresses the religious faith that Jesus Christ is the Savior and the Lord of this world. His power encompasses pain and those who suffer. He gives up on no one. In him we can see God's kindness. The sign of the cross stands for a life path which did not end in the palaces of the mighty. *For the Son of Man came not to be served but to serve, and to give his life a ransom for many* (Mk 10:45). When they want to arrest him, he does not draw a magical sword. He surrenders himself to his enemies. He descends into the realm of the dead. There he breaks the diabolical chains and takes the sting out of death. From there he comes back to life. The Chosen one of God has triumphed once and for all. *Where, O death, is your sting?* (1 Cor. 15:55). We have been celebrating the resurrection of Jesus Christ ever since. That is also what the cross stands for.

But the cross of Jesus does not go unchallenged in our world. The cross on the dome of the St. Nicholas Church also fell among the ruins of Potsdam in 1945. Thirty-six years later that church was consecrated again. So this is also the story of a small resurrection. The cross has been raised again alongside Atlas and Fortuna.

Let us listen again to the Gospel of this service: *You know that among the Gentiles those whom they recognize as their rulers lord it over them, and their great ones are tyrants over them. But it is not so among you; but whoever wishes to become great among you must be your servant, and whoever wishes to be first among you must be slave of all. For the Son of Man came not to be served but to serve, and to give his life a ransom for many* (Mk 10:42-44).

Is this the description of a Christian special way? It certainly begins with the order in the house of God. Anyone who insists on being first in here is violating the rules. Because if we accept Jesus as the Lord who made himself a servant to all, we will align our actions with the well-being of our neighbor and not with our own claim to power. Jesus's cross stands for people bowing only to God, and to nobody else in this world. They stand up straight and refuse to bend. They put themselves in the service of a message in which the love of God is connected with love for their neighbors. It is the responsibility of the churches to act on Jesus's behalf, and to draw attention to the splendor of the gospel through the word and the sacrament.

Jesus recommends a different path not just against tyrannical leadership, but also against every practice of power: people must become helpers for one another. A political program cannot be derived directly from this, not before and not after elections. Political elections give power that is limited in time. Whoever runs for office is ready for responsibility and wants to gain and execute the necessary power for it.

But Jesus's instructions do apply to the political realm too. When there is someone in the center of our world and of our faith who is not concerned with leadership but with service, then this is not without consequences for the exercise of power. We need people with integrity and reliability also in politics who bow to God, but otherwise stand straight and remain unbending. We need responsible people who are willing to extend their hand to those in need so that the strong and the weak can achieve their goals together.

Power is not an end in itself. It serves our collective life. It is exercised to solve the problems of a country and to take responsibility beyond its borders. This results in a clear priority of common tasks before personal goals. Political tasks are more important than the combinations of political colors. The topics that move people weigh heavier than the names that concern them. People's worries deserve to be taken seriously. The expectation that the necessary reforms will be realized in the spirit of social justice is accompanied by the hope that this will be met with a convincing response.

People want to be taken along on the difficult path that must now be mastered. I see an opportunity in the message of the October 3, 2005. It is the opportunity to gain trust once more and to find common solutions. People expect honest answers and want to be involved when it comes to remaking our fatherland.

The cross of Jesus Christ, capricious Fortuna, and Atlas's burden of political responsibility remain in tension with each other in the urban fabric of Potsdam. It is up to us to give this relationship a distinct direction. Jesus's guidance can help us with that: *but whoever wishes to become great among you must be your servant, and whoever wishes to be first among you must be slave of all. For the Son of Man came not to be served but to serve, and to give his life a ransom for many* (Mk 10:42-44).

Amen.

Appendix 2

Bishop Johannes Hempel (Sachsen)

Sermon on Rom. 15:7

[St. Mary's Church, Berlin, October 3, 1990]

> "Therefore, accept one another, just as Christ also accepted us to the glory of God."[1]

Dear Sisters and Brothers, honored guests!

Today—on this day which stands out for our people and country, on this Day of German Unity, with its great significance for us and our European neighbors and even beyond them—we once again hear and contemplate the word of God.

"Therefore, accept one another, just as Christ also accepted us to the glory of God."

The Apostle Paul exhorts us with these words. Christ our Savior accepted us! This is the message. Jesus Christ the Son of God and our Lord is with and among us as who he is: supremely independent and sometimes mysteriously hidden, merciful to us, but also admonishing, judging us if need be. That is who he has been during the past decades. It is who he is today and how he wants to stay, because that is who he is. Independent, merciful, critical. And he wants us to treat each other like that: In inner freedom, in the merciful love of Christ, in truthfulness.

1. If we try this approach, we must give thanks to many people, and through them, we must give thanks to God. The citizens of our country live on in our memory who protested on the streets of the cities in the fall of 1989 at high personal risk, among them a striking number of women, making it clear that they had had enough of the conditions at the time. We remember the prayers for peace in many churches and we remember the groups of young adults on the margins of society and sometimes the margins of the church, who developed new concepts of human rights and a better future. We remember certain artists whose clear language in public could not be misunderstood, as well as certain

representatives of the churches. We testify, still amazed, to the momentous significance of the political changes in the Soviet Union which shaped our path through the last few months, but also to the determined realism of the former allies in the last few weeks.

We thank the federal government for its commitment and persistence when it comes to solving the upcoming political problems. And we thank our outgoing government for being active and staying active under difficult conditions. Last but not least, we thank the many people in Germany who kept the connection to us alive for decades, by visiting us faithfully and sending material aid.

But all of that could not guarantee the unity of Germany. We turn our full attention to God and thank him for beginning to solve the riddle of his different leadership of the two parts of Germany in the last forty years. He kept the churches of our country alive in spite of external strains and in spite of our weakness, and he brought them closer together. God animated and blessed the connection between Christians in the West and the East through the power of his gospel. His eyes are on us, attentive and trusting. So it was and so it remains.

2. "You should accept each other."

We do also have worries today. Many people do not feel accepted today, not by others and not by God. There are all those without employment and all those who are starting anew, but are held back by the lack of work orders. Many people do not see any chance of retraining, or they have grown old and worn out after decades in our country. We now know much more about the ecological and economic crises of our country, and it weighs heavily on us. We think of the spidery fingers of the State Security (*Staatssicherheit*) and its murky legacy that we want to overcome. We are dismayed that Jewish congregations and Jewish citizens are being reviled and insulted once more. We hope that the relationships that have grown up with the churches in Eastern Europe and in the Soviet Union, whose value we highly appreciate, will not be displaced by new contacts and duties. There are new tensions within our congregations and with the church leaders because the chosen paths to unify the German churches had to be taken too quickly and without sufficient inclusion of the congregation's base. We are preoccupied by the West German superiority in almost all areas: many people longed for it, but many also fear it. Will anything remain of our way of living and thinking, which emerged in and despite the GDR, or will everything change?

To accept each other as Christ did and because Christ did will still be a challenge, and maybe a bigger challenge even after this day of agreement. It will be accompanied by effort, patience, and sometimes disappointment. The path we start following today needs our commitment. Our success will continue to be piecemeal. God will help us to move forward.

3. "Christ accepted us. This will bring glory to God."

Christ is not simply constantly here "for us" and "with us." He remains merciful as well as critical, not from a distance but up close. Because he is present, hope does not die. After all, beneath the daily march of activity, urgent decisions, rethinks, crisis talks, uncertainties, and partial successes, hope flows like clear water. "Yet those who [a]wait for the Lord will gain new strength" (Isa. 40:31) is the motto for the coming year, which will—or so they say—be another difficult one.

We hope that we will be revitalized by a society in which we do not have to lie and can instead find the courage to be truthful, even if the truth is unpleasant. We trust that many people will put all their efforts into gradually overcoming the economic difficulties and that the rule of law which will now also have to be implemented here will help them in that. We expect that in time we can solve the social and political tensions, and that the strength to accept those who think differently will grow among us. We sincerely ask God that we should not forget about the poor in our communities and the poor and those without rights in this world, but assist them even when our own prosperity slowly increases.

The churches in Germany are coming together. We have the opportunity and the duty to listen to each other keenly and without bias, and to respect our different gifts and paths, and to concentrate entirely on preaching the gospel and serving the people. We trust that the spirit of God will free us—church leaders and congregations—from new blindness or new habituation, and give us a renewed sense of obedience. The October 3, 1990, will now be an important day to remember in recent German history. The word of God outlasts the times. We will be carried through time by the knowledge that Christ is at our side, independent, merciful, critical.

"Now may the God of peace Himself sanctify you entirely; and may your spirit and soul and body be kept complete, without blame at the coming of our Lord Jesus Christ." (1 Thess. 5:23)

Note

1 For the sake of better coherence with the German original text, we are using following Biblical translation here: New American Standard Bible (2020).

Appendix 3

Bishop Dr. Christian Stäblein (Berlin-Brandenburg)

Sermon on Mk 8:1-9

[St. Peter and Paul, Potsdam, October 3, 2020]

Dear congregation—in front of your screens at home or here with me at church, isn't it amazing? Everyone will get their fill of good words today. There will be words of courage about unity and departure, and words of manna about food in the desert and what it really means to be united: It's only 10:30 a.m. in the morning, and we are almost sated with good words, but baskets full of them are still arriving, so now we have this beautiful story about the multiplication of the loaves. What are we going to do with it then, when we're already practically full to bursting with good messages? What are we going to do with that lovely story? I have three ideas in mind, following today's motto: "Germany is one thing: many things." Along the same lines, I want to say: "Good news is one thing: many things."

My first idea:

We enjoy the story. Really? Yes! I suggest we enjoy that story for a moment. It tells us how life is supposed to be.

People get enough to eat. Unexpectedly. No one is overlooked.

And that is how it should be, here and everywhere. Every region gets its turn. The people who live in villages which are said to be on the margins, and also all the people in our capital, who are supposedly always visible anyway, but then no one really looks into those flats in the back alleys, other than a few speculators. In this story with Jesus everyone is seen, and every life story is heard. Everyone eats their fill. There are even baskets full of food left over. #westillfoodleft, we could post, or maybe #wehavespaceandevenmore. And so this is a story to enjoy. I want to emphasize this, because we should not forget that this is a fascinatingly beautiful story we are celebrating today. And we should not forget this among all the other things which should be said on this day. Thirty years of German unity, that means baskets full of stories about reunion and new beginnings, and it means baskets full of enriching each other and finding new paths, baskets of courage and joy in freedom, Brandenburg courage, Saxon courage, Thuringian courage, Berlin and East German courage. We could just sit here patting our bellies full of good stories. And they are still coming in one after another. In my opinion, one of the good stories is the story of the municipality of Staaken, right on the border between Spandau and Falkensee. West Staaken belonged to Brandenburg, west in the east or east in the west. Anyway, they had been separated for a long time, and then West Staaken in the east was reunited with East Staaken in the west. It's so beautiful that it's almost confusing. And that's how it should be after thirty years of German unity; people should be getting confused between east and west, since they're not fixed or separated anymore. Either way, in the church of Staaken you can find a beautiful wall painting. It shows varied Protestants and Catholics throughout history gathered around the cross. The painting is called "Reconciled Unity." The name suits it. A mission for our future, clearly. Stories of unity, there are baskets full of them, and do not forget today to enjoy them too. "Germany is one thing: many things. And yes, faith does one thing: it fills us up in many ways."

My second idea: After you've enjoyed this story you might get annoyed, that's also part of it, of course, it's also part of the story about Jesus and the multiplication of the loaves.

Is it really true everyone gets to be full or at least to be seen? Or was it just good luck that Jesus was there? Since then, and even today, the reality is: People are not getting enough, they are hungry all the time, everywhere in this world, in our country, in our midst. And the hunger to be seen is insatiably great and unequally met. #theillusionofbeingfulltogether

Should we post that?

And then, there is something else that's very weird. The story of the miracle doesn't tell us how the multiplication of the loaves actually works. It is in fact not explained in this story. It is told in a simple and matter-of-fact way. Jesus gives thanks, he breaks the bread and his disciples hand it out. The end. Enough for everyone. But what's the trick, or rather, what's the secret? There is a gap in this story. Well, we can fill the gap, we can close it. We can do that with trust, for example. Nobody is scared in that story and where nobody is scared, where everyone is full of trust, everyone gets enough. For exactly that reason. No one needs to snatch or grab from others or hoard anything. That's a nice way to fill the gap. #noonehastohoardyoucantrust

Even in the middle of a pandemic.

Another way to fill the gap is sharing. Where people share, everyone gets enough. That is the miracle of our life and daily life, again and again. Where people share, you don't end up with less, you end up with more. Especially here in Brandenburg I hear and experience those stories all the time about how people used to be good at sharing, and how difficult it can be today sometimes. Sharing. It is an open secret about how to fill the gaps.

But why is that gap in our story? How is it possible that everyone gets enough?

My third idea:

It is concerning the question what we are going to do with this story today. Maybe we should just do what the story itself says. They live. The disciples don't ask a lot of questions. They just do what has to be done. And they do it at exactly the right moment. They hand out the bread. The miracle happens because people perform, they step up, as we would express it these days. They step up just like the courageous people here in the East thirty years ago. They didn't worry about themselves. For three days, we're told at first, the crowd had nothing to eat. Well, the comparison with a burning refugee camp seems obvious these days. Three days with barely any supplies. Sometimes that means: Just do it, now, just do it Europeans. Dear congregation, is it that simple? Or is that too simple? Of course it is a long process, and we know it from becoming one in this country, from becoming one in Europe too, let alone becoming one in this world. A long process. So it's essential, it's like the most basic ingredients that nourish us, to have stories like this about Jesus. And to do what we do these days with stories—we share them. Especially with those who are being jailed at the moment for justice and freedom, those we cannot hear, whether they're in Belarus or in Hong Kong. To share the story with them, the story in which everyone gets enough to eat and no one gets overlooked by Jesus. And that he has confidence in us to share and to live it. Can we do that? Of course we can, at least from time to time.

And surely we can do what Jesus does first in this story. What's that? He gives thanks, of course. We are giving thanks today. To all those on the path of unity. We are giving thanks to the courageous and also the hesitant people, and to those who just do what has to be done. To those who warn us to remember the past, and to those who share their memories. Still one story after another keeps coming in. We are giving thanks to everyone in the name of God. Giving thanks in God's name does one thing: It makes us open to each other. #openforgodjustbebrave

We could post this right now. And then go on and collect baskets full of stories about it. #openforgodjustbebrave

Amen.

Notes on Contributors

Olaf Blaschke is Professor of Modern and Contemporary History at the Historical Department at Westfälische-Wilhelms Universität Münster.

Ruth Conrad is Professor of Practical Theology at the Faculty of Theology at the Humboldt University in Berlin.

Maren Freudenberg is a scientific associate at the Centre for Religions Studies (Centrum für Religionswissenschaftliche Studien) at Ruhr Universität Bochum.

Roland Hardenberg is Professor of Social and Cultural Anthropology at the Goethe University in Frankfurt am Main. Since 2017, he has also been the director of the Frobenius Institute for Research in Cultural Anthropology.

Jan Hermelink is Professor of Practical Theology and Pastoral Theology at the Faculty of Protestant Theology at Georg-August Universität in Göttingen.

Linda Gale Jones is part of the research group Ethnographies, Cultural Encounters and Religious Missions in the Iberian World (ECERM) at Universitat Pompeu Fabra in Barcelona.

Hanna Miethner is a research assistant at the chair for Practical Theology at Humboldt University in Berlin.

Julian Millie is Associate Professor of Anthropology and Indonesian Studies at the Faculty of Arts at Monash University in Melbourne.

Paul Post is Professor Emeritus of Ritual Studies at the Department of Culture Studies at Tilburg School of Humanities and Digital Science at Tilburg University.

Tahera Qutbuddin is the AlBabtain Laudian Professor of Arabic in the Faculty of Asian and Middle Eastern Studies at the University of Oxford, and Professor of Arabic Literature Emerita in the Department of Near Eastern Languages and Civilization at the University of Chicago.

Marileen Steyn is a PhD student in the Department of Practical Theology & Missiology at the Faculty of Theology, Stellenbosch University, South Africa.

Max Stille is executive director of NETZ Partnership for Development and Justice, Wetzlar, and member of the Young Academy, Heidelberg Academy of Sciences.

Abdulkader Tayob is Professor of Islam, African Publics and Religious Values at the Department of Religious Studies at University of Cape Town.

Cas Wepener is Professor of Practical Theology in the Department of Practical Theology & Missiology at the Faculty of Theology, Stellenbosch University, South Africa.

Index of Names

The index follows the articles and hence the respective author's choice of transliteration.

'Abd al-Raḥmān III al-Nāṣir (Umayyad caliph of Cordoba) 12, 173, 178–81, 184, 188
Abraham 74–5, 78–9
Abu Bakr 169
Adam 74–6, 78–9, 82
'Alī ibn Abī Ṭālib 12, 158–69
Antoun, Richard 67
Arendt, Hanna 170
Asad, Talal 68, 70, 128, 132
Attab ibn Warqa' 169

al-Bashir, Omar 49
Bell, Catherine 146, 174, 181
Bendel, Alois 30–3
Borthwick, Bruce 67
Bowler, Kate 109–11
Buc, Philippe 175
Butler, Judith 149

Coleman, Simon 109–10, 135

al-Dhahabī, Muḥammad 176–83
Davies, Douglas 149, 152
Deedat, Ahmad 73, 80
Demombynes, Gaudefroy 184
Dibelius, Otto (bishop) 90
Doutté, Edmond 183
Durkheim, Émile 66, 132, 183

Ehrler, Joseph (bishop) 22, 29

Frings, Josef 21

Geertz, Clifford 66–9, 71
Gordhan, Pravin 51
Gorman, Amanda 152
Graham, Billy 29
Grimes, Ronald 146–7

Hagin, Kenneth 110
al-Ḥasan b. Muḥammad 178
Hajjaj (Umayyad governor of Iraq) 159
Hempel, Johannes (bishop) 96–8
Heubner, Heinrich 28
al-Ḥimyārī, Ibn 'Abd al-Mun'im 177, 179–82, 187
Hirschkind, Charles 67–70, 130, 135
Hitze, Franz 21
Hofacker, Ludwig 22
Hofbauer, Clemens Maria (bishop) 21
Hölscher, Lucian 26
Huber, Wolfgang (bishop) 93–5
Husayn, Prophet's grandson 170
Huizinga, Johan 149

Ibn 'Abbād of Ronda 65
'Iyāḍ ibn Mūsā 177

Jaeger, Lorenz (bishop) 26, 30
Jesus 19, 20, 22, 24, 29, 40, 45–6, 48, 55, 93–7, 112, 120, 122

Katongole, Emmanuel 56
Khan, Nouman Ali 74
Khomeini, Ayatollah 63
Kögel, Rudolf 29

Lanham, Richard 162
Leppich, Johannes 29
Lichtenberg, Bernhard 25
Luther, Martin 39, 89–90

Madonsela, Thuli 48
Mahmood, Saba 69, 132–4
Makgoba, Thabo (archbishop) 5, 39–57
Malinowski, Bronisław 66
Mandela, Nelson 42, 47
al-Maqqarī, Aḥmad 12, 176–88

Mbeki, Thabo 44
Moses 171
Motlanthe, Kgalema 44
Muhammad (Prophet) 11–12, 65, 74–5, 78–9, 82, 156, 159, 162–3, 166–8, 171, 175, 182–4, 186–7
Mundhir b. Sa'īd al-Ballūṭī, 12, 173–7

Ong, Walter 158–9
Osteen, Joel 8–9, 105–22

Quss ibn Sa'ida 160–1

Rahman, Fazlur 80
Ramaphosa, Cyril 43, 52–3
Roberts, Oral 110–11
Rushdie, Salman 63

Sailer, Johann Michael (bishop) 22
Schleiermacher, Friedrich D.E. 21, 29
Schulz, Dorothea 67
Sinitiere, Phillip 105, 107–12
Sounaye, Abdoulaye 67
Stäblein, Christian (bishop) 98–9
Stoecker, Adolf 29–30
Sufyan, Abu 159

Thomas, Dylan 151–2
Turner, Victor 41, 43, 56–7, 176, 181
Tutu, Desmond (archbishop) 5, 39, 41

Umar ibn al-Khattab 168
Uthman 169

Van Beek, Wouter 151
Von Galen, Clemens August Graf 25–6
Von Ketteler, Wilhelm Emmanuel (bishop) 21

Wadud, Amina 71
Wasil ibn Ata 159
Wichern, Johann Hinrich 20
Wittgenstein, Ludwig 70
Wulff, Christian 91

Ziyad 160
Zuma, Jacob 40, 43–4, 47–52

Index of Subjects

action 3, 10, 40, 42, 45, 118–19, 122, 130, 132, 135, 164, 169, 188, 194
ethical action 47, 50, 55, 100
symbolic action 66, 176
aesthetic(s) 3–4, 12, 14, 43, 67–8, 92–3, 156–8, 185
agency 108, 110, 115–16, 127, 133–4
listener's agency *see* listening
altar call 135
apartheid 5, 41–2, 70, 72–3
audience (*see also* listening/listener) 48, 50, 52, 67, 95–6, 108
audiences' attention 93
audiences' interest 33
authority over audience 170
effects on an audience 117
feeling of familiarity 118
online audience 10
virtually audience 113
authority/authorities 3, 4, 11, 23, 28, 65–6, 82, 106, 171–2
biblical authority 106
charismatic authority 107
institutionalized authority 68
orator's authority 168, 170
sacred authority 185–6
awakening 21–2

balāghah (*see also* oration; speech) 64, 78
Bible/biblical 8, 20, 27–8, 106, 112–14, 118, 121–2, 151–2
biblical exhortation 110, 196
biblical norms *see* norms
biblical terms 42
biblical themes 53
biblical text(s) 58, 94, 97, 99
biblical tradition 95
bible-believing Christian 109
Hebrew Bible 89
blessing 80, 110, 163–4, 171, 179, 185
calvinism 22
catechesis 151
celebration 8, 74 (*see also salāt al-istisqā'*)
Day of German Unity 91, 95, 98, 100
feast-day celebration 12
'id ul-fitri celebration 129–31
wedding celebration 130
charisma 4, 14, 30, 107
charismatic authority *see* authority
charismatic Christianity *see* Christianity
charismatic church *see* church
charismatic leadership 105, 122
charismatic preacher 108
Christianity
charismatic/neo-pentecostal Christianity 114, 134
eastern Christianity 70
church(es)
Action Chapel (Accra) 39
African Independent Churches 39
Anglican Church/Anglicans 5, 39–40, 49
bible-based church 112
Catholic Church 22, 24, 29, 32–4
Catholicism/Catholics 4, 21–3, 25–6, 31–2, 99, 200
charismatic church 105, 107
Lakewood Church (Houston, Texas) 8, 107, 122
Lutheran Church 90
mainline churches 39
megachurch 8–9, 105–8, 117, 119
neo-pentecostal church 39
Old Catholic church 24
pastor-focused church 105, 107
Protestant Church 26, 28, 89–90, 93, 96–9
Riverside Church (New York) 39
St. George's Anglican Cathedral (Cape Town) 39, 44, 49, 51, 56
St. Mary's Church (Berlin) 96
St. Nicholas Church (Potsdam) 90, 93

state-church law 1, 7
Zion Christian Church (South Africa) 39
colonialism 68, 70
communitas 41, 56–7
congregation 2, 6, 10, 33, 71–2, 92, 95, 107, 114, 118, 183–4, 188, 197–8
content
content analysis 43–4, 106, 113
content of *khuṭbah* 66
content of sermon 5, 8–10, 20, 22, 40–5, 50, 56–7, 92, 112, 114, 117–19, 136, 164, 167, 183, 185

dars (lesson) 64
da'wa (Islamic predication) 133
dhikr (remembrance) 64

economy 54, 69, 94, 111
education/educational 27, 31, 49, 74, 107, 122, 128, 130, 133
embodiment/embodied 55, 70, 111, 119–22, 128, 131–2, 134–6, 163
embodied participation 127, 129
embodied performance *see* performance
embodied ritual *see* ritual
emotion/emotional/emotionalizing 4, 9, 12, 99, 109, 112, 118, 122, 129, 133–6, 150, 176, 181, 183–4, 188
contagiousness of emotions 184, 188
dialectic of emotions 183, 188
emotional community 174, 182
emotional experiences 183, 185
emotionality as a performative act 120
emotionalizing effects of religious speech 3, 117
emotional response 134–5, 186
ethic/ethical 43, 46, 52–4, 63, 68, 70, 74, 81, 95–6, 109, 135–7, 170
ethical action *see* action
ethical decision 64, 75, 80, 82
ethical living 45–6, 48, 50–1
ethical teaching 12, 156
events
national events 89
pedagogical events 128, 132–3
popular events 91
preaching events *see* preaching
religious events 31
example(s) 46
from the Bible 106, 117, 120, 122
from everyday life 115–18, 122
exhortation 168, 184–8
biblical exhortation *see* Bible
homiletic exhortation 179
moral exhortation 5–6, 63–76, 78, 82–3
Qur'anic exhortation *see Qur'an*

faith, faithful 8, 10, 46, 66, 81, 106, 111, 114–16, 121–2, 164, 166
faith community 41–2
faith teaching 109
innerfaith 22
fatwa 69
fiqh (jurisprudence) 69

gender 71, 128, 149
gender stereotypes 26–7
gender-based violence 52–3
glossolalia (speaking in tongues) 106, 108, 135
gospel 19
health and wealth gospel/prosperity gospel (*see also* theology) 3, 8, 106–10, 112, 115, 116, 121–2

hadith 69, 75, 77, 79–80, 163, 175, 181, 185–7
health 9, 46, 106, 109–11, 114, 117, 120, 122
healing 106, 108
health and wealth gospel *see* gospel
Holy Spirit 8, 33, 106, 108, 110–11, 121–2, 134–5
homiletic(s) 19, 31, 40, 54, 92, 179
homily 64, 169

Imam 70, 72
inclusion/exclusion 1, 3, 7, 14, 93, 106, 197
Islam/Islamic 67, 91
discourse of Islam 5–6, 63–83
Islamic calendar 128
Islamic jurisprudence 71
Islamic studies 64, 71
medieval Islam 65
pre-Islamic culture 158–61, 170–1
Sunni 69, 159, 168–9, 173
Shi'a 69

Jews 23, 25
jumuʿah (Friday worship) 77

kalām (dialectical theology) 70
khuṭba(h) (*see also* preaching; sermon) 2, 5–6, 12, 63–7, 69, 77, 156–7
  khuṭba(h) exhortation 69–71
  khuṭba(h) studies 65–9
  online-*khuṭba(h)* 72
  pre-*khuṭbah* 5–6, 63–4, 70–2, 74, 77, 82
  pre-*khuṭbah* talk 63, 74–9, 82
  khuṭbat al-istisqāʾ/rain rogation *khuṭba(h)* 12, 173–91
knowledge 71, 158, 164–5, 198
  cultural knowledge 9, 136
  religious knowledge 1, 3, 131
  ritual knowledge 10
  shared knowledge 130–1

language 152, 159, 170–1, 185
  body language 120
  language ideologies 134
  language of Jesus 48
  liturgical language 148
  ritual language 144–8, 151
  religious language 15, 92, 100, 145–8
  sacred language 147–9
  symbolical language 144
  theological language 97
liminality 41, 43, 56–7
  preliminal rites 178, 181
linguistic(s) 6–7, 10, 105, 119, 181
  linguistic strategies 113, 122
  linguistic style 106–7, 112, 117, 119–20
listener/listening
  agentive listening/listener's agency 9, 127–34, 137
  female listening 134
  ideology of listening 135
  incidental listening 9, 130–1
  listening body 134
  mere listening 132–3, 135, 138
  non-agentive listening 9, 131–2, 137
  pious listening/listener 127–8, 130, 132–3, 135, 137
  routine listening/listener 9, 127–32, 134–7
  unintentional listening 129
liturgy/liturgical 12, 43, 134, 144, 168
  islamic liturgical orations 12
  liturgical language *see* language
  funeral liturgy 148
lutheran *see* church

madhhab (legal school) 175, 187
madrasah (religious school) 73
manual 31
mawʿiẓah (moral exhortation) *see* exhortation
Mecca 75–6, 78–80, 160, 166
media/mediatized 119, 121–2
  media celebrity 107
  mediatization 13, 66–7
  new media 62, 66
  popular media 1
  preaching as media form 133
  social media 14, 44, 131, 137
Medina 11, 78, 156, 166, 169–70
metaphor/metaphorical 75, 78–9, 82, 96, 99, 152, 159
mnemonic 158–9
mosque 6, 11, 51, 64–5, 71–3, 75–83
  Bridgetown Mosque (Cape Town) 73
  Claremont Main Road Mosque (Cape Town) 71
  Masjid al Ḥarām (Mecca) 81

norms, normative, normativity 3, 6–10, 14, 28, 91, 96, 100–1, 106, 114, 116, 133, 136
  biblical norms 27
  normative values/norms and values 1, 145
  normativity and popularity 2–3, 6–7, 9, 14, 91, 122
  normative practice 79
  political norms 91
  religious norms 2, 132
  social norms 2

online viewers 112, 120–1
orality, oral
  oral culture 157–8
  oral milieu 156, 158
  oral society 160
  orality-rooted speaker 159
  rhetoric of orality *see* rhetoric
oration (*see also balāghah*; speech)

Qur'anic exhortation 182
Qur'anic recitation 74–6, 165, 171, 182, 185–6
Qur'an(ic) quotation 76, 80, 162, 169, 182, 187

religion/religious
cross-religious 2
religious communication 148
religious communities 3–7, 71
religious knowledge *see* knowledge
religious language *see* language
religious norms *see* norms
religious speech *see* speech
religious pluralization/plurality 4, 91
religious traditions *see* tradition
religious studies 14
religious institutionalization 65
religious values *see* values
religious rhetoric *see* rhetoric
religious utterances 174
religious obligations 136, 181
religious resources 100
rhetoric/rhetorical 10–12, 14, 157
political rhetoric 94, 97
pop-cultural rhetoric 3
religious rhetoric 92–4
rhetoric of hope 118
rhetoric of orality 156
rhetoric of reflection 96
rhetorical means 6, 96–7
rhetorical skills 71
rhetorical strategies 9, 112–13, 118, 121–2
rhetorical style 106–7, 112, 117, 119
ritual(s)/rites
collective rituals 130, 181
disaster rituals 143, 145
embodied ritual 171, 174, 187
funeral rituals/rites 66, 148–51
preliminal rites of separation 178, 181
(rain) rogation rituals/rites *see salāt al-istisqā'*
rites of affliction 174, 176, 181, 184, 187
rites of passage 41, 74, 176
rites of separation 178–83
ritual agency/agent 174, 182, 184, 187
ritual ambiguity 145, 149
ritual ceremony 175
ritual complex 174, 176, 183, 187
ritual criticism 11, 145, 150
ritual drama 174
ritual efficacy 187–8
ritualization/ritualizing 11, 146, 174–6, 181–2, 184
ritual knowledge *see* knowledge
ritual language *see* language
ritual speech *see* speech
ritual studies 11, 144–6

Sacred, the 145, 147, 150
sacred text 4, 185
salāt al-istisqā' (rain rogation ritual/rites/ ceremony) 12, 173–8, 181, 183–5, 187–8
sermon (*see* also *khuṭba(h)*; preaching)
ad hoc sermon of pious counsel 160–3
as a public oral discourse 176
Catholic sermon 4, 32
Christmas sermon 5, 39–62
effects of sermons 31
Friday sermon *see khuṭba(h)*
online sermon 107
performance of the sermon 43, 49, 56–7
popular sermon 89
printed sermon 20, 22, 31
sin/sinner 12, 21–2, 53, 92, 110–11, 114, 161, 179–81, 184, 187
societas 5, 41–2, 56
speech (*see also balāghah*; oration)
battle speech 160, 168–9
interactive speech 12, 156
motivational speech 116
political speech 20, 91, 93–5, 160, 168–9
public speech 1, 92, 120
religious speech
local patterns of religious speech 1
ritual dimensions of religious speech 5, 11, 145, 152
ritual embeddedness of religious speech 3
ritual speech 13, 148, 150–2, 176, 185–6, 188
Sufism 69–70
sunna(h) 79, 171, 175, 187
symbol(s)/symbolical 119, 144, 149
sacred symbols 151–2
symbolic action *see* action
symbolic system 66–7

Symbolism 150–1
synagogue 51

tadhkīr (reminder/remembrance) 64
taqwā (consciousness of God) 12, 162–3, 165–7 (*see also* piety)
television 8, 33, 56, 91, 105, 111–12, 120–1, 131
televangelist 113
television ministry 105, 111
theology
incarnational theology/theology of incarnation 43, 45–52, 54–6
neo-pentecostal theology 106, 110
practical theology 19, 92
predestination theology 109
prosperity gospel theology (health and wealth theology) 108–9
Protestant theology 19
theology of hope 46, 54, 56–7
tradition(s) 4–7, 14, 148
Arabic literary tradition 157
biblical tradition *see* bible/biblical
Christian tradition 25, 39, 92
homiletical tradition 40
local tradition 3, 75, 79
neo-pentecostal tradition 105
prophetic tradition 79
religious tradition 7, 11, 15, 91, 133, 146
textual tradition 69, 133
traditional style of preaching 97, 133

Umayyads 12, 150–60, 169–70, 173, 175, 178

value(s) 3–8, 10, 63, 68, 70, 96, 101, 106, 114, 145, 170, 184
bourgeois values 26–7
Christian values 40
civic/civil values 26, 28
common values 8
commercial values 10
ethical values 95
middle-class values 108
national values 53
(socio-)political values 7, 89
religious values 67, 69, 101
values of society 89, 91, 93
virtue 163, 165–6

worldviews 67–9, 106, 114
worship 25, 46, 76, 81, 96–7, 101, 113, 118–22, 150, 157, 163–4, 167
Friday worship 12, 71–3, 77
worship practice 135

www.ingramcontent.com/pod-product-compliance
Lightning Source LLC
Chambersburg PA
CBHW052111300426
44116CB00010B/1624
9781350408883